D0250862

*American Lives*

# Gang of One

*Memoirs of a Red Guard*

FAN SHEN

University of Nebraska Press, Lincoln and London

© 2004 by Fan Shen
All rights reserved
Manufactured in the
United States of
America ⊗
Library of Congress
Cataloging-in-
Publication Data
Shen, Fan, 1955–
Gang of one:
memoirs of a Red
Guard / Fan Shen. p.
cm. – (American
lives) ISBN 0-8032-
4308-1 (hardcover:
alk. paper)
1. Shen, Fan, 1955–
2. China – History –
Cultural Revolution,
1966–1976.
3. China – Social life
and customs – 1949–
4. China – Biography.
5. Chinese Americans
– Biography.
I. Title. II. Series.
CT1828.s46 A3 2004
951.05'6 – dc22
2003017901

ISBN-13: 978-0-8032-
9336-6 (paper: alk. paper)
ISBN-10: 0-8032-
9336-4 (paper: alk. paper)

This is what life is made of:
Fire
Earth
Metal
Wood
&
Water.

*Lao-tzu* (6th century BC)

# Contents

# Preface

I am a first-generation immigrant and a proud American. I came to America in January 1985 as a graduate student. Like most immigrants to America, I brought with me little money ($100 to be exact) but a big ambitious heart. In the next six years, I studied very hard, supporting myself with a scholarship and odd jobs at a restaurant and a bookstore. To complement my formal schooling, I also took every opportunity to visit various institutions that make up the vital parts of American society, in order to study and understand the country that I admired. I sat through church services and court trials, visited farms and state penitentiaries, toured TV stations and newspapers offices, and volunteered in retirement centers.

I received my master's degree in a year and a half and my Ph.D. in five years. Today, I have a happy family life and I teach as a professor at a beautiful college in southern Minnesota. Happy as I am, I still often wake up in the middle of the night and find myself reliving my tormented past, a life full of struggle and despair, and yet, a life that sharpened my determination to succeed and made me appreciate the opportunities in the land of the free.

&

It took me a long time to make up my mind about whether to write this book and to divulge the secrets that I had harbored in my heart for many years. The decision was agonizing because the book will almost certainly upset my parents; it may even cause them to regret that they had ever given birth to me. Having been revolutionaries all their lives, they will be angry and hurt because I have committed the ultimate crime as a revolutionary: I have rebelled against the Great Leader, Chairman Mao, and have become an anti-revolutionary despite their lifelong teachings.

Without a doubt, my "treachery" will be unbearably painful and disappointing to my parents, since they had every reason to believe that I would grow up to be a perfect revolutionary, having been born and brought up in a family full of dedicated revolutionaries. Both my grandfather and granduncle were revolutionaries who fought against the Qing (China's last dynasty) and the foreign devils. My parents were life-long communist revolutionaries who fought against the Japanese and the nationalists in World War II. And they had decided that I would be a revolutionary even before I was conceived. At their wedding ceremony shortly after the founding of the People's Republic, my parents vowed in front of the portrait of the Great Leader and a roomful of guests that all their children would follow the Great Leader, and declared that they had chosen a revolutionary name for their first baby. "Fan," my given name, means "ordinary—one of millions of working people," because only the working people could be true revolutionaries. I was brought up in the "Big Courtyard," the headquarters of the People's Liberation Army at the west end of Beijing, and was sent, at the age of three, to the Flying Wing School, an elite boarding school for the children of communist officials. From the moment I entered the kindergarten there, I had been taught all the right thoughts, all the thoughts a little revolutionary needed to know: love of the Great Leader, love of communism, and hatred of capitalism. And before each class, we sang revolutionary songs. From the very beginning, I was a diligent and dutiful student and had a gift for revolutionary words. My parents and my teacher told me so when they read the little revolutionary essays I wrote in the second grade. The teacher read the essays to the whole class, and later my mother mentioned proudly that with my gift I could one day become a high-ranking Communist Party official.

Yet, despite my gift for revolutionary words and the best efforts of my parents and teachers, my tree did not blossom with revolutionary flowers as expected. In this long process of indoctrination, something went wrong and an "evil power" sneaked into my mind and controlled my thoughts, a power that was greater than that of the golden words of the Great Leader. Even at a young age, I recognized the "evil" thing right away—it was called "personal ambition" at the purgation sessions and had been condemned most rigorously over and over again. It was the most dangerous thought a revolutionary could have, I was told—a thought that goes against everything a true revolutionary is supposed to stand for. A true revolutionary should be completely selfless, free of personal ambition, and should obey only the call of the Communist Party and the call of the Great Leader. But I was powerless against the "evil power" because I wanted to have a successful life. I began to play at being a perfect little revolutionary while deceiving all the people around me and working only for my personal ambition. Although I was shouting slogans to sacrifice my life for the Great Leader and to be a selfless, name-less solder for the revolution, I had no intention of doing so at all; even worse, I deliberately used those revolutionary slogans to further the goals of my ambition. In doing so, I rebelled against even my own given name: I was not content to be "Fan," one in a million, and not content to accept the fate that the Great Leader and the Communist Party assigned me. But I could not help it and will not apologize for it. I did it in such a de-ceiving manner because that was the only way "I," my individual spirit, could have lived.

Apart from the pain that I would cause my parents, there is another reason I hesitated to write this book: it is the embarrassment and shame that I felt when I reflected on what I had done during the years of the Cultural Revolution. I felt embarrassed and ashamed not because I had succumbed to the command of personal ambition and had used decep-tive means to advance my personal goals, but because I had participated in a number of cruel and destructive actions while playing the little revo-lutionary. No doubt readers will find some of my actions cruel and de-testable. They are indeed cruel and detestable, even though I did them mostly when I was still a naïve revolutionary who was taught that no ac-tion against an enemy was too cruel. They will remain a painful chapter in my life.

In addition to the pain to my parents and to the shame to myself, there is yet a third concern that agonized me about writing this book: it is the potential danger such a book poses to my family and friends still in China, even though this is a purely personal story and not an account of a historical event or a commentary on China today. To mitigate possible trouble with the authorities there, I have changed some people's names in the book, and I want to hereby declare unequivocally that nobody—not my parents, not my friends, not my teachers—but myself is to blame for my becoming a little anti-revolutionary and for all the statements I made and the actions I took in the book.

I am deeply indebted to many people for my survival and my eventual victory, but I want to dedicate this book especially to these friends Gu Junde, Master Peng Yulin, Master Nan Boqin, and Clever Zhao, friends from my childhood and young adulthood who provided subtle catalysts that had changed the course of my life in significant ways. It is sad that none of them will ever see this book (they are all dead), but they are at least partially responsible for its existence.

# Acknowledgments

First of all, I want to thank countless friends in the Big Courtyard in Beijing, in Shaanxi Province, in the 5702 factory in Xi'an, in Lanzhou, in Tanggu, and in Tianjin. I would not have survived without their friendship and help.

Some people, though, deserve to be singled out by name—Judith Blatchford, Dan and Mary Louis Meissner, Paul Olson, Linda Pratt, Lynette Reini-Grandell, Julie Rodakowski, Gail Sauter, Kathy Schatzberg, Ann Whelan, Warren and Ginny Wong, Virginia Wright-Peterson, my parents, my sister, and my brother. Their love, friendship, and aid have helped me through countless troubled times. As for my parents, I hope I will bring no more trouble to them.

I want to thank Michael Wreen, my good friend, Bob Silverstein, my able agent, and especially Ladette Randolph, my insightful editor, for their numerous and invaluable editorial suggestions.

Finally, I want to thank my wife, Zhang Wei, for her love, which made the completion of this book possible.

# *I* Fire

# 1 "Burn the Old World!"

"Wowu—Wowu—Wowu"—the cicadas on the poplar trees outside my window had been singing their labored, slow songs for hours, and for all that time, I had been lying restlessly on a wet reed mat, sweating and waiting impatiently for my father to hum his way out the door. The summer had started unusually early in 1966. With sultry air pouring in through the open window, the apartment seemed hotter by the minute. Although I never liked the torturous naps, my suffering on that day in May was particularly keen because I was afraid that I would miss out on a most important event of the Cultural Revolution to be held at my school that afternoon.

I don't know how many times I craned my neck over the desk and glanced at the old rusty wall clock, which had an ugly rooster scampering around its face to indicate the hours and minutes. The rooster must have been distracted by the bewitching songs of cicadas or the sweltering heat and forgotten its duty. For all the monotonous songs I had suffered through since my last glance, the silly creature had barely budged a measly step each time I looked up. Twelve is not an age of patience.

Even though my father, Col. Shen Nang, knew the Cultural Revolution had begun and that a big event was happening that afternoon at my school, he still insisted on living our old daily routine, which included a mandatory afternoon nap. I felt the whole world was flying by while I was imprisoned in my room, wasting time listening to the silly songs of cicadas.

The ugly rooster on the rusty clock finally strutted to five minutes to two. I heard the off-key notes of "The Red Army March," which was my father's favorite song. It became louder in the hall and then faded at the front door. Shortly after, I heard the long-awaited "Da, da, da—Da," a coded knock at the door. I rushed over and threw the door open, and was so glad to see the square figure of my friend Baby Dragon standing at the door. On the floor by his feet stood a bulging green army satchel.

"Are you ready, Fan Shen?" he asked, beads of sweat hanging from his fat chin. He lived in the same apartment building and must have been waiting outside for a long time.

"They've already started, hurry!" He panted and wiped his wet hands on his shorts.

"Shhh, don't wake up my sister," I said. "She'll give us a lot of trouble if she wakes up." My sister was two years younger than I, and was an avid reader. She would certainly get mad if she knew what I was about to do to her books. Rushing around the room noiselessly, I pulled most of the books from the shelf and stuffed them into a canvas satchel. Heaving the heavy bag over my shoulders, I could feel the straps cutting deep into my flesh, but I paid no attention to the pain. I nodded to my friend, and we walked swiftly out the door.

It was a short walk from our apartment building to the schoolyard. We soon reached the low stone wall surrounding the soccer field of our school. As we walked along the wall, we could hear loudspeakers broadcasting a revolutionary march inside the wall and see a fog of velvety black flakes of ash gently falling down in the air. My body reacted excitedly to the sound of the revolutionary march and my steps quickened automatically. "Hurry up," I shouted to my friend, who was trailing behind. As soon as we rounded the corner, I saw a spectacular sight at the center of the soccer field: a giant heap of books, almost two stories high, was engulfed in flames and sparks, which whirled and danced toward the sky. Around the fire, dozens of people, mostly my fellow students, were busy throwing books onto the blazing heap. I had never seen a big fire before, and the sight of the orange flames and the smell of smoke in the air made my heart pound with excitement. The shrilling revolutionary march pouring from the loudspeakers and several gigantic red banners strung across the spectator stand added to the excitement of the scene. The banners bore the slogans of the Cultural Revolution and the purpose of the current fiery campaign:

"THE NEW SOCIETY WILL BE BUILT ON THE ASHES OF THE OLD!"

"BURN THE FEUDAL RELICS!"

"BURN THE SENTIMENTAL BOURGEOIS CULTURE!"

In the stands, sitting below the giant banner, a large group of younger students were clapping their hands and singing the Great Leader's song "Harden Our Hearts."

Baby Dragon and I walked to the edge of the fire. The heat was so intense I could feel it bake my face. I set the bag down on the gray ash-

covered ground and pulled out the first book from the bag. It was entitled *A Doll's Adventures*, a children's classic I had read a dozen times. I
hurled the volume as far as I could and watched with satisfaction as the
book landed, burst into flame, and quickly disappeared in the fireball.
Beside me, in the style of throwing grenades, Baby Dragon pitched in
three thick hard-covered volumes in quick succession and set off three
small explosions of black ashes and sparks.

"What are they?" I asked.

"That infamous feudal relic—*The Dream of the Red Chamber*," Baby
Dragon replied breathlessly. He bent down again to scoop another heavy
set of books out of the satchel.

"Don't throw everything in at once," I cautioned. "Save some fun for
later."

Baby Dragon straightened up and grinned. We both watched happily
as the pages of his famous eighteenth-century novel curled up one by
one, blackened, and then danced as glowing embers and charred flakes.
Looking around, we watched other people pitching in books. Despite
the heat and sweat, everybody was smiling and the whole scene was like
the Lantern Festival held once a year on this soccer field.

A few feet from us, a small girl, perhaps four or five, toddled forward
with a big book. "Go on, Little Flower," urged her father, a man with
thick glasses. "Yes, Little Revolutionary, go on!" I shouted to the little
girl. She heaved the book toward the blaze with all her might. But the
book was too heavy and it plopped to the ground just outside the reach
of the flames. The girl made a helpless step toward the book but was
scooped up by her father.

"Allow *me*," Baby Dragon said. He had always liked to perform such
little heroic acts. Pulling down his shirt to shield his face from the heat,
he crawled on all fours toward the fire and bravely extracted the volume
from the edge of the fire. He flipped over the volume and, with false sadness on his face, showed me the title. It was a collection of two years'
worth of issues of *The Young Scientist*, bound in black leather. He knew
the volume would be of some interest to me, since I was considered a science whiz in our school.

"Should I?" he opened his mouth wide and asked.

"Does it have a red cover?" I asked back. And we all knew the answer.
Only the Great Leader's books have red covers and thus the right to live.

"No red cover, no pardon!" I said, smiling and pointing to the fire.

"Yeees, Comrade Shen!" Baby Dragon said in an exaggerated revolutionary tone and gave me an army salute. He turned around, clutched the heavy book in both hands, rotated on his heels as if beginning a hammer-throw, and flung the book to the top of the bonfire.

"Good job!" said a familiar nasal voice behind us. With the voice, the angular shape of our friend Snivel emerged, his usually sallow face glowing with sweat and his eyes shining with wild excitement. Aided by the heat, the streams of mucus under his nose—for which he was famous throughout school—were longer than usual and already extended past his parched lips. He was a year older than we, having failed the third grade once, but he was a street-smart kid and a good friend who knew how to have fun. He dropped on the ground two bundles of books tied with twine.

"Burn! Burn! Burn! Let's burn the whole world!" he said and sniffed at the smoke as if savoring the delicious aroma of a freshly roasted Peking duck. He kicked the strings loose, picked out a hardback book, and balanced it carefully on one foot.

"Watch this, Fan Shen!" he said. He took a step forward, flicked his leg, and kicked the book high in the air. Its arced trajectory made it look like a small missile. When it came down, it slammed into the ashes and generated a whooshing boom and an impressive mushroom cloud of burning embers.

Following Snivel's example, we kicked the books high and enjoyed their explosive landings. Volume after volume, books went up in flames. The warmth of the flames had an intoxicating effect on all of us, and we worked tirelessly to stoke the fire to make it go higher and higher. The giant fire gave me a sense of power, a power so invincible that I felt as if we could extend it without limit and conquer the world tomorrow, as the revolutionary slogans said.

The bonfire burned the whole afternoon and into the night. Its flames sometimes looked like a red hand waving in the inky evening sky, beckoning and enchanting us to bring more books to it. We obeyed its command. Baby Dragon and I went back home one more time and brought more books to it. I burned everything on my bookshelf. Even though I loved books as a child, I loved the fire and the revolution more. The teachers told us that except for the red-covered books, almost all the other books were bourgeois (we learned the word "bourgeois" in kindergarten and knew it was a very bad word) and must be burned. I even burned some of my father's technical books. I figured that he probably would not be mad at me because he had not used those books for years and had once mentioned selling them.

I got home that night around midnight, thirsty, hungry, and tired, but still feeling warm and excited from the fire. My parents were waiting for me in the hall when I entered, and from my father's face I thought I was in big trouble. He must have found out that I had burned some of his technical books. "I was out doing revolution at school," I told them right away, hoping to ward off their anger. "We burned all the bourgeois books today. And we have started a big revolution." Surprisingly, my parents' faces cleared up and they did not scold me for coming back so late. The word *revolution* seemed to have a magical effect on them. Upon hearing the word, my father said it was all right and he did not need those technical books any more and my mother smiled and said that she was proud of me for burning all those bourgeois books. "Let me cook some egg noodles for the hungry little revolutionary," she said and tenderly rubbed my head. Revolution, I realized that night, had made me their equal, their comrade. My sister did not speak to me for two days for burning her books, but I made it up to her by giving her my favorite pen that my aunt Zan Mei brought back for me from Moscow.

My parents were naturally proud that I became a revolutionary at a young age. They were proud that I carried on the family tradition. The tradition started with my paternal grandfather, Shen Tiansheng, who joined the Boxer Rebellion in 1900 when he was not yet fourteen. He was born in the south in a big poor peasant family with eight children (he was the second son) but moved to Beijing during a famine in the 1890s. He became a pushcart driver as soon as he turned eleven to help support the family. When the Boxers rose up and killed foreign missionaries in Beijing, he and his older brother joined their siege of the foreign embassies in the downtown. They fought bravely for two months, until the rebellion was crushed by the troops of eight imperialist countries. When Beijing was lost, his brother was captured and beheaded by the Russian troops, but my grandpa escaped to Shanghai, where he settled down and was married. Through hard work, he eventually became a postmaster and made a comfortable living. In 1938, after the Japanese invaded China, he secretly joined the Communist Party and began providing intelligence to communist guerrillas who were fighting the Japanese. Just before the end of World War II, he was arrested by the Japanese. "They tortured Grandpa and put Grandpa on the tiger bench and broke one of his legs," my mother told me. "He fainted twice, but he was so brave that he did not say anything, just like those heroes in movies." Grandpa was later rescued by his friends, who had connections to local gangsters. After the communists took over the country in 1949, he became a deputy mayor of Shanghai. When he died of illness in 1958, he was honored with a state funeral, and even the Great Leader sent a personal wreath, which was a point of pride for my parents. "I'd be happy to die any day," my mother said jokingly one day, "if only I could get a wreath from the Great Leader."

My father's revolutionary career started even earlier, at the age of twelve. When the Japanese bombed Shanghai and started invading southern China in 1938, my grandfather took my father on a secret journey out of the city. They traveled in a donkey cart all night, passed several Japanese checkpoints, and arrived at a mountain village by dawn. There, after a breakfast at a country inn, Grandpa left my father with two "uncles" and returned to his family in Shanghai. The two "uncles" were actually officers from a communist guerrilla organization. They took my father to a guerrilla camp deep in the mountain that day, gave him a small rifle, and made him a soldier. For the next seven years, my father fought the Japanese with the guerrillas and did not see his family until the end of the war. Although he told me very little about his fighting, I knew he fought bravely in battles. In the closet in his bedroom, I was very excited one day to find a small pamphlet printed by the army entitled "The Stories of Shen Nang: An Army Hero" and learn that my father had been wounded twice, awarded several medals, and promoted to captain when he was barely eighteen. "He was the youngest colonel in the Big Courtyard when we moved here in 1959," my mother told me proudly.

My mother also joined the revolution young. She was born to a comfortable intellectual family in Shanghai. Her father, my grandpa (whom I never met), was a professor of Chinese literature in Tongji University in Shanghai, but he was paralyzed during a treacherous trip out of the city during a Japanese air raid. He and his students were hiding in a rice paddy for four days in the pouring rain when he suffered acute rheumatism and was carried back by his students. He never got out of bed again and died fifteen years later. Impoverished after my grandfather's illness, my mother and her older sister, Zan Mei, left the family and joined the Communist Army together in 1948. My mother was fifteen. Like my father, she became an ardent communist and worked selflessly for the Communist Party. In the army, she worked as a radio operator, and was eventually promoted to be a lieutenant. Right before the end of the civil war that led to the founding of the People's Republic of China in 1949, my mother met my father in the army, and found him a perfect match as a revolutionary.

Both my mother and my father were the kind of true revolutionaries that I often read about in books, the kind of people who do not hesitate to sacrifice anything personal for the cause of the state and the Party. When I was still young, mother told me, without any regret, that she often had to leave me in the middle of breastfeeding to rush to work. "You cried so hard and so pitifully that your nanny cried with you too," she said, smiling and very proud. She was a revolutionary first, and a mother second. And she's proud of that, as all revolutionaries were in those years. "Your father is an even better revolutionary," she said with real admiration. "He was an army inspector when you and your sister were born, and when I was giving birth to you, he went away on business and came back when you were a month old. I walked two miles by myself to the hospital to give birth to you." As a good revolutionary, she accepted such sacrifice as simply something a revolutionary must do.

I knew these family stories since the very beginning of my memory, so I did not feel strange at all when I officially joined the revolution at my young age. On the day we burned all the books, I was full of enthusiasm and hope. I was glad that my revolution, for which I had been prepared for years, had come, and I jumped into it with all my youthful energy and conviction. I had no doubt that I, as my grandpa and my parents had done in the previous revolutions, would become a hero in this revolution.

**"Long Live the Red Terror!"**

Chairman Mao, the Great Leader, officially launched the Cultural Revolution in his May 17 proclamation in the *People's Daily*, calling for the masses to smash the five-thousand-year-old Chinese culture and to rid the country of any foreign influence, in order to build a brand new communist culture. "Power to the Red Guards!" said the Great Leader. "Expose and destroy the hidden enemies who have been sleeping among your ranks!" ordered the Great Leader. Overnight, people young and old all rose at the summons of the Great Leader. After the giant bonfire, the fire of the Revolution spread fast and wide throughout the Big Courtyard.

No one could have imagined that such chaos was possible in the Big Courtyard, whose buildings were most stern-looking and whose life, for adults and children alike, was highly regulated. Situated at the west end of the long and wide Eternal Peace Boulevard that runs from east to west through the whole city of Beijing, the Big Courtyard is an enclosed compound with high, solemn gray walls that housed the headquarters of the People's Liberation Army. A square park with short pine trees divides the Big Courtyard evenly into two parts: the residential area on the south and the business area on the north. The south side is a self-sufficient and orderly community, with sixteen identical four-story apartment buildings neatly arranged in four blocks, a hospital, a shopping complex, a huge public dining hall where all my friends and I bought our meals with food coupons since we were in first grade, and the Flying Wing School, which I attended since I was three. This is the whole sphere of my childhood and I never knew any freedom growing up in such an orderly place. Every minute of my life, from the moment I was awakened in the morning to the moment I was put to bed, was carefully planned by my parents and teachers. I was not allowed to go outside of the gray wall that encircled the Big Courtyard and I never played with children outside. Nor was I allowed to go beyond the little park lined with trimmed pine trees to the north side, which is called the "Little Forbidden City" and is guarded by soldiers. The north side always seemed to me like a ghost city with clean and quiet and empty streets leading to the three cheerless, dark-green office buildings on the right, and to several smaller brown buildings known as generals' quarters on the left.

But in just a few days, the call of the Great Leader turned the quiet and orderly Big Courtyard into a big boiling cauldron, and the normal life that I had been living was shattered. The adults in the Big Courtyard and the senior students at our school formed various Red Guard teams and began writing big-letter posters and holding all kinds of rallies around the clock. My school was closed the day after we burned the books, and we were told to join the revolution. I was overjoyed. No school and a revolution! Nothing could be better! I especially enjoyed the freedom that I suddenly gained from my parents: they became so busy attending meetings that they were hardly home during the day and were forced to allow me more freedom to come and go, as long as I went out to read revolutionary posters and did not forget to take my sister to the public dining hall to eat.

Having been brought up in a very strict family, I took full advantage of my newfound freedom and went out every day to read posters or to simply get away from the apartment. No more torturous afternoon naps! For many days, I roamed the Big Courtyard with my friends and stood among adults reading the innumerable sensational and entertaining posters. At the outset of the revolution, the posters were hung in neat rows in my school's classrooms and auditorium, but soon they spread out onto any space available. The larger ones were posted on the walls and windows of residential buildings or hung from long ropes strung among the pine trees in the park, and the smaller ones on lampposts and tree trunks. At first, most posters were serious debates among various Red Guard "fighting teams," all of which bore impressive names like "Red Iron-Fist Corps," "The Crimson-Terror Battalion," and "The Scarlet-Blood Regiment." It was a totally confusing war of words for a twelve-year-old like me. For all I could make out, all the Red Guard teams claimed to be fighting for the Great Leader, but they could not agree on who were the hidden enemies that the Great Leader wanted them to expose. Oddly, they seemed to find the hidden enemies in other Red Guard teams, and they seemed to hate each other so much that they called each other "guards of capitalist dogs" and wanted to chop their opponents with "ten thousand knives" as if they were worse than Japanese Devils. It is truly amazing, when I think back on those posters, that the Red

Guards used so much paper and ink to fight each other when they were all comrades under the Great Leader. But in those days, nobody saw the ridiculousness of the fight among Red Guard factions.

I certainly did not. For quite a few days, I racked my young brain reading the confusing posters and trying to detect who the real enemy was. But the more I read, the more confused I was and, finally, I lost interest in the debate and turned my attention to more entertaining posters, which started to appear more often. These were amusing exposés of the dirty pasts and corrupt lifestyles of members of the opposing factions. One such poster gave a graphic account of a young school nurse's affair with an older officer; another detailed the collection of fine clothes and furs that our school superintendent had; and a third exposed a math teacher who had a taste for imported beer and cigarettes. All of these would be silly and insignificant charges today, but were considered grave bourgeois offenses in those days. The poster which drew the largest crowd exposed a shocking incident about the former chairman, Liu Shaoqi. When he visited Indonesia, the poster said, he was invited by Sukarno, the president of Indonesia, to watch naked women bathe in a specially designed pool with secret observation windows. To this day I don't know if these stories were true or not, but in those days, I believed everything in the posters.

The first few weeks of the revolution went breathtakingly quickly and except for a few hours of sleep each night, I was hardly home, not wanting to miss any exciting event of the revolution. During the day, with all the seriousness of a little revolutionary, I entertained myself by reading sensational stories that grew more bizarre each day. Since the big-letter posters had made all the buildings open for inspection, my friends and I were allowed into the formerly tightly guarded "Little Forbidden City" and into those dark green office buildings to read posters. But the real fun was at night. I wolfed down my dinner at the dining hall as quickly as I could and ran out with my friends to see "struggle rallies" at my school where "capitalists and their running dogs" were paraded and humiliated. Night after night, my friends and I sat in the front row and took in the drama: our old math teacher, with dignified white hair, crying and begging for mercy; the superintendent of my school, a middle-aged woman, getting her face painted black by Red Guards; and a senior student wearing a Red Guard armband collapsing and falling off the stage after tearfully shouting revolutionary slogans.

Not long after the Great Leader's proclamation, the sultry summer temperatures rose exponentially in Beijing, and so did the intensity of the revolution. The attendance at the nightly "struggle rallies" swelled quickly from a few dozen to several thousand. In late June I attended three massive "ten-thousand-man" rallies, which brought Red Guards from all over Beijing to the Big Courtyard. A gigantic open stage was hastily constructed on the soccer field just for these rallies.

The first mass rally was against General Luo, the former Chief of Staff of the People's Liberation Army, who the Red Guards said was a hidden traitor. As usual, before the rally began, my friends Baby Dragon and Snivel and I worked our way through the legs of adults and found a perfect spot directly in the front of the stage. Sitting in a sea of red—red flags, red armbands, red banners with slogans—I was very excited and was very eager to do my part to fight the enemy who had been hiding in the army for so many years. When the rally started in the early evening, the general was brought onto the stage by two Red Guards amid a deafening roar of revolutionary slogans. He wore white casts on both his legs and could not stand on his own. "He tried to jump out of a second-floor window, pretending to commit suicide," a nearby member of the Red Guard told us.

The general was planted in a chair on the stage, but the guards had scarcely released their grip and turned their backs when the old man collapsed and slumped to the ground. In the sharp bluish floodlight, his face had turned ghastly white, like a piece of tofu.

"He is playing dead!" Baby Dragon shouted.

"Pull him up! Pull him up!" Snivel and I shouted.

"Pretending to be dead won't save your skin!" the man who just gave us the information on the general yelled at his white, lifeless face.

A soldier with a red armband strutted over and splashed a glass of cold water on the ashen face on the ground, but the general barely moved. The soldier bent down and pulled the general's head up by the hair. We clapped our hands and laughed at the distorted, ugly face. The old man moaned and his jaws flapped mechanically as if he were drowning, gasping for air.

"He knows how to put on a show," our informant said to us and we all laughed.

"Don't try to fool us," I shouted to the old man. "Stand up and face the people!"

The soldier propped him up on the chair again. From where we stood, we could almost touch the general's blanched face. His face was so haunting in its pallor that many nights after the rally I could still vividly see the sunken eye sockets, the bluish lips, the chalky skin wrapped around a skeleton, the sweat-soaked dusty green uniform, the half-torn insignia, and the trembling hands. Of course, as I gazed at the ghastly figure, I felt no pity.

Now that the target of the rally had been stabilized, the meeting began. As with all such rallies, it began with thunderous slogans bellowed from loudspeakers. Like a row of gigantic black toads, the loudspeakers formed a semicircle around the edge of the stage, barely three yards from our faces. The sound from them was so powerful that I could feel each syllable strike my face.

"CONFESSION OR DEATH!"

"LONG LIVE THE RED TERROR!"

"LONG LIVE THE GREAT CULTURAL REVOLUTION!"

We raised our fists and shouted with the loudspeakers. The shouting served its purpose. It got our blood boiling and we got more and more angry at the enemy sitting before us. One after another, people read indictment papers and we shouted more slogans after each one. We were halfway through the rally when the old general again slipped off the chair and slumped to the ground.

"He's playing dead again!" My friends and I shouted. "Get him up! Get him up!"

A soldier walked over and tried to pull him back onto the chair. He then frowned and checked the old general's pulse. "He's dead!" he shouted to the people in front of the stage. "He's really dead!"

We did not believe him. Several people went on stage and checked again. But it was true. The man was dead—probably from a heart attack.

We did not feel sorry for him, though. Revolutionaries, as we were taught since childhood, should feel no mercy for enemies. In fact, we became angrier at him for dying so soon. The rally went on with even greater fervor for another hour, and I, along with all the Red Guards, shouted slogans at the dead body on the chair, denouncing the general's treacherous final act of escaping the revolution prematurely. It was the first time that I saw a dead man, but I did not feel the terror of death, for the fervor of the revolutionary fire around me had temporarily removed the possibility of fear.

The target of the second "ten-thousand-man" rally was the mayor of Beijing, Peng Zhen, and the rally was more fun than the first. When the mayor was brought on stage, he wore a cream-colored Western suit splashed with red paint and a paper stove-pipe hat that was as long as his body. His wife, a fat, nondescript woman, was wearing a ridiculously tight red dress. The dress was slit up the side to expose her red underwear, and through the tear we could see her plump white thighs. She was also wearing high-heeled shoes which were obviously too small for her feet. During the rally, several Red Guards shaved half of her head in a "yin-yang" fashion and made her walk about the stage like a prostitute. As she staggered on the high heels and wagged her half-shaved head this way and that, she looked monstrously comical. We roared with laughter. The mayor and his wife were smart people and they did everything they were asked to. Both of them knelt down before us and knocked their heads loudly on the ground, like grandchildren kowtow to their grandparents during Chinese New Year. The audience was amused by their obedience and satisfied that they bowed down before the people. As a result of their complete submission to the will of the people, the mayor and his wife survived the rally without much bodily harm. Strangely, the rally ended with everybody in a jocular mood.

The target of the third massive rally was General Hei, deputy commander of the army. This was a much more serious rally and had none of the comic atmosphere of the previous rally. From the very beginning of the rally, we found that we were faced with a hardcore enemy who refused to submit to the will of the revolutionary people. As soon as he was brought on stage, General Hei refused to bow down before the people. He was a large and powerful man and when two Red Guards tried to press his head down, he struggled fiercely to keep his head up. Finally, amid deafening slogans from the loudspeakers, an angry Red Guard member leaped onto the stage, slapped the general, tore off his red insignia, and stripped him to his underwear. We all cheered and applauded.

"That's right!" Snivel shouted. "Teach him a lesson!"

"DEATH TO THOSE WHO REFUSE TO BOW DOWN BEFORE THE PEOPLE!"

"DOWN WITH THE HARDENED ENEMY GENERAL HEI!"

The two announcers shouted angrily over the loudspeakers, and we all raised our fists and shouted with them. Blood dripped from the old man's mouth. The general was shocked by the blows and by the thunderous shouting of thousands of voices. He ceased to struggle and let his head be pressed down, but people were not satisfied. "Give him an airplane ride!" someone shouted in the audience. "Yes, an airplane ride! An airplane ride!" we all shouted in chorus. Following popular demand, the three Red Guards on stage twisted his arms back like the wings of an airplane and forced him to bend over until his face almost touched the ground. In just a few minutes, his face became a giant purple raspberry, and a long strand of saliva extended from his mouth onto the stage floor. Despite the airplane ride, General Hei was tough and did not beg for mercy, and he got more for his stubbornness.

After the rally, he was paraded around the Big Courtyard in his underwear. A Red Guard tied a rope around his neck and led him around like a dog. We followed him all the way and prodded his sides with sticks whenever he slowed down. I felt no guilt at all when I thrust my stick into the man's bruised legs and arms to get him going. I was a good revolutionary then.

In addition to these grievous and dramatic "struggle rallies," there were massive jocular rallies, where we sang and danced around bonfires and soldiers fired small rockets and firecrackers to celebrate the Great Leader's latest decrees. Worship of the Great Leader reached a fever pitch at those rallies. One rally, for example, which took place right after the rally against General Hei, was to celebrate the occasion of Chairman Mao's sending a case of mangos, a gift he received from the tropical province of Hainan, to the Red Guards of Beijing. The mangos, people proclaimed, were symbols of the Great Leader's love of and trust in the Red Guards. Some people immediately made wax replicas of the mangos and sent them to cities across China, where they were enshrined. Thousands of people shed tears visiting and bowing to them. Even then, it seemed kind of comical to see people bow down before the wax mangos installed in the lobby of my school, but I did not dare to say anything. I do not know what happened to the real mangos and have often wondered about them. No one dared to eat them, that is for sure. Were they permanently preserved in some way? Were they put in large glass jars filled with Formalin preservative? I had seen roundworms preserved in such jars in the nurse's office in my school. Or did the mangos eventually rot? When they rotted, did people dare to throw them away? Would that be considered disrespectful to the Great Leader? I knew, of course, even at the age of twelve, that these were childish questions that should never be asked.

One afternoon, however, the thus far joyful revolution took a sudden turn for me when I saw my first bloody body. This was the first time that I sensed the terrible dark side of the revolution and began to experience a fear of its brutal force.

It was another of those humid afternoons, after the workers had sprayed the poplar trees with lime-water for the third time in as many months in a vain attempt to eradicate the cicadas. Baby Dragon, Snivel, and I had just sat down in the public dining hall to eat lunch when we heard a commotion outside and saw many people running in the direction of the "Little Forbidden City." I threw down my chopsticks and ran outside.

"What happened?" I asked, after flagging down a young boy who trailed a group of older boys.

"A body, a dead man. Someone . . . jumped off . . . a building," stammered the boy, quite out of breath.

I went back in and shouted to my friends: "Let's go. A man jumped off a building."

The front of the dark green office building was packed with people by the time the three of us arrived. Most of the crowd was youngsters our own age. Despite the crowd, there was not a sound to be heard. Everybody was still and was staring at a twisted lump lying motionless on the concrete. The man must have landed on his head, for it had half disappeared into his neck. Dark blood soaked his brown uniform. His hands were tied behind his back. Since he was facing down, I could see only the back of his head. His white hair, sticky with blood, stood up like the needles on the back of a porcupine.

"Who is he?" Baby Dragon whispered.

"General Hei," answered a tall, skinny young man who did not bother to turn his face as he spoke. I remembered the old man's agonized demeanor when he was paraded in his underwear a few days before. It was so recent that I could still remember how it felt when my stick struck his thigh.

"No need to pity him," a soldier with a red armband said to break the spell of silence. "He was a hidden enemy of the revolution. This is what he deserved in the first place."

The young boy who had informed us of the event at the dining hall stepped out of the circle and inched up to the body. He had a stick in his hand. Very carefully, he thrust the stick under the chest of the dead man, and using it as a lever, he pried the body up and over. My heart fluttered uncomfortably as one side of the body slowly rose. I averted my eyes when the body flipped over. I heard the people gasp. When I turned my eyes back, I saw the most terrible sight: the dead man's face, smeared in dark purple blood, was completely flat—the nose, the eyes, and the mouth were flattened as if they were slits drawn with crayon on a dark purple sheet of paper. What made the horrible face more frightening were two white teeth, which stuck out and gave it a sinister grin.

Neither my friends nor I waited to see the body removed. Nor did we return to the dining hall to finish our meal that afternoon. For many days after that, I did not go near the green building. Even from a distance, I seemed to be able to see the dark stain on the ground and to smell the stench of violent death.

I tried to tell myself not to be troubled by the ugly death, though. After all, the Great Leader had said that "Revolution is not a dinner party, not painting or embroidery, and cannot be gentle and polite," and we should not pity the enemies who were beaten or humiliated to death by revolutionary people. Still, the sight of the horrible grinning face left a terrible image in my mind that would not go away. I began to feel afraid, for I knew that I had played a role in the old man's death and that I would be punished one way or another. I did not admit to my friends that I was afraid of ghosts, but for months after the death of the old general, I always carried a rock in each of my hands whenever I walked in dark places at night, and braced myself for a fight with the general's ghost.

## 3 "That's My Piano!"

General Hei's death is not the only event that still troubles my sleep these days. I was involved in another event that not only resulted in a death which left an indelible guilt in my heart, but also changed my life in subtle ways that became clear only many years later. It started on a stuffy morning when Baby Dragon barged into my room without our customary coded knocking.

"Get up! Let's go! Quick!" he said. I was lying on a wet mat, trying to cool down from the heat. This was two weeks after General Hei's death and I had been avoiding going to struggle rallies where people like General Hei got beaten.

"What's the rush? Your house on fire?" I asked, swinging my legs slowly from the reed mat to the floor to sit up. I thought he was going to drag me to another of those struggle rallies.

"*Military campaign*, top secret!" he said impatiently.

He used the buzzword *military* to get my attention. I knew anything having to do with military always set Baby Dragon on fire. For as long as I could remember, Baby Dragon had liked fights, even though he was clearly less than adept at fighting; he threw his arms about like drumsticks and often took more hits than he gave. His ambition was to be an army general. His feeling that his destiny was a glorious military career was rooted, first of all, in his given name, *Long*, which means "dragon." Dragons are the best fighters according to Chinese legend. Even the fact that he was born in the Year of the Snake, and not the Year of the Dragon, did not discourage him from associating himself with the fabled firedrake. "A snake is actually a *little dragon*," he used to explain to me in all seriousness. "People with a dragon in their names often end up as generals, like Marshal He Long, who was also born in the Year of the Little Dragon."

"What military campaign? Who's the *general*?" I asked, playing along with him.

"It's a campaign to search the house of a big capitalist," he said very seriously. "As a matter of fact, my sister is the general. I just saw them leave and she told me where they were going."

That finally got my attention. Baby Dragon's big sister, Dragon Sister, had recently joined an elite Red Guard organization, the United Red Action Committee, whose teenage members were all children of military officers from the Big Courtyard. To distinguish themselves, they all donned green army uniforms, white basketball shoes, two-inch-wide Sam Browne belts, and elaborately embroidered red silk armbands. Sweeping through the Big Courtyard on shining bicycles, they had become known as the "Reddest" group, "so Red that we have turned purple," as they described themselves. Their fame, however, rested not on their distinctive outfits, but on their famous battle cry—"Long Live the Red Terror!"—and their merciless attacks on anyone they identified as anti-revolutionaries, bourgeois, or traitors.

"Are you coming or not? We are already late." He was genuinely exasperated now.

I needed no more prodding. I slipped on my rubber shoes and said, "Let's go."

It was around noon when Baby Dragon and I arrived by bus at a house in the old residential district just behind the Imperial Palace. It was an area lined with narrow alleys and older houses with traditional square yards. Thirty or forty people, mostly high-school-aged youths like Baby Dragon's sister, had already gathered around the corner. A long row of shining bicycles rested neatly against the wall. True to their image, these youths of the Red Action Committee all wore green army uniforms and red silk armbands with golden trimming, their sleeves all rolled up. Their trademark white basketball shoes gleamed conspicuously in the sun. I was quite impressed by their uniforms.

As Baby Dragon and I joined the group, I could feel the palpable excitement of the crowd. Some of the Red Guards carried clubs, while a few others had wide army belts in their hands. Dragon Sister had already divided them into four groups and was issuing the final order: "Group One, attack the front door. Group Two, guard the back door of the yard. Group Three, guard the family members to prevent them from hiding anything. And Group Four, search the house. There will be no mercy for the enemy. Let's do this for Chairman Mao. Long Live the Red Terror!"

"LONG LIVE THE RED TERROR!" everybody around me echoed.

After the battle cry, the white shoes broke into a run in different directions, and I followed one group to the front door.

A rough-faced young man with long curly whiskers led the group. He went up the steps and shouted: "Open the door! The Red Action Committee!" and with that he raised his club and struck the heavy black-lacquered door.

And strangely, as soon as the club touched the door it swung open, as if someone had been waiting inside for an anticipated visitor. A gentleman, around fifty-five, in a white silk shirt and cream-colored, impeccably pressed dress pants, materialized in the doorframe. He had a broad smile on his face and his arms were outstretched to greet us.

"Comrade Red Guards, welco—"

Before he could finish the sentence, however, Whiskers had slapped him sharply across the face. "Fuck you bourgeois!" he snarled. "Why *tamade* were you so slow to open the door? Don't give me that fake smile! Were you *tamade* trying to hide anything? I'll *tamade* teach you to respect your Red Guard Grandfathers!"

The Chinese national curse word *tamade*, the very worst thing one could say to someone, sounded even more slimy than usual in his street accent. He swung his fist at the man again. The man tried to fend off the blow with his arm, but did not dare to try too hard, evidently afraid of disappointing the attacker and thus inviting more blows. The fist caught him flush on the nose. The man staggered backward, still trying to smile. All of a sudden, I felt sorry for the man. I did not like Whiskers's cruelty, even though it was done to an enemy.

"Get the fuck out of the way!" Whiskers thrust his club into the man's chest and shoved him aside.

People poured into the yard. The old man's face seemed to have frozen into a distorted smile as I passed him. A dark bump was beginning to rise over his right eye, and a thin red trickle dripped slowly from his nose onto his white silk shirt.

The rectangular yard, paved with oversized pale green imperial bricks, was large and peaceful and cool—a sharp contrast to the dusty and sultry street outside. The tall stonewall, covered with green vines, seemed to rise indefinitely above its top, keeping the cool air inside. A footpath of large granite slabs led to a trellis of grapes and through it to the main house. On the right side of the trellis, under a gigantic oak tree that must have been a hundred years old, a flower garden bloomed. Beside it stood a small marble table and four marble stools. A delicate white porcelain teapot, two teacups, an open magazine, and a plate of fried peanuts were spread out on the stone table. The scene was like a picture of The Fairy's Peach Garden that I had read about in a book.

"Damn the bourgeois!" a girl walking before me muttered, her long ponytails under the army cap slapping prettily against her hips. She strutted toward the marble table. "During the Cultural Revolution he still dares to hide here and enjoy his bourgeois life!"

Suddenly, with one broad sweep of her stick, she smashed the teapot and the teacups, sending the white fragments showering down on the blooming peonies and azaleas. Peanuts flew everywhere. Two chickens dashed out from nowhere and started pecking at them feverishly. "We'll cook the chicken later," she said to Baby Dragon and me, and we smiled back at her.

The veranda in front of the main room was adorned like a life-sized dollhouse, a set of four red wicker chairs and a tea table neatly arranged in a semicircle. The door leading to the living room was wide open. I followed the bouncing long ponytails and the swinging hips onto the veranda and then into the house. As I crossed the threshold, I nearly brushed three silent figures—a woman with two girls huddled half hidden behind the door.

Obviously, they were the rest of the family who had been rounded up by the Red Guards. A tall young man with acne was guarding them with a club. The woman had large eyes and smooth skin, and was perhaps no more than forty-five years of age. Her nose was small compared to her large round face. The taller girl beside her was almost a carbon copy of her mother, except she was a bit slimmer. She nestled tightly against her mother's bosom, and kept her eyes on her feet. She was crying.

It was the younger girl's demeanor, however, that strangely startled me. Never before, in life or in movies, had I seen such arresting and unsettling features. Instead of the round and mild features of her mother and sister, her face was sharp and angular, and yet strikingly beautiful. She had a high-bridged nose, pointed chin, tight pale lips, very large and fiery eyes, and eyebrows which curved sharply upward like two Turkish swords. Hers was not a beauty that would inspire me to love and tenderness; rather, it was a beauty that seemed to intimidate and mock plain-looking people like me. With a silent hatred, she swept her eyes toward me, and I immediately felt uncomfortable and I became very conscious of myself. I looked down and avoided her eyes.

But my downcast eyes gave me more reason to feel uncomfortable when I saw her bright white socks and polished black leather shoes—

the kind I had seen on an imported foreign doll that my sister once had. They contrasted sharply to my dirty brown rubber shoes with their ugly canvas tops streaked with dried sweat. As much as I tried to put on an air of indifference, I could feel my legs wobble a little as I walked past the girl, as though I were walking on a balance beam. I was glad when the two people behind me walked into the house and sheltered me from those contemptuous and beautiful eyes.

There was a loud thud in the next room, as if a wall were being knocked down, followed by a string of cursing and laughter. The sitting room which I just entered was already a mess. The thick Oriental rug that covered three-quarters of the room with two golden, fire-breathing dragons chasing each other's tails, was strewn with paper and dirty footprints. The doors of the large glass cabinet standing at the far corner of the room were open, and a young man was taking out shiny glass goblets and pitchers and putting them on the end table. At the left corner of the room, the girl with the long ponytails was kneeling on a stool and was having trouble prying open the cover of the grand piano. "Does anyone have a screwdriver?" she yelled, but no one paid attention to her. On the big leather couch along the windows, I located my friend Baby Dragon, who was trying to turn it over to search underneath. I quickly past him and went toward a side door. I had become conscious again of the flaming eyes behind me.

I got out of the large sitting room as soon as I could and found myself in a spacious and cool side room. It was evidently the library. The room was lined with magnificent bookshelves, standing from floor to ceiling. In the middle of the room were a gigantic mahogany desk and several leather chairs. Several people were searching the bookshelves, taking the books off the selves, leafing through them, and dropping them on the carpet. Dragon Sister was pulling out the desk drawers. I looked around and found some large picture books. On the cover of one was a painting of a naked woman with large breasts. Having never seen a naked woman before, I felt blood surge to my cheeks as I casually looked at the book. The fat foreign woman was lying on a couch, with one hand supporting her head on the pillow and the other casually draped by her waist. Grabbing two or three other books and laying them aside—I did not want to appear to be interested only in the book with the naked woman—I sat down on the carpet to examine the book with the naked woman. I could not read it, however, because it was in a foreign language, so I flipped through the pages looking at the pictures. Many of them were of naked or half-naked women.

"You shouldn't look at that," a young man with a Sam Browne belt said to me as he snatched the book away from me. "These are bourgeois books and we will burn them later." He hurled the book onto a pile in the corner of the room.

I soon picked up another interesting book. This one was also in a foreign language, but it had a lot of colored photographs of the native peoples of Africa. Some women had large wooden plates inserted into their lower lips, making them look a bit like ducks. All of the women wore nothing on their upper bodies and the pictures showed every detail of their sagging, wrinkled breasts. Although most of them wore some sort of straw skirt, a few had nothing. They often were not facing the camera, much to my chagrin. I grabbed the picture book and started to look for other picture books that had naked women.

"Look what I found here!" exclaimed Dragon Sister, startling everybody in the room.

We all gathered around the mahogany desk. Lying at the center of the desk were three large glittering yellow bars. None of us had ever seen a gold bar before.

"The bastards told me that they had given the government everything, but they hid these in this hollowed-out book," said Dragon Sister proudly. "It felt very heavy when I took it out. Obviously they were saving these in expectation of returning to the old society."

"How much do they weigh?" asked the young man with the Sam Browne belt.

"One hundred ounces, it says here." A girl with the short combat-style hair pointed to the small numbers and foreign letters on the bar.

Sam Browne Belt said, "Let me see how heavy they are," and grabbed a bar and grimaced to the rest of us. "They say gold is the heaviest thing on earth."

Following everyone, I took the bar in my hand to feel the weight. It was cold and smooth and heavy.

"Now, listen, everyone," said Dragon Sister, wrapping up the gold bars in their original oilpaper. "Look very carefully at everything. There's got to be other things hidden in these rooms. Tear everything up. Look inside the sofas, under the floor, inside the walls. We have to confront the bastard with these gold bars and see if he will make a confession of other criminal possessions."

"Let's not forget the attic and the ceiling and the yard," suggested Sam Browne Belt. "Last week, we dug up an old landlady's yard and found a big jar full of silver dollars. All of the bourgeoisie have hidden treasures."

"I'll be the interrogator," Whiskers volunteered. Several of us followed him to the outer room. He walked swiftly to the door, pulled the gentleman out, and without a word, slapped the gentleman hard several times. "We have just found your gold," he said slowly, smiling. "Now, tell me where your other treasures are, or I will extract your oil and make a sky-lamp out of you." He raised his hand again, poised it in the air, and then slowly swept it across the man's face, as if to wipe the blood from his face. But suddenly he struck again with his backhand and the man moaned. I could almost feel the man's pain and I cringed at the man's cry.

Covering his face with both hands, the man said in a weak voice: "Don't beat me again, Red Guard Grandpa! I'll tell you everything! There is something in the mattress that I have forgotten to mention. I am so sorry that I have forgotten about it." Following his tip, Dragon Sister found a small silk pouch in one of the mattresses, which contained three gold rings and a diamond ring. But the new discovery made us believe that there had to be more.

We searched for two hours, tearing up everything, including the wallpaper. By the time we all gathered in the living room to pool together what we had found, it was already getting dark outside. On the oak coffee table were the spoils of the battle, and they were quite impressive: three large gold bars, sixty four one ounce silver dollars (found in a small jar in the chicken coop), three gold rings, a diamond ring, two pairs of jade bracelets, five American hundred-dollar bills (which I found hidden in a picture book), three bank passbooks with a total deposit of sixteen thousand yuan, and two gold chains, found in the woman's bra during a body search. There was also a small handgun, which was found wrapped in oilpaper in a jar of rice. Carefully putting everything into a canvas satchel, Dragon Sister turned to the gentleman, who sat on the ground with his wife and daughters near the front door.

"You bourgeois bastard," she said sternly to the gentleman. "You have committed the crime of trying to hide a gun and a large amount of gold and silver, and we are sure that these are just the tip of the iceberg. We must take you to our headquarters. I am sure that once you are there, you will remember more things that you have forgotten now. Take him to the truck!"

"*Please*," said the old man, putting together both of his hands and making a kowtow, "I swear to Chairman Mao that I have confessed to all the money that I have, and may the Five Thunders in Heaven strike me in half if I've lied to you. I have always been loyal to the Great Leader and his revolution . . . ." His hands, stained with the dried blood from his nose, trembled visibly.

"Get the hell up!" Whiskers kicked his thigh viciously. The man keeled over in pain. "Don't play chicken with us. It won't work. We know how sly you are."

Two young men grabbed his arms and pulled him out the door. "I am a revolutionary. I came back from America to serve the Great Leader. The Great Leader invited me. Ask . . ." the old man pleaded as he was half dragged through the garden. The tall girl started crying again, holding on tightly to her mother, who also started sobbing. Only the younger girl was silent. She sat still and glared at us.

"Take the piano away," ordered Dragon Sister. "Put it in the truck. Put all the light things in the truck, too. The rest will be sealed. The three of you," she pointed to the mother and daughters in the corner, "from now on you can stay in the servant's room by the front gate. The main house will be sealed until further notice."

"Can we take a few clothes with us?" asked the mother timidly.

"No," Dragon Sister answered without looking at her. "All the things here belong to the public now. You cannot touch anything here. You will have to learn to live like the laborers now."

People had already started to carry things to the truck. Eager to get out, I joined a group of young men and pushed the piano toward the entrance. Whiskers directed our complicated operation of easing it out the door. The piano was bulky and heavy and it got stuck in the doorframe. Whiskers got mad and gave the piano a hard kick.

"That's *my* piano! You can't take it away!" A strange voice suddenly came from nowhere and for a moment surprised and confused us. We looked up to see who dared to oppose the Red Guards.

"That's *my* piano," the young girl in the corner said again. Her voice was not loud, but it was clear and piercing. She was standing now, her hateful eyes peering at all of us with the piano. For a moment, we just stared at her, not knowing what to say.

"What did you *say*?" Whiskers finally found his voice. He moved to stand in front of the girl and stared down into her pale face. "*Your* piano? Say that again? You still fucking want to play the role of the little bourgeois girl?" He looked back at us, and several young men chortled loudly. "What's your name?" he turned back again and asked the girl.

"Li Ling," the girl said clearly, looking at Whiskers's face.

"Well, Li Ling, my bourgeois girl, I'm sorry to have to tell you that the piano is the people's piano now. We will chop it up and burn it for firewood tonight, and you are welcome to come and dance with us at the bonfire." He savagely banged his club several times on the cover of the piano to emphasize his point, leaving deep dents on the previously spotless black paint. "If you dare to say another word, I will damn well teach you to respect your Red Guard grandpas."

Cackling, he waved his hand in front Li Ling's face, as if to slap her. His comrades again laughed. The girl bit her lips and said nothing. But her fiery eyes still fastened on the face of Whiskers.

Standing behind the piano and holding a large picture book under my arm, I felt a strange urge to strike Whiskers and knock his teeth out. I imagined myself sneaking up behind him and kicking his knees very hard and sending him writhing on the ground. But I was not courageous and I made no move.

The woman grabbed the young girl's arm and pulled her closer.

"I knew you wouldn't dare to repeat that," said Whiskers. He smiled wickedly at the girl, and then waved at us to get moving.

We started again and pushed the piano out, but all the while, I felt certain that those large eyes, burning with hatred, followed me; I seemed to feel them boring into me as I ashamedly walked away. My legs started to wobble again.

Two days later, while eating dinner in the public dining hall, I asked Baby Dragon whose house we had ransacked.

"He is just a surgeon at the Beijing University Hospital," said my friend. "His dad, however, was a big capitalist, who used to own two textile factories in Shanghai. Everybody knew they had a lot of money. The father died ten years ago, so the son had inherited his father's capitalist hat and had to suffer the consequences. By the way, did you know that the man died after they took him to Red Action Committee headquarters that night?"

I felt an upsurge in my stomach. But I tried to remain calm, even nonchalant. "No. How did he die?"

"They did some really silly things to him when they got there," said Baby Dragon, taking a bite of a steamed bun. "They beat him with army belts first, and when he did not give any new information about his hidden treasures, someone—you remember Whiskers?—he cut open his belly with a surgical knife and poured a bottle of soy sauce into his guts. The man screamed like a pig. And then they poured a bucket of hot pepper water on his face. He rolled on the floor and jumped up and down, with his guts spilling out, and the guys just stood there laughing. Finally the man fell down the stairs, cracked his skull, and died that night. The guys there had a good time, although my sister thought it was a bit too cruel."

I felt sick; in my mind I had the image of the small, sharp surgical scalpel slicing open the man's flesh, revealing bluish, snake-like intestines.

Baby Dragon was not the sort of person to let horrendous pain and torture affect his appetite. Having swallowed the first bun and taken the second, he added in the tones of a pseudo-adult: "But of course, nothing is too cruel for an anti-revolutionary." He took a big bite and picked up a piece of pork with his chopsticks. "By the way, don't tell anyone about this. They told the people outside and his family that he committed suicide by jumping out the fourth-floor window. Just the death of an enemy. No one will care if we don't say anything."

I nodded and buried my head in a bowl of rice. I did not want this conversation to continue. This kind of revolution made me sick. The torture and killing of the doctor seemed extremely cruel and senseless. It seemed that Whiskers and his comrades tortured and killed people not for any revolutionary purpose, but for the pure enjoyment of it. Deep down in my heart, I knew this was not the kind of revolution that the Great Leader wanted and I told myself that I should stay away from Whiskers and his likes in the future.

I hid the large picture book with naked women that I took from the girl's house under my bed, for fear that my parents would see it. Only when there was no one at home did I dare to take it out and look at it.

Several weeks later, I went back to the house to see what had become of the woman and the girls, especially what had become of Li Ling, the younger girl. In the once cool and quiet yard I found, instead of the mother and the girls, six poor families living noisily in various rooms. The yard was littered with garbage and several naked children were playing on the marble table under the oak tree. There was no trace of the mother and her daughters. One of the new residents, a tall and fat woman who was the head of the local residents' committee, informed me that, after the death of the doctor, the mother tried to hang herself in one of the rooms, but was discovered in time by a Red Guard.

"To commit suicide is an anti-revolutionary act, you know," said the woman. "It won't be easy for her to try the same thing again. She is now sweeping the streets under guard everyday. We can't let the anti-revolutionaries get away so easily."

I slipped out of the yard very disappointed and wandered into the maze of the narrow side streets of the old city. I had a vague hope that, by chance, I might run into the young girl, even though her eyes had made me so uncomfortable that I knew I would not have the courage to speak to her.

I walked aimlessly for two hours and found no sign of the girl. Finally, tired, I decided to walk through the Jingshan Park to Tiananmen Square and from there take a bus home.

Near the gate of the former Imperial Park, however, I suddenly saw Li Ling. She was swinging a big bamboo broom and sweeping the street with her mother and sister. A young man with a red armband was guarding them. For a few minutes, I stood on the corner and watched her from a distance. She seemed very small with that large bamboo broom she was holding. I thought for a moment of walking past them, just to have a good look at her. But then, her head rose and her big eyes swept in my direction. I turned quickly around and walked away. I walked randomly for half an hour, not being able to muster enough courage to walk back to see her. After taking a long detour, I finally decided to go back to the park's gate. I tried to focus my eyes on the ground and walk fast, as if I were in a hurry to go somewhere. But, as I turned the corner toward the gate, she and her mother and sister were no longer there. I felt sort of relieved. Maybe it was better not to see her after all. On the bus home, I thought that I should forget about her, for a girl of her family background could only bring me a lot of trouble, and that I should never go back to her house again. Indeed, I never went back to try to find her, but, despite my decision, fate had arranged other places I would meet her again.

## 4  The Great Wall Fighting Team

On September 1, I went to school to see if it would open as it had in previous years, and I found out quickly—even without reading the notice at the gate—that the school would not open this year. In fact, most of the teachers and school officials were gone. Some, like my math teacher Mr. Tian, a plump old man who spoke with a woman's voice, had been arrested by the Red Guards as anti-revolutionaries and had been locked up in the basement of the school. Others, the "problem-free" ones, had joined the Red Guards and were devoting their time to revolutionary activities. Besides, most of the classrooms had been taken over as headquarters by various Red Guard organizations and were no longer available for schooling. Walking through the building, I visited a few headquarters and learned that any group of three or four like-minded individuals could declare itself a Red Guard fighting team and claim a classroom as its headquarters. That gave me an idea.

Later that day, while we were eating lunch at the public dining hall, I told my friends that I was forming a Red Guard team called "The Great Wall Fighting Team" and showed them the team's seal, which I carved out of a large square rubber eraser with my father's razor blade. "As long as you have a seal," I said to my friends, "you are a legitimate Red Guard team and you can claim a classroom as your headquarters. Anybody want to join me?" As I expected, I found four eager recruits on the spot.

After examining our official seal, the school's deputy principal gave me some red silk armbands bearing the words "Chairman Mao's Red Guard" and a key to a classroom on the third floor. Proudly wearing the brand new armbands, we marched to our new headquarters. On the door, Snivel painted "Great Wall Fighting Team Headquarters" in large red letters. We pushed the desks and chairs to one side, and sat down and had our first meeting. "Before we start," I said, "Let's give each of us a good title. Like the political bureau of the Communist Party. We won't be a proper revolutionary team without titles. I will be commander in chief. Baby Dragon, you are vice–commander in chief and since you like fighting, you will be our minister of defense. Snivel, you are good at stealing things and you should be our chief of logistics. Kangaroo, you do good calligraphy and you will be our secretary-general; and Sparrow, you have been drawing pictures since kindergarten and you'd better be our chief of propaganda."

Everybody was happy with their impressive titles. We then debated hotly about what to do next and we settled on a campaign to attack the former chairman Liu Shaoqi. We would draw cartoons to ridicule him.

The next morning we went into action with great enthusiasm. "Campaign Number One" went smoothly at first. Snivel, chief of logistics, managed to break into the supply room of the school and brought back brush pens, bottles of ink, rolls of paper, and a bucket of glue. Sparrow, chief of propaganda, copied the cartoons we found in Red Guard newspapers onto large posters. That afternoon, when the cartoons were done, we all went down and posted them on the stretch of wall in front of the school building that commanded the largest audience. Since the wall was facing a busy street, it did not take long for the cartoons to attract a small audience. Watching people gather around our handiwork—and especially seeing two girls giggle at our funny drawings—I felt proud that we had made a contribution to the revolution at last. "The Great Wall Fighting Team," said one of the girls. "Do you know them?" The other girl shook her head. I wished that I had the courage to step in front of them and say to them, "We are the Great Wall Fighting Team," but I was too shy to do that. Still, it was a very sweet moment for me and my friends.

But the fruits of our hard work did not last very long, and unexpected trouble began the next day. Early next morning, my friends and I went to the school building to enjoy our artistic work again and were shocked to find that our posters were all gone, covered up with another team's posters. The team that covered our posters was called "The Fearless Red Rebels."

"Who are these bad eggs?" Baby Dragon asked angrily. "Should we tear up their posters now?"

"Wait a while," I said, "Those adults are reading them. You can't destroy revolutionary posters in broad daylight."

"But we can't let these bad eggs get away with it," said Kangaroo. "I know them. It's Three Twirls's team. They are from the seventh grade. His father is the head of 'Chairman Mao's Iron Soldiers.' That bastard!"

I had heard of Three Twirls, who was famous for the three twirls on his head and for making trouble for teachers.

"Let's go back and draw more cartoons," I said to my team. "We will give them a taste of their own medicine tonight."

That night, when the schoolyard was completely deserted, we sneaked back in, tore down the enemy posters, and plastered up our own. Feeling avenged, we went home happily. "Now we have to find a way to defend our posters," Snivel said as we were about to separate and go to our own homes.

"Don't worry. I have a perfect plan," said Baby Dragon, our chief of defense. "You will see tomorrow morning."

The next morning, we found out that the perfect plan he devised consisted of the chief of defense himself sitting on the third-story windowsill and leaning halfway out, looking for anyone approaching the wall with a bucket of glue and a roll of paper. "If I see the Fearless Red Rebels coming," he told us, "I'll blow a whistle and we will all go down to confront those bad eggs."

Toward noon, the Chief's effort paid off. He spotted Three Twirls and a friend approaching our posters and blew the whistle at once. We all ran downstairs right away and were just in time to line up in front of our posters before they reached them. Three Twirls walked over with his friend and immediately found out that his posters had been covered. "Who the hell covered our posters?" he cursed loudly and spitted to our posters. "Who is this Great Wall Fighting Team?" He reached out his hand as if to tear down the last page that bore our signature.

Baby Dragon stepped in front of him and said: "Are you trying to tear down a revolutionary poster?"

Looking at the five of us, Three Twirls drew back and smiled. "I was just trying to take a closer look at the signatures on the poster. Who is the Great Wall Fighting Team?" he turned around and asked his friend.

"We are," said Baby Dragon proudly.

"So you are," said Three Twirls, spitting on the ground. "I'll remember you people and don't you forget me." He turned around with his friend and walked away.

For the whole afternoon, we waited nervously for him to come back, but he never did.

But Three Twirls did not forget us. The next morning, we found out that not only did Three Twirls's team cover our posters with theirs, but they had attacked the Great Wall Fighting Team viciously in their posters. "The Great Wall Fighting Team is a Den Full of Hidden Bourgeois

Snakes!" said their headline. "We have discovered," the poster went on to say, "that Fan Shen's father and Baby Dragon's father formed an anti-revolutionary clique who plotted against the revolution at their Sunday chess games." It was a venomous lie. Standing around their posters, Three Twirls and three of his Fearless Red Rebels were smiling at us.

Shaking with anger, Baby Dragon moved to Three Twirls but I took hold of his arm. We could not win a fistfight with them; they were bigger than we.

"Let's go," I said to my friend in low voice. "Remember: Ten years is not too long to wait for revenge. Confucius said that."

Back at our headquarters, I said to my team: "The Fearless Red Rebels has declared war on us. We have a real enemy now. We will let them see who the real owners of that wall are."

"Yeah," said Baby Dragon hotly. "If they want war, then they'll have it."

An intense war of posters had begun that day. It was a meaningless war when I think of it today, but we took it very seriously then. At three o'clock the next morning, Baby Dragon and I sneaked back in school and plastered our posters over Three Twirls's posters. "Revolutionary People, Beware the Wolf in Sheep's Clothing," said the headline of our poster. "Three Twirls Exposed as a Hidden Enemy of the Revolution!"

The next morning, it was our turn to smile at our enemy as Three Twirls read our posters with utter disgust. Since there were adults around, he and his friends could not do anything to our posters. This was the kind of revolution I enjoyed. Revolution to me had become a game and I devoted myself eagerly to playing it.

Several days later, we saw Three Twirls's posters covering ours again: "Latest News: Kangaroo's Mother a Former Thief and Snivel Still Wets Bed at Night!" They had resorted to ridiculous personal attacks.

We sneaked back again that night and covered their posters with our own personal attacks: "Rise Up, All Red Guards: Defeat the Fearless Red Rebels! Down with the Ugly Head of Three Twirls!"

The war of posters went on for nearly a month. Gradually, the guerrilla warfare with the Fearless Red Rebels evolved from covert operations into open hostility, from covering up each other's posters at night to throwing rocks at each other whenever we met in the vicinity of the posters. I became a little worried at this point because they were bigger kids and I did not like getting beaten up. But fortunately, before any one of us got hurt, a turn of events suddenly put Three Twirls out of action and handed us an unexpected victory.

One morning, we went to the school gate, expecting to see some fresh posters from Three Twirls, and were surprised to find our posters still on the wall. Beside our posters, a small poster from the Fearless Red Rebels delivered stunning news: "Yesterday, Chairman Mao's Iron Soldiers have discovered that Old Three Twirls had lied on his application form to join the Communist Party; he was not from a poor family as he claimed. He was, in fact, from a rich peasant family. As a result, the Iron Soldiers have expelled Old Three Twirls. And in accordance with our revolutionary slogan—*as the father is a reactionary, so is the son a bad egg*—the Fearless Red Rebels have decided to follow the example of the Iron Soldiers and expel Three Twirls." The poster also declared a truce with the Great Wall Fighting Team.

The sweetness of our victory, however, did not last long for me and my friends. Our posters stayed on our now undisputed wall for more than a week, uncovered and no longer read, and we started to get bored. We missed the thrill of the war with Three Twirls—the lookout, the nightly reconnaissance, the surgical operations of tearing down our rival's posters and putting up our own. I even missed the ugly head of Three Twirls.

It was not until after the National Day of October 1 that I found a new adventure for our team. One morning I noticed a poster at our school signed by Dragon Sister, who was the commander of the Red Action Committee. "An Urgent Appeal to All Red Guards in the Big Courtyard," said the poster. "Come to the Aid of the Red Action Committee, to Help Defend the Great Leader at Beijing University!" I had heard that there had been some clashes among Red Guard teams in Beijing University, and this sounded like a good opportunity for us to see some real action rather than creating useless posters.

"Our real battle has finally come," I announced to my friends later that day and explained the content of the poster. "We've got to help Baby Dragon's sister. Let's go to Beijing University tomorrow and help out."

"Of course we will go and help Dragon Sister. But how long are we going to stay there?" asked Snivel. "What should I say to my parents?"

"I think a few days," I said. "Tell them that we are going to a Red Guard meeting there."

In those days, Red Guards attending meetings were provided with free food by the city and since we were staying with Dragon Sister, it was not too hard to persuade our parents to let us go. As soon as we all got permission, the five of us set out by bus for Beijing University. I proudly carried a red banner bearing the name of the Great Wall Fighting Team. Thinking this would be a game like the one we played with Three Twirls,

I went with a light heart, not knowing the real danger that we were about to face. The journey took more than two hours and we arrived around noon at the No. 15 building at Beijing University. It was a gray three-story student dormitory, serving as the headquarters of the Red Action Committee. In an office on the ground floor we found Dragon Sister, who gave us a warm welcome. "We want to see some fighting," said Baby Dragon to his sister right away. "Where is the fighting?" "Don't worry," said Dragon Sister. "You'll get your fighting soon enough. Let me show you around first and then I'll send you to the frontline."

Following Dragon Sister, we walked around the building, passed a small lake, and came up to a check point at a two-lane cement road lined with ancient Chinese cedar trees. "The south side of this road is our territory," said Dragon Sister. "The north side is controlled by our enemy called 'Mao's Vanguards.' In the last few weeks, they have attacked us several times and have taken three buildings away from us."

"Over there," said she again, pointing to a gray building whose windows were mostly broken and sealed with bricks, "is the No. 12 Building. It was attacked twice last week and four people were injured there. They need reinforcements badly. That's where I am going to send you. Chunky will be here soon. He's the commander of that building."

While we waited for Chunky to come over to collect us, Dragon Sister told us more about him; he evidently was a legendary fighter for the Red Action Committee. "He used to be a star on the University track and field team, and now he's our fiercest fighter against the Vanguards," Dragon Sister said proudly. "Last week, when the Vanguards attacked, he guarded one entrance by himself and bravely fought four Vanguards; he wounded two of them with a spear. All Vanguards are afraid of him. He inherited the revolutionary spirit from his father, who was the Chairman of the Poor Peasants Association in his village. Chunky told me that when he was six, he saw his father shoot the village landlord and his wife like dogs at the riverbank. That's how he learned to deal with enemies without mercy."

Chunky showed up soon. He was a big man wearing a loose red T-shirt and brown pants with the cuffs rolled up to his knees. I was very impressed by the size of our commander's body. His bulging chest muscles, large nodular hands, and short, veiny shins all gave me the impression of a man of great strength. "Five of Chairman Mao's young soldiers! Welcome!" he said with a broad smile and gave each of us a firm tap on the shoulder. "I heard you want to see some fighting," he eyed Baby Dragon, who nodded eagerly. "Well, let's go and see some fighting then."

He led the way and we followed him eagerly.

Taking a short cut through a soccer field, we arrived at the No. 12 Building shortly. "Let's see the cannons first," Chunky said. "They are on the third floor. Then we will go around and meet other Red Guards here." The "cannons" turned out to be large slingshots made of V-shaped crude forks from a young cherry tree and two bicycle inner tubes. A pile of broken red bricks was the ammunition. A tall man, whose dark oily skin glistened with sweat, was adjusting the length of the inner tubes. "That's Water Buffalo," Chunky said. "He is the leader of this squad. Our best shooter." Downstairs, we saw a small group of students erecting a barricade of dismantled desks in front of an entrance. "See that skinny young man with a big white porcelain pipe in his mouth?" Chunky asked. "He's Smoking Devil, the smartest fighter we've got. The one with the spear is Whiskers." I recognized the rough-faced young man immediately. He was practicing his spear by repeatedly stabbing a figure drawn on a door. An unpleasant feeling swept through me. I thought of the images of him slicing open the doctor's belly and pouring soy sauce into it. Other people probably did not know that he had killed someone in such a cruel fashion.

Our tour ended in a large room on the second floor, where we saw two young girls and a young boy in one corner, perhaps just a bit older than my friends and I, sitting by a microphone. "That's our propaganda team," said Chunky. "They are from Beijing Drama School. We have a loudspeaker on the roof."

It was obvious that the large propaganda room also served as a make-shift kitchen. On a table in another corner stood a big basket of steamed buns and a pile of bowls and chopsticks. Chunky went over there and gave each of us a steamed bun and a salted cucumber. "Here's your din-ner," he said, and bit into a bun himself. "Eat and be ready to fight." We were all hungry and the dinner tasted very delicious.

For the next two days, the war was a war of loudspeakers across the "38th Parallel," the narrow cement road that separated us from the Vanguards. I spent most of my time with the propaganda team. Broad-casting day and night, we took turns reading articles attacking the Van-guards, calling them reactionaries, running dogs of capitalist bureau-crats, traitors of communism in disguise, and any combinations and permutations of pejorative descriptions that our young brains could dream up. Our accusations were fully returned by the Vanguards' loud-speaker perched on the roof of the No. 13 Building, just fifty yards away across the 38th Parallel.

On the third day after our arrival, however, the action for which we had been waiting finally came. At seven o'clock in the evening, just before sunset, the Vanguards' loudspeaker challenged the Red Action Committee to a "peaceful debate" on the 38th Parallel at eight o'clock. I thought it was kind of bizarre to talk about peaceful debate when we knew they were trying to attack us. But Chunky thought about it and decided to accept the challenge. I knew he must have been thinking of some plan of attack when he made the decision. After announcing the decision, he walked around the building and began picking his "debate team." We all volunteered eagerly. In order not to miss the action, Baby Dragon and I followed Chunky throughout the building and begged him again and again. "We will obey all your orders . . . we are not as young as you think . . . we have plenty of fighting experience," we said. "We once defeated a larger team called the Fearless Red Rebels."

He finally gave in after we badgered him for an hour. "You two can go," he said. "But you must walk behind Water Buffalo and Smoking Devil and let them protect you. Dragon Sister will kill me if something happens to you."

At eight o'clock, just after dark, we watched fifteen people from the other side walk to the 38th Parallel. "All right," said Chunky to us. "If it comes to fighting, we will have no mercy on the enemy. Now, before we go out to meet them, let us recite the words of the Great Leader." We all knew which passage he was referring to. It was the famous "Harden Our Hearts" that had become the battle cry of the Red Guards:

> Harden our hearts,
> Fear not sacrifices,
> Overcome ten thousand obstacles,
> To achieve the ultimate victory!

All the Red Guards in the building joined us as we recited, and our voices reverberated through the building. While we made our war pledge, we could hear clearly the recitation of the same passage by our enemies. I felt both proud and nervous as I walked out with the other "soldiers." We all carried concealed weapons like stones and sticks, just in case. The two teams lined up along the center of the concrete road, about two steps apart. It was a strange "debate." As soon as we arrived, and without a starting signal, everybody began speaking. In no time, the debate degenerated into a furious shouting match. "Down with the traitor Vanguards!" "You are traitors yourselves!" people shouted at each other. I felt confused and stupid. With all the shouting around me, I could not hear a whole sentence that my opponent was saying. Fortunately my opponent was a tall and pretty girl, and her lovely face fascinated me. The girl's mouth was moving passionately and was calling me a little anti-revolutionary, but I did not care. I was staring at her soft white neck heaving up and down and at her bosom—her shirt opened a little at the collar. A warm feeling swelled in me and I got the stupid and wild idea that I should ask her name.

Our lines inched closer as people tried to out-shout each other, and then someone threw a punch. "They hit me!" a man shouted. I looked around and saw two Vanguards in green raincoats pull out baseball bats and start to swing wildly. Obviously they came prepared to fight, too. Someone screamed. I heard a thumping sound, which I imagined came from a bat meeting a human skull. Then out the corner of my eyes, I saw the pretty girl in front of me whip a bicycle chain out of her pocket and whirl it at me. I instinctively ducked and wheeled about. The chain scraped my scalp, caught some of my hair, and gave me a quick ripping tug and a creepy sensation. I sprinted into the darkness. I was a quick runner and felt the wind whizzing in my ears as I ran. I could hear shouting, cursing, and the whooshing of baseball bats all around me. "Defend the revolution with blood!" a woman's voice shouted in the dark.

I stopped in the safe shadow of a poplar tree and turned around. I could see shadow figures whirl around one another along the road and someone lying under a street lamp. "Long Live Chairman Mao!" I heard Water Buffalo shout and saw his large body rush forward. I felt ashamed of myself for staying in the shadows while my comrades were fighting. I tried to move but my legs were twitching violently with a will of their own. They did not care what I wanted, even though I knew I should be brave. I recited under my breath the Great Leader's golden words and ordered my legs to stop shaking: "Harden our hearts, fear not sacrifices, overcome ten thousand obstacles, to achieve the ultimate victory!" But my legs would not listen. I hit my legs with my fists and repeated the Great Leader's words, which I heard always brought courage to soldiers. But my legs were no soldiers.

It seemed a long time before my leg cramps subsided and I was able to drag my legs forward to rejoin the fight. But before I reached the road, a whistle blew in the dark. At the sound, the Vanguards disentangled themselves and retreated into the inky night. I saw a large figure running past me and recognized the shape of Water Buffalo. "Withdraw! Withdraw!" he shouted. I ran after him. When I neared the building, I heard an ominous thump against the wall, then another, and another. The other side had started their artillery bombardment. At the building entrance, Smoking Devil and Water Buffalo reached down and pulled me up the barricade. As soon as I climbed up the jumbled desks, a brick slammed into the wall and shattered just inches above my head.

"Damn it! Fire the cannons!" I heard Chunky shout upstairs.

Shortly afterwards, I could hear a flurry of dull thuds and crashes in the darkness. Amid the bombardment of bricks, our loudspeaker, which had been broadcasting Chairman Mao's song "Harden Our Hearts," began blasting the latest battle communiqué at full volume, condemning the other side's treacherous attack.

On the third floor by the No. 2 Cannon, I found Baby Dragon. He was busy helping out. He seemed to have suffered some injury to his chin, for he had a bloody bandage on it. But Baby Dragon did not seem to notice it. His eyes glowed with the delight of a puppy who had just retrieved his first bird.

"Did you see me fight, Fan Shen?" he asked. "I shot one of them with my slingshot, right in the face. I saw blood run down his face. But I didn't see the brick coming at me."

In the command room, Chunky tallied the casualties. The most serious casualty was a boy from the Drama School. He had been hit on the head with a baseball bat and was barely conscious. Chunky sent two guards to carry him to the hospital. Five other people, including Smoking Devil and Baby Dragon, had been hit by rocks. The loudspeaker from the Vanguards claimed that nine people on their side had suffered severe injuries. Half an hour later, the loudspeaker reported that one of the injured, the leader of the debate team, who had been hit on the head by a shot-put ball, had died. Hearing this, Chunky chuckled proudly. I knew he had always carried a shot-put ball in his pocket as a weapon. Whiskers, however, was also recognized as the hero of the battle: his bricks found three enemy heads. Our great victory was broadcast to the whole campus that night and Dragon Sister came over and told us that there would be a celebration the next day. Despite my personal cowardice (of which only I myself knew), I was pleased that we had played a good game of revolution and we had won. That night, very tired, I slept soundly on the floor and had a sweet dream of being welcomed as a hero by the Great Leader into the Great Hall of the People.

The next morning, however, before dawn, I was rudely awakened. Sitting up, I saw soldiers with rifles all around us. In the darkness, they rounded all of us up swiftly and escorted us off the campus. Standing in the chilly wind, we were ordered to disperse immediately or be arrested. "Why are you driving us out?" I asked a soldier.

"Because the fighting here last night has been declared illegal by the Central Committee of the Communist Party," he said. "Some enemy attacked Red Guards last night and the Great Leader has ordered us to arrest the enemies."

I was a bit confused. I thought we had fought a brave battle for the Great Leader. The soldiers must have mistaken us for the Vanguards, who must be the enemy they were after. We could not have been the Great Leader's enemy because we fought with the best Red Guards, like Chunky, who was Red to the core. "We are the good Red Guards," I told the soldier. "It's the Vanguards that you should arrest." But the soldier would not listen. "We have orders to clear you all out. If you don't leave right now," he said, pointing his gun at us, "I'm going to arrest you as anti-revolutionaries."

We stayed around the school gate until noon but it seemed pointless. The soldiers had sealed the school and would not recognize us as the good Red Guards. "You'd better go home now," said Dragon Sister finally. "I'll come and get you back when we straighten things out here."

"Good-bye, young men," Chunky came over and said to us warmly as we boarded a bus home. "You were good fighters for the Great Leader." We beamed at the compliment and I waved our red banner outside the bus window as it pulled away. I saw Water Buffalo and Smoking Devil wave their banners in return. Suddenly, my eyes became moist. Although I was with them for only a few days, I felt a strong bond between me and these fearless and loyal Red Guards. Even Whiskers, who was sitting under a tree, seemed less detestable to me then.

The next day, we settled back in the headquarters of the Great Wall Fighting Team and waited for Dragon Sister to call us back. But instead of the word to call us back, some extremely disturbing news about our battle at Beijing University arrived. That evening after dinner, I returned home from the dining hall to find my father, his face ashen, reading the *People's Daily*, the Party newspaper. "It's good you came back yesterday," he said. "The newspaper said that some enemies had infiltrated Red Guard organizations at Beijing University and had been trying to instigate internal fighting among the Red Guards. You did not join the fighting, did you?"

"Of course not, we were too young to fight," I lied.

After my father was done with the paper, I picked it up and read the editorial. "The enemies in Beijing University have miscalculated as all enemies do," said the editorial. "Our Great Leader and wise commander Chairman Mao has anticipated, and in fact has encouraged, this scheme of the enemies in order to destroy them with a single decisive blow . . . Last night, the invincible People's Liberation Army soundly defeated the scheming enemies and arrested all of them. Once again it has proved the indisputable truth: any enemies who dare to challenge the Great Leader's revolution will be crushed like eggs on a stone."

Reading this, I thought that the enemy to whom the paper referred could not be anyone but the Vanguards and I was delighted that they had been arrested by the People Liberation Army. Late that evening, I went to Baby Dragon's apartment to tell him the news about Beijing University, and I found him crying.

"Chunky and my sister have been arrested," he said tearfully before I could ask why. "They say they are the scheming enemies of the Great Leader."

I was shocked. That was the most terrible crime a person could be charged with. "That's impossible," I said. "They are Red Guard heroes. Chunky loves the Great Leader. How could he be an enemy?"

I went home that night very disturbed and saddened. The Revolution had become a thoroughly confusing affair, and I no longer knew who the good guys were. I did not even know if I were still a true revolutionary. How could I be, since I fought on the side of the "scheming enemies"? I could not figure out why they arrested Chunky and Dragon Sister, who were the most loyal Red Guards that I knew. I was beginning to doubt that the Great Leader was as great as I thought; he did not even know his most loyal Red Guards and he arrested them as enemies. The doubt, I realized right away, was a dangerous thought, and I buried it immediately deep in my heart and never mentioned it to even my closest friends. But buried as it was, the doubt never went away, and like dripping water upon sandstone, it began to wear away, bit by bit, everything I was taught to believe about the Great Leader and the revolution. This is perhaps the start of my rebellion against the Great Saint, whom I had been worshipping all my life.

# 5 "Revolution Means Chopping Life"

The disastrous retreat from Beijing University seemed to be the harbinger of a run of back luck that descended upon our proud Great Wall Fighting Team.

I knew the word "revolution," *ge ming*, literally means "chop life," but I had thought it meant to chop the life of enemies like General Hei, not the life of comrades. But revolution has a funny and strange way of turning comrades into enemies. In a few short weeks following our retreat, the Cultural Revolution had turned against many of its most ardent proponents, the Red Guards themselves. After her arrest, Baby Dragon's sister was charged as an anti-revolutionary and quickly sentenced to seven years of hard labor; Chunky, the most decorated Red Guard commander, was declared a class enemy and sentenced to ten years in prison. I later learned that he was severely tortured on the "Tiger's Bench" in prison, with his legs strapped to a bench at the knees while bricks were added under his heels; his legs were so severely mutilated that he was crippled for life. Whiskers, the other hero of the fight at Beijing University, was bludgeoned to death by a rival gang of Red Guards during a brawl. The Cultural Revolution had begun to chop the lives of revolutionary Red Guards as cruelly and as quickly as it had the earlier capitalists.

The bad luck also gripped the Great Wall Fighting Team, and it started with Sparrow, our buck-toothed propaganda chief. One morning in February of 1967, Baby Dragon charged into my room and told me terrible news: "Sparrow's father's dead," he said. "He hung himself from a pine tree in the park last night."

"Why?" I asked.

"They said he was declared a traitor yesterday by some Red Guards."

"Is that true?"

"I don't think so," said Baby Dragon.

We went over to Sparrow's home, which was in a building just a block from ours. But there was little we could do to console our friend. A few days after his father's death, Sparrow and his family were told that they could no longer live in the Big Courtyard and had to move out immediately. They soon moved to the other end of the city and I rarely saw Sparrow afterward.

A month later, the horrible hand of revolution struck Kangaroo, our secretary-general. For several days he did not show up at the Great Wall Fighting Team headquarters, and we went to look for him. At his apartment, we found the door was sealed and nobody was living there anymore. "Why did they go?" we asked around. "They left two days ago, at night, the whole family," a neighbor boy told us. "Kangaroo's father is a fake Party member and he's not an officer any more." That's all we found out about his sudden disappearance.

Several weeks later, I got a letter from Kangaroo, which was mailed from a state farm in Xinjiang, a remote region where China's emperors used to exile their prisoners. He sounded cheerful enough in the letter, telling me about the white mountains and herds of sheep and drinking horse milk on the farm, but I knew life must be hard for him now that he was the son of a disgraced father. I wrote back immediately and told him that we would visit him someday. After that letter, however, I never heard from him again.

I missed both of these friends very much. With Sparrow and Kangaroo gone, the once noisy and joyful headquarters of the Great Wall Fighting Team became quiet and empty and seemed to have lost much of its fun. I went there less and less and began spending more time at home, trying to find books to read.

But the bad luck did not stop with Kangaroo. About two months after his disappearance, the mysterious hand of revolution struck again, this time at my family.

On a Sunday night, I came home with my sister from the public dining hall and saw Aunt Zan Mei and my mother huddled outside the back door (we lived on the first floor), talking tensely in low voices. They did not seem to notice the chilly wind and the light rain that was falling on them. I had not seen Zan Mei, my favorite aunt, for several years. She was wearing a thin black coat and had a large coarse gray shawl tightly wrapped around her neck and chin, as if she were trying to hide her face. Her small, twinkling eyes, which she used to squint and which became teary when she told jokes, were dull and furtive. With a cry of joy, I ran out to greet her, but my mother blocked me before I could get near her.

"Go back inside," she ordered sternly, pushing me and my sister in. "I have something serious to discuss with Aunt Zan Mei." With a faint smile, Aunt Zan Mei nodded at me.

Aunt Zan Mei was a carefree, generous, and humorous person. Large and boisterous, she smoked incessantly and knew all about different liquors. She had visited my family many times with her three children. Each time she brought numerous gifts, including swan eggs, beef jerky, Tibetan butter, pine nuts, and countless jokes from Qinghai Province, where she and her husband worked. Her husband was the director of a naval plant—a torpedo-testing center—on Qinghai Lake, and Aunt Zan Mei was the chief of supplies at the plant. Once she brought two large nylon bags of giant sea crabs, which she steamed, and our two families had a crab feast. I never had better crabs than those brought by Aunt Zan Mei. It is many years later and I still haven't.

Through the window I watched Aunt Zan Mei talking to my mother and impatiently waited for Aunt Zan Mei to come into the house. The cup of tea that I had poured for her was getting cold. But fifteen minutes later, Aunt Zan Mei had gone without coming into the house.

"Where did Aunt Zan Mei go?" I asked as my mother came in.

Her face was the color of ashes. "Don't ask," she said. "And don't tell anyone she was here. She escaped from Qinghai by herself. The Red Guards have seized their home and have beaten her husband with iron bars. They are looking for her now. She hoped to hide here for a few days, but how could we let her? I told her we were in trouble too and she must find some other place."

I did not know where Aunt Zan Mei went. I was sad that my mother did not allow Aunt Zan Mei to stay with us, but I did not blame her for her cold-heartedness. I understood why she closed the door to her sister: a revolutionary must draw a line between herself and a relative who has been declared an anti-revolutionary, in order to save herself and her family. But still I hated my mother for sending Aunt Zan Mei away on that terribly cold night. Where could she go? A few months later, I learned that her husband had been killed, thrown into a lake by the Red Guards; my guilt became nearly unbearable, and has remained with me to this day. Aunt Zan Mei was eventually arrested and sent to a labor camp in Qinghai, but fortunately, she survived the Cultural Revolution.

Just two days after Aunt Zan Mei left, more trouble descended upon my family. Coming home late one evening after going out with Baby Dragon, I found the apartment eerily dark and silent. The front door was wide open and no lights were on. My father and my sister were normally home by this time. I walked in cautiously and turned on the light in the hall.

I heard my mother's voice unexpectedly: "Turn off the light! Go to your room!" That alone told me something very serious had happened. My mother was an ardent revolutionary and had been working late at her job in the Museum of Natural History since the beginning of the Cultural Revolution. She was rarely home before I was in bed.

"Why can't we turn on the light?" I asked my sister.

"Shhh, Mother is afraid that the Red Guards might come back again if they see the light." Her scratchy voice told me that she had been crying.

"Why? What happened?" I asked.

"A Red Guard team called 'Chairman Mao's Iron Soldiers' was here this afternoon. They took Father away and said he was an anti-revolutionary."

My father an anti-revolutionary! I was shocked to hear the ridiculous charge, and was very angry. How could my father, who had joined the Great Leader's Communist Army at the age of twelve, be an anti-revolutionary? He was an army hero with many medals! He may have been slow to join the Red Guards, but he had always taught me to be loyal to the Great Leader.

"Why did they say Father's an anti-revolutionary?" I asked my sister.

"They say he tried to harbor a fugitive and wanted him to tell them where Aunt Zan Mei went."

"But how could he know," I said. "She went away by herself." But I knew how things were in those days. One could not argue with the Red Guards. They were the law.

That night, my father did not come home; nor did he in the next three nights. My memory of the next three days is hazy. I slept a lot, only vaguely aware of whether it was day or night, for my mother had forbidden me to turn on the lights at night. For the first time in my life, I felt fear. If my father were an anti-revolutionary, then I would be a little anti-revolutionary. That was the logic of the day. I could barely think of the fate that was awaiting me. I knew too well how little anti-revolutionaries were treated. I still remembered very well the little girl with her mother and sister sweeping streets with a huge bamboo broom. Of my friends, only Baby Dragon came over once and left very quickly. I knew he was afraid of being seen visiting a little anti-revolutionary.

The day after my father's arrest, my mother suffered a nervous breakdown. For the next few days, she did nothing but sob hysterically, and point at the wall and scream: "Damn relatives! Damn relatives! They are nothing but trouble!" She blamed the whole thing on Aunt Zan Mei. Once in the middle of the night, she came into our room and hugged my sister so hard that she squealed. The next moment, she pushed her away with a disgusted look on her face as if she had hugged a dirty piglet by mistake.

On the morning of the fourth day, my father came home, but only briefly. He was brought back by the Red Guards to collect some clothes before he was sent to a labor camp. Pale and hungry, my father said nothing to us. If he had been a man of few words, the ordeal had turned him into a virtual mute. For many years after that, he trusted no one, not even his children. After my father left, my mother was sent to a different labor camp. She was allowed to come home once a week to check on us.

Those were the darkest days in my life. In a few days, I had gone from a proud Red Guard to a little anti-revolutionary and a social outcast. My friends no longer dared to come and see me, nor did I want to see them. Feeling ashamed and fearful that other Red Guards might attack me, I did not want to go out anymore and spent most of my days in the apartment with my sister.

With my parents gone, I became the man of the house and had to learn quickly the basic skills of survival. I learned to cook barley porridge for my sister and me, and to wash clothes and to clean the apartment. As days went by, I was amazed that I was doing so well with cooking and housework and was proud that I took care of my sister as a big brother. I guess I have a natural-born survival instinct, like a mouse. The mouse always survives, and even prospers in his small way, because he is the most tenacious of all creatures, even though he is probably also the most unfortunate and most despised animal.

After two long months in the labor camps, both my father and my mother were temporarily released. The Iron Soldiers could not find enough evidence to charge them as anti-revolutionaries, so they were released as "comrades who needed further education," which meant that they were still considered "problematic." But despite the shadow still hanging over their heads, my parents' release immediately made all the difference in my world. I again became a little revolutionary. The day after my parents came home, I put on my Red Guard silk armband once more and joined Snivel and Baby Dragon in the headquarters of the Great Wall Fighting Team. Again, I tried to do the kind of revolutionary activities that I had done before, reading posters, attending struggle rallies, etc. But I soon found that the experience of being a little anti-revolutionary for two months had changed my attitude toward revolution permanently.

The ordeal deepened my doubt about the Great Leader and the Cultural Revolution. I started to realize, though still vaguely, that there was no real meaningful purpose to the Cultural Revolution and there were no real enemies. The Great Leader himself probably was as confused as I was, and he did great wrongs to people like Chunky and my father, who would have gladly given their lives for him. Why he had to sacrifice the lives of his most devoted followers, who worshipped him like a god, is a puzzle for which I still do not have an answer. But one thing I knew for sure: I no longer cared about the meaningless revolution. Outwardly, though, I had to continue to participate in the revolution and to act as the little ardent revolutionary I had been before.

Besides deepening my doubt about the whole revolution and the Great Leader, the ordeal did one other thing that helped foster my future rebellion against the Great Leader. In those boring and dangerous days when I was alone with my sister in the house, I wished more than ever that I had some of the "bad" books that we had burned at the big bonfire, those novels of foreign knights, dragons, monkeys, and monsters! I knew it was a dangerous wish, but I did not try to suppress it. It was only an empty wish, though. All libraries had been sealed by Red Guards since the beginning of the Revolution and all bookstores had been empty except for a few shelves of Little Red Books, and so thoroughly had we burned the "bad" books that I did not see a single novel in any of my friends' homes.

But the Chinese have a saying: "Wish and it will be done." Just a week after I was "released" from the prison of my apartment, my dangerous wish was suddenly fulfilled unexpectedly.

## 6  The Forbidden Books

One day after breakfast, tired of going out to read wall posters that had become tasteless to me, I took out the big picture book with naked women that I had taken from the doctor's house and tried, for the hundredth time, to entertain myself with those stimulating pictures. Flipping through it slowly, I thought of what had happened to the owner of the book and to the little girl who had become a social outcast because of her father's death. I was so engrossed in my thoughts that I did not hear Baby Dragon slip into the apartment and sneak up behind me. We never locked doors then.

"Ha! A *bad* book!" he exclaimed, pointing to the half-naked woman on the page. His voice almost knocked me off my chair. I could be in serious trouble if other people found out I had the book. Angrily, I closed the book and shoved it under my bed.

"Hey, don't you try to hide it from me," he said, seeing the flames in my eyes and trying to calm me down. "I can get you a hundred books like that if you have the nerve to keep them, all bad books."

"You have bad books?" I asked, my heartbeat still trying to find its regular rhythm. "We burned them all, remember?"

"Well—not all, I'm afraid."

"You kept bad books? How dare you?" I tried to assume the tone of a little revolutionary, but he knew me too well to be fooled. "Where?" I finally asked.

"In a secret place," my friend said proudly. "Want to get some? I'll take you there if you allow me to look at this book."

"Deal," I said. "But only after you show me your books." I decided to play along.

"All right, meet me at the No. 1 bus station at seven o'clock tonight. Bring a flashlight and a big bag."

We got off the bus at Goldfish Street that evening. The street was flooded with amber light from the street lamps and bustled with evening shoppers. We walked briskly through the commercial district, and then abruptly stopped at an alley barely wider than a pickup truck. "Drum and Gong Alley," said the rusty sign on the gray brick wall. At the corner of the alley, Baby Dragon gave me one of those over-the-shoulder glances that American spies in trenchcoats constantly give in Chinese movies. Having made sure that we were not being followed, Baby Dragon sauntered in. I followed him and even mimicked his poor imitation of a Hollywood spy.

We walked to the end of the alley and found ourselves in front of a marble doorway so grand and elaborate that it seemed entirely out of place among its decrepit neighbors. The door was secured by a large rusty padlock shaped like a bottle-gourd. Above the lock, two long red strips of seals crisscrossed each other. It was too dark to read the words on them but we knew they must have been put there by the Red Guards.

"This is it," Baby Dragon whispered.

"What is this?"

"One of the storehouses of the old Red Guards. Used to be a famous actor's studio. When he killed himself, it became the warehouse for everything of any worth that the Red Action Committee had confiscated—everything not taken home by the Red Guards themselves, that is. Radios, records, things like that—they are all gone. But there are still a lot of books. I was here with my sister once."

I wondered whether the piano they took from the girl's house was here. But one thing I did know was that we had to find a way to get in.

Baby Dragon thrust his head out of the doorway to make sure no one was coming into the alley. About ten yards from the doorway, there was an elm tree by the wall. With much effort, both of us climbed up the tree and slid alongside the wall into the yard. Under the half moon, the yard was desolate but blanketed with a very faint white light.

The padlock on the door of the house easily yielded when Baby Dragon inserted his screwdriver in it and hit the handle hard with the palm of his hand. The door groaned and creaked as the wooden hinges ground against each other. We switched on our flashlights and walked into what appeared to be a large living room. A large heap of books as high as our hips took up two-thirds of the room. Dust and cobwebs were everywhere.

"There you are," said my friend. "Take as many as you want. But we have to be quick. I hope we will not be caught as thieves."

"Want to be a hooker and a saint at the same time?" I said, stepping on the edge of the pile. "But don't trouble your conscience about this. *Stealing books is not theft*—Confucius said that."

The room smelled faintly of "666" brand pesticide and the dust made breathing difficult. As if by pre-arrangement, we started scavenging in different directions. Like a groundhog, Baby Dragon burrowed through the books quickly, throwing the ones he did not want backwards between his legs. His task was simple; he was looking for one kind of book only.

"Slow down, will you?" I said, sneezing several times. I pulled my shirt over my mouth to make breathing easier. "You are going to choke us to death with dust."

"Hurry up! If you see any good military biographies, or anything about wars, let me know, will you?" Baby Dragon said, without raising his head or slowing down.

Unlike my friend, I did not know exactly what kind of book I was looking for. I recognized a few Chinese classics: *Investiture of the Gods*, *Journey to the West*, *The Romance of the Three Kingdoms*, and *The Dream of the Red Chamber*. They had been condemned as symbols of feudalism and I had seen them burned at our bonfire in the Big Courtyard. But the most condemned books now had the most appeal for me. I threw them all into my satchel.

"Look what I found!" Baby Dragon cried. He straightened up and waded through the books to me. Sweat was dripping from his chin and his wet shirt stuck to his chest. He shined his flashlight on the book in his hand. "Look at this, Fan Shen! Have you ever heard of *The Golden Lotus*? It's the WORST of the bad books."

I knew of the book, from overhearing remarks whispered by older Red Guards. In fact, I then remembered, Smoking Devil had said that this was the most pornographic book in the whole of Chinese literature. My heart sped up. I touched it with both excitement and apprehension.

"We have to keep this a top secret. Never, ever, tell anyone about this book," Baby Dragon said gravely, as he slid it carefully into my bag. I nodded. Both of us knew how deadly the consequences would be if we were found to be in possession of such a book.

It did not take long for us to fill our bags. Besides the few Chinese classics, I found six volumes of great works of Western literature in Chinese translation. I glanced quickly at the authors and recognized only two names, both Russian—Leo Tolstoy and Anton Chekhov. Nevertheless, I put the six heavy volumes into my bag.

Just as we stepped out of the room, we heard noises outside the front door. Some people were coming our way. We could see the light from their torches reflected on the leaves of the elm tree.

"Shit," Baby Dragon muttered. "Get back in the room, quick."

*Clank! Clank!* Someone rattled the rusty lock against the front gate. "Who has the key?" a sharp-pitched voice asked.

"Wait a minute, here is the key," another voice said.

The yard door was unlocked and pushed open. Through the glass window, we could see people in red armbands enter the yard and walk toward us.

Baby Dragon tugged at my sleeve with his wet hand and we retreated to the inner room. We heard someone yell:

"Hey, the door is unlocked. Someone is in here."

"Catch the thief and fry him!"

We heard people laugh and enter the outer room. I was conscious of the coldness of my shirt sticking to my back as I crawled behind Baby Dragon into the bathroom. Climbing on top of the toilet, Baby Dragon pushed the small window open. It squeaked loudly.

"Someone's in there! Catch the thief!"

"Catch the thief!"

Throwing his bag out the window first, Baby Dragon pulled himself up to the windowsill swiftly and dove out head first. I pushed my bag up to the sill, but its bulging mass got stuck in the window frame. Grabbing an overhead water pipe, I swung myself up and kicked the bag hard with both of my feet. The glass shattered and the bag dropped out.

"He is in here!" several voices shouted. "Don't let him get away!" "Catch him and light him up on a lamppost!"

That was no empty threat. The Red Guards had done worse with anti-revolutionaries. I had to get out at all costs. As shadows and torchlight appeared on the bathroom floor, I climbed up with all my strength and dove out. I landed on my bag on the ground and rolled to the side. As I scrambled to get up, I saw that I was in a large alley now and not far ahead of me was a well-lit main street.

"Quick, the thief is outside! Go around the house!" people shouted in the house.

"Let's go," Baby Dragon said, emerging from the shadows and pulling me up. A torchlight shone suddenly from the bath window behind us and someone shouted: "They are here!" At the sound, Baby Dragon took off for the main street. I too jumped up, grabbed my bag, and ran for my life. As I ran, I could feel something wet on my left hand and knew I was cut, but I couldn't care less as long as I got out of this alive. Fortunately, the main street was still full of shoppers and no one paid any attention to two teenagers darting in and out of the crowd.

The cut on my hand required five stitches and I had to make up an elaborate lie to explain it to my mother. But it was worth it. I hid the books under my bed and, for several months, read them day and night. I read the Chinese classics first, and then steadily worked through the great works of Western literature.

Of the Chinese classics, I liked *Journey to the West* the best. It is the story of an omniscient monkey who rebels against the Jade Emperor in Heaven. I liked the free spirit of the monkey, who was my kind of hero— fearless as well as mischievous. Obeying no authority, he peed in the Buddha's hand, stole royal wine from the Jade Emperor, and, after getting drunk on royal wine, let loose the Emperor's horses and wreaked havoc in Heaven. Later on, in my rebellion against the Great Leader, I often thought of myself as a monkey battling the omniscient Jade Emperor.

Of the Western authors, I enjoyed Stendhal and Jack London the most. If the Monkey book stirred up my nature of rebellion, Stendhal and Jack London sowed the dangerous seed of ambition that would permanently "ruin" me as a little revolutionary. Both Stendhal's *The Red and the Black* and London's *Martin Eden* have a common theme that touched my heart: their characters are passionate and tenacious, driven to pursue a dream and to rise above their appointed fates. I knew I should not, but more than once I cried when reading those novels. I admired the character of Martin Eden especially and wished that I would become someone like him, overcoming countless failures to achieve success at last.

The "dirty" book *The Golden Lotus*, however, was a disappointment. It was an abridged version, with frequent blanks in the text, indicating that words, sentences, or whole passages had been deleted. The censors had purged the book before the flames had their chance. I burned most of the books as soon as I had read them, for fear of being discovered by my mother. The only books that I could not bring myself to destroy were *The Red and the Black* and *Martin Eden*. I taped them to the underside of my bed frame and would read them over and over again. The seeds of ambition they sowed in me had taken root and would blossom in the coming years, and would pitch me into a long and harsh battle against the fate that had been assigned to me by the Great Leader, a fate that few people dared to change.

## 7 The Great Leader Meets the Red Guards

During the time I shut myself up in my room reading forbidden books, a significant change had occurred in the Cultural Revolution. In the summer of 1967, the second year of the revolution, the Great Leader issued a decree to unite all warring factions of the Red Guards and instill in them the spirit of the old Red Army. "From now on," the Great Leader proclaimed, "China will become one big barrack and everyone will be a Red soldier." The Red Guards rejoiced at the Great Leader's instruction and began implementing the scheme immediately.

Rallies were soon held everywhere in Beijing. Firecrackers exploded in the sky, drums shook the dust from the beams of the two-hundred-year-old houses, and the Red Guards shook hands with all the rival teams, and submitted to the military training provided by the People's Liberation Army. One day, when I emerged from my apartment and went to the headquarters of our fighting team, I found the sign bearing the proud name of "The Great Wall Fighting Team" had been taken down. "You came just in time," Snivel said. "Here is your new armband. Now all the Red Guards in Beijing wear the same armband." Instead of the words "Red Guards of the Great Wall Fighting Team," the new armband bore the simple words: "The Red Guards of the Capital." I could tell from Snivel's face that he shared my sadness that the Great Wall Fighting Team was no more. But Baby Dragon was not too concerned about the change. "The Revolutionary Committee has told us that we are going to start military training next week," Baby Dragon said excitedly. "And we are going to learn to shoot real rifles. All the Red Guards from the Flying Wing School will be in one regiment. Guess who's the commander of the regiment? Snivel's father!" I looked at Snivel and he smiled.

A platoon of soldiers led by Snivel's father came to our school and started our training. We were taught to goose-step in formation and we practiced target shooting with obsolete rifles from World War I. The training was rigorous and kept us busy and tired. I guess that was exactly what the Great Leader had in mind: to keep the Red Guards busy and under tight control so that they could no longer run the streets as a lawless mob, thus giving him the chance to put the country back in order.

To show his support for the united Red Guards and his appreciation of what they had accomplished for him (whatever that was), Chairman Mao began inspecting the Red Guards at mass rallies in July. It became the highest honor of a Red Guard to see the Great Leader in person, and millions of Red Guards from all over the country flocked to the capital to wait for their chance to see the Great Leader. For weeks, tens of thousands of them camped out in every available space in Beijing, with more arriving daily. In the Big Courtyard, a tent city was set up in the park, which housed three thousand Red Guards. Newsreels of the Great Leader inspecting the Red Guards were shown repeatedly on the open-air screen at one end of the park and we had all seen the movies several times. People in the films seemed so happy that most of them jumped about like frogs in mating season and, beside themselves, they wept with joy. We were told that the Red Guards in the Big Courtyard might get a chance to see the Great Leader, too.

But no one knew when such a mass inspection rally would take place, and we were told to be ready at a moment's notice. "My father said we'd better move to the tent city now," said Snivel one day. "Otherwise, we may miss out on seeing the Great Leader." I was not too crazy to see the Great Leader, but as it was expected of every Red Guard, I went along with my friends and settled down in the tent city. My parents, of course, had no objection to my living there in order to see the Great Leader.

During most of August and September, we waited day and night, not daring to stray too far from our tents.

To keep our spirits high, company commanders organized rigorous training exercises for us during the day, mostly goose-stepping in formation; in the evening, they conducted endless classes and contests, in which we studied and recited the Great Leader's "Three Old Essays" and "ageless poems." Everybody was required to write reports to express his appreciation of these works, and the most effusive essays were displayed on company bulletin boards around the tent city. Since I had a little talent for words, I became a star in these contests. All my upbringing as a revolutionary seemed to have finally paid off here: I wrote several revolutionary articles, full of embellished hyperbole and studded with numerous quotations from the Great Leader's works. Even though I did not believe a word of what I wrote, I basked in the glory. On several occasions, I was invited to read my articles to the company at the evening meetings, and afterwards, to post the essays prominently on the bulletin board.

But it was in one of these essays that I made a mistake that was almost fatal and that nearly ruined me and my family. It taught me an unforgettable lesson on just how dangerous the revolution was to a careless foot soldier.

One evening, just after I had proudly placed my latest article on the bulletin board, an elaborate celebration of the Great Leader's poem "On Climbing the Lu Mountain," a sharp cry from behind startled me: "Look at this!" a young man with a Sichuan accent cried, pointing to the bottom of my article. "Look at what it says! It attacks the Great Leader! It's ANTI-REVOLUTIONARY! Watch him, don't let him get away! I must report it at once!" With that, he dashed toward the company headquarters.

Everybody around the bulletin board froze at his words. A deadly silence fell over the crowd. Looking at the end of my own article, I shuddered and my feet became weak and numb and my head dizzy. Something cold, like a hairy spider, crept down my spine. The customary slogan "Long Live Chairman Mao!" at the end of the article read, "No Live Chairman Mao!" It was in my own handwriting. It was a careless slip of the pen, but I knew how deadly the offense was. The Red Guards had killed people for lesser crimes.

Baby Dragon and Snivel, who were with me earlier, had slipped into the crowd. A small circle of people formed around me, murmuring and nodding. I was alone at the center. An invisible line had been drawn between me and my former comrades. Everybody had drawn a line between themselves and me. It was the loneliest moment of my life.

Commander Duck Egg of the 134th Company—so-called for his shining bald head and his peculiar, almost addictive fondness for preserved black duck eggs—immediately reported the serious incident to the commander of the regiment. Duck Egg was another of those whom the mysterious hand of the Revolution had plucked out of the mud, rinsed clean, and made to shine briefly as a hero. An illiterate cook before the Cultural Revolution, he was very proud of his current position and his revolutionary instincts, and was always alert to any sign of covert class struggle between good revolutionaries and hidden enemies. That evening, with my essay in hand, he looked like he had finally found concrete evidence of the class struggle that he always tried so hard to detect. He pushed me into the tent that served as the headquarters of the regiment.

"Look at this!" he said loudly as soon as we stepped in the tent. He handed the paper to Commander Qi of our regiment, who happened to be Snivel's father. "It is so vicious an attack on the Great Leader that I can't even repeat what is written here. It is too venomous to be a casual mistake. We have to call a mass rally against him immediately and hand him over to the police." I shuddered at each of his words.

Commander Qi's face dropped as he read the paper. He clearly recognized my name. And he must have recognized the danger to himself, too. I was his son's best friend and we were inseparable companions on the Great Wall Fighting Team. If I were declared an anti-revolutionary, his son would be implicated, and he himself might be as well.

"Let me handle this," Commander Qi said, pausing to weigh his words carefully. "I will investigate this personally and then decide what to do. You have done a good job, Commander."

That evening, while I was writing the confession ordered by Commander Qi in his tent, my mother stepped in. Commander Qi had notified her. As soon as she saw me, she rushed over.

"How could you be so stupid? You *have ruined* your parents! You . . . you . . . you . . . ," she screamed at me, bitter and resentful tears oozing out of her small puffy eyes. "You are not my son if you did this!" With a sudden rage, she seized a heavy ruler from the table and swatted me across the forehead. She raised the ruler again to give me a second hearty swipe, but Commander Qi quickly stepped between us.

"Please, Comrade Zan," he said, taking her arm and leading her to a chair. "Sit down, please. Fan Shen, why don't you step outside while I talk to your mother?"

I waited with a heavy heart outside. Even though I resented my mother for not protecting me, I knew I had done something that was likely to harm her irreparably. My parents' revolutionary careers could have been completely undone by my blunder. Half an hour later, my mother came out. She seemed to be relieved. "Commander Qi does not think your mistake is intentional and will not charge you with anything," she said. "But you will have to write a long and heartfelt self-criticism and read it to your company." As we walked back to my tent, she reached out to hold my arm. "You must remember, everything you do affects the people who care for you. This is a good lesson for you. Our family cannot afford another political blunder." I took my arm away. I felt betrayed.

After reading a long self-criticism at a company rally, I made five copies by hand and posted them on various bulletin boards in the tent city. Although at the next meeting Commander Qi told the company that the matter was closed, the injury that my heart had suffered from the event has never completely healed.

The marching order came at one o'clock in the morning on October 15. In darkness, we boarded a column of army trucks, which then rumbled through dim streets for more than an hour before stopping on a side street. Beijing's autumn nights were already chilly, and a small but steady breeze made us shiver when we stiffly climbed out of the open trucks. Despite the large number of people who soon filled the entire street, it was unusually quiet. We were soon assembled into companies and led off by the commanding officers.

The columns moved silently but swiftly through the dimly lit streets. After looping around the old city for some time, my company suddenly stumbled out of the maze of streets and marched into the capacious expanse of Tiananmen Square. I could see dozens of columns like my own streaming into the Square from all directions simultaneously.

As vast numbers of people squished and pummeled each other, my column slowly made its way toward the Monument of the People's Heroes. Contours of the buildings surrounding the world's largest square were starting to become visible through the bluish morning mist. The Gate of Heavenly Peace, the first of a series of gates built to guard the Forbidden City, loomed in front of us with its gigantic portrait of the Great Leader above the lofty gate where emperors used to hang the heads of executed prisoners. By the time the sun was visible above the flat roof of the Museum of History, my company settled in front of the Monument of the People's Heroes, about five hundred yards from the Gate of Heavenly Peace. From our central location, I could see that the whole square was jammed with people, who formed a two-colored ocean of brown uniforms speckled with red banners and red armbands. The next day the *People's Daily* reported that 1.2 million Red Guards attended the rally.

The wait was long. Some people said the Great Leader would appear on the Gate of Heavenly Peace at ten. Ten o'clock passed quietly. The loudspeakers mounted on each of the lampposts throughout the square broadcast songs whose lyrics were popular quotations from the Great Leader's Little Red Book: "Harden Our Hearts," "A Revolution Is Not a Dinner Party," and "Young People Are The Morning Sun." People hummed along with the loudspeakers. The sun had risen, bright and warm, and despite our fatigue and lack of sleep, we were in high spirits.

After sitting on the hard ground for several hours, however, my butt started to hurt. I could hardly stretch my legs without kicking the persons around me. Baby Dragon and Snivel were playing cards, so I had to try to find something entertaining for myself to keep from falling asleep.

I looked at the people around me and suddenly noticed that Commander Duck Egg had been summoned to a meeting and his bag, containing his lunch, lay on the ground across the narrow passageway from me. A naughty thought immediately occurred to me. I was a timid person in general, but once in a while, I would do something silly and bold, and this was one of those times. I stood up on the passageway, stretched my arms several times, yawned once or twice, turned around, and sat down on the wrong side of the passageway, squarely on Commander Duck Egg's bag. I could feel the boiled eggs give way and the steamed bun flatten under my weight. A surreptitious sensation of joy radiated throughout my body. Having crushed Commander Duck Egg's food, I inched away, pretending to be puzzled at what I was sitting on. I was glad that nobody paid any attention to me.

By noon, the sky had turned cloudy and breezy. Tired of sitting and singing, people began unpacking their lunches. Having had nothing to eat since supper the night before, I munched heartily on my steamed bun and waited for the little drama to begin.

Commander Duck Egg returned from his meeting and sat down to open his lunch. I peered sideways in the direction of the shining head, eagerly anticipating the impending explosion. He soon extracted the flattened bun and crushed eggs from his bag and instantly bellowed: "What?! WHO STEPPED ON MY LUNCH?" His eyes bulged as he showed the crushed eggs to us. We looked up at the commander with sympathy. But the eggs and the bun were in such comically sorry shape that Baby Dragon and a few other insolent people started to laugh. Innocently, like everybody else, I also laughed, but I made sure that I did not laugh any harder than the others. It was a perfect little revenge for what he had done to me.

By two o'clock, the festive atmosphere had faded. Lunch was over and the sun was in hiding, and the people were now subdued, talking in groups of two or three in low voices. From time to time, I saw a white canvas stretcher carried by two medics thread its way through the crowd toward the edge of the square. There are always people who faint at such rallies.

By four-thirty, a plump young woman sitting in front of me passed along a rumor that the rally had been postponed till tomorrow afternoon, because the Great Leader was still in an important meeting. At five-thirty, the loudspeakers began playing "Sailing the Ocean Depends on the Helmsman," which seemed to confirm the plump woman's ominous rumor, for the song was always played at the end of a mass rally. Hearing it, some people sighed and began packing.

Then, all of a sudden, without warning, all the loudspeakers broke off in the middle of "Sailing the Ocean Depends on the Helmsman," and started "Red Is the East," and we all knew what it meant. It was the signature song that always accompanied the Great Leader's appearance. We saw people closer to the Gate of Heavenly Peace jump up and start to wave their Little Red Books and shout, "LONG LIVE CHAIRMAN MAO! LONG LIVE CHAIRMAN MAO!" The waving and shouting spread like a tsunami through the entire square. The shouting was deafening. Everybody around me shot up, waving and shouting, jumping up and down, trying to get a glimpse of the Great Leader over the hundreds of thousands of waving Little Red Books. The plump woman who had started the rumor not long ago wiped her eyes and sobbed loudly. Being a head shorter than the adults in front of me, I could see nothing. Baby Dragon and I tried to jump up to get a glimpse of the Great Leader, but that did not help either. The great Imperial Gate was too far from us; I could hardly make out the small moving specks on top of the gate. Waving mechanically and softly saying "Long Live Chairman Mao," I resentfully watched the spirited jumping bodies all around me. I felt I was being cheated. But I also felt guilty that I was not excited. With the presence of the Great Leader, I was supposed to be excited, as all true revolutionaries should be. I was supposed to think of all the great things that the Great Leader had done for China and of his plump benevolent face on posters, and then get tearful as many people around me did. I did try to do that, to imagine all that I was supposed to imagine, but my pulse did not go faster and tears did not come to my eyes. Nothing happened at all. The presence of the Great Saint stirred up nothing in me. I kept wondering if everybody around me was genuine in his happiness to see the Great Leader, although he was only one of the small black ants moving on top of the Gate of Heavenly Peace. Looking at my friends, I felt almost certain that I saw tears sparkle in Snivel's eyes—along with the ever-present free-flowing snot on his face. Beside him, Baby Dragon jumped tirelessly as if he were fueled by an inexhaustible battery. What made them so excited, having seen next to nothing?

"Stretcher! Stretcher!" Several voices around me shouted. The plump woman, who had spread the rumor and who had hopped and shouted and cried like a victim of torture, had risen—or rather fallen—to the occasion. She had fainted from excitement. Two medics soon squeezed through the passageway and hoisted her up on a stretcher. They carried her above people's heads and moved gingerly toward the edge of the square. As they passed, everybody's eyes followed her with admiration and respect: few accomplish such a heroic feat. The stretcher finally disappeared into the crowd, and people returned to jumping and shouting, and I joined in too, this time with greater energy. I was hoping that by giving it all the energy I had, some great emotion would flow into me so that I could at least get some tears into my eyes to show my friends. But then another idea hit me, which was even better. I jumped up one more time and let out the loudest cry that I could manage, "Long Live Chairman Mao!" and then I went limp and dropped to the ground and closed my eyes.

"Stretcher! Stretcher! Fan Shen has fainted!" I heard Baby Dragon's voice. I was soon picked up by many hands and put on a stretcher. I began to float over people's heads. I must say it was most pleasant to be carried out like a fallen hero in a moment like that. I kept my eyes shut and enjoyed every minute of the long ride. When I opened my eyes once my joyful journey came to an end, I found that I had been laid on the ground next to the fat woman, and was surrounded by Baby Dragon and Snivel and Duck Egg. I was very satisfied to see the admiration in Commander Duck Egg's eyes, but I had to close my eyes right away so that I would not laugh out loud and give myself away.

I listened to the shouting around me for nearly half an hour. And then, suddenly, the thunderous shouting stopped. In a moment, the loudspeakers switched to "Sailing the Ocean Depends on the Helmsman" to signal the end of the rally, and then a voice ordered the crowd to withdraw from the square in an orderly fashion. I was lifted up once more and carried out of Tiananmen Square. Again, I enjoyed the gentle ride back to our trucks. It was past five in the morning when the trucks stopped at the tent city in the Big Courtyard. Few people spoke on the return journey: obviously they had neither energy nor voice left. And throughout the journey, I kept my eyes and mouth shut to be consistent with my role as an exhausted fallen hero.

When the newsreel about the most recent inspection of the Red Guards by the Great Leader came out two weeks later, I finally saw what I had missed on that historic day. I saw the Great Leader slowly wave his white fleshy hand, his plump face expressionless, as if he were unaware that a million people, including his vice chairman behind him, were waving their Little Red Books and shouting "Long Live Chairman Mao!" The face looked completely emotionless, even a bit irritated. But seeing that face, people at the movie got excited and teary all over again, which puzzled me greatly. What did they see that I didn't? Some people in the front rows shouted "Long Live Chairman Mao" every time he appeared on the screen. One woman in the audience sobbed uncontrollably throughout the movie. From her voice, I suspect it was the same woman who had fainted so heroically before me at the rally.

Watching the movie, I felt certain that at that very moment, on the lofty Gate of Heavenly Peace amid the waves of the brown and red ocean, the Great Leader was planning something new for the Red Guards, who seemed to irritate him with all that shouting. Perhaps he will give us more military training, I thought. I could not have known, of course, that within a few months, what he had in mind would change my life completely. He would send me on a long, arduous, and miserable journey, along with thousands of his loyal former Red Guards. Like the monkey's journey, mine was to a deserted land in the west, thousands of miles away from the capital, and like his, it was a journey filled with battles against local monsters, and finally against the Jade Emperor himself.

Does the road wind uphill all the way?
Yes, to the very end.

*Christina Rossetti*

# *2* **Earth**

# 8 The Journey West

It took me many years to figure out the possible reasons why the Great Leader sent me and millions of Red Guards to remote villages to live as peasants, which caused great destruction to the rural economy and brought enormous misery to our young lives. It must have been another of his schemes to tame the Red Guards and to solve the urgent issue of unemployment for millions of city youths, because most of the factories were shut down during the Cultural Revolution. But, of course, he did not say anything like that when he ordered us to the countryside in January 1968. What he said was, "All the Red Guards should go live among revolutionary peasants for the rest of your lives and to learn the spirit of the old Red Army through hard labor." Whatever the true reason, the scheme failed completely, for few of us became true revolutionaries with the spirit of the old Red Army, and nearly all of us eventually escaped the miserable countryside and returned to cities.

But in 1968, nobody dared to question the Great Leader's word and his wish was taken as an order from God. It became a national movement, and within a few weeks millions of Red Guards were sent to rural areas. Some of them went willingly, but many others, like me, went reluctantly. I was ordered to go with the first group because of my family problem, and the Revolutionary Committee told me that I was in special need of education by revolutionary peasants.

In early February, Commander Duck Egg, representing the Revolutionary Committee, informed me that I had been chosen to be sent to Shaanbei, one of the poorest regions in the country. "Congratulations, Fan Shen. It's a great honor from Chairman Mao," he said to me, "that you are among the first Red Guards to settle down in Shaanbei. It's a priceless opportunity to learn from revolutionary peasants. Our company is honored to have one in the first group." I did not believe the lofty words he bestowed upon me, and I knew that Duck Egg had chosen me either because of my essay with that misspelled slogan or because he found out that I was the one who spoiled his lunch.

"Could you give the honor to someone else this time?" I asked without much hope.

"No," said Duck Egg firmly. "The Revolution Committee has discussed it thoroughly and because of your family background, we feel that you are the best choice to go first."

I knew it was useless to argue with Duck Egg, so I went home and pleaded with my mother. "But you have to go," said my mother. "Think of your family. If you don't go, your father and I will be in more trouble, and we can't afford to have more trouble than we already have. You have to follow the command of the Great Leader." I disliked the way she used lofty revolutionary words to talk to me, but I knew she was right: I dared not disobey the Great Leader's order.

On February 23, with a heavy heart, I left Beijing on an overcrowded train. But what made leaving Beijing so hard was not that I would leave my parents or that I was barely fourteen and had never left home before, but that neither of my two remaining friends from the Great Wall Fighting Team came with me. To avoid my fate, a few days after I was chosen, Baby Dragon left the Big Courtyard quietly and joined the army through the "back door," that is, with the help of his father. Soon afterward, Snivel left the Big Courtyard, too. His father, who was now the chairman of the Revolutionary Committee, found him a job as an office clerk in the railroad yard.

On the crowded special train whose passengers were all former Red Guards, however, I soon found something to cheer me up. Not long after the train started, I discovered, sitting not far from me, two former Red Guard friends whom I had met during the battle at Beijing University. Meeting Smoking Devil and Water Buffalo was a godsend. I hit it off well with them and decided to go to the same village they did. The official in charge of the train thought it made no difference whether I went to one village or another and agreed to give me permission to transfer to my friends' village. It did not take me long to realize how lucky I was to have found these resourceful friends, who would become my guardians and teachers later.

The train ride from Beijing to Xi'an was long and wearying. The black steam engine huffed and puffed westward for two days and two nights before finally dragging us into Xi'an, an ancient capital of many dynasties.

When the train stopped, I waited until the compartment was nearly empty before I dragged down the two bags I brought with me and got off the train. The scene on the platform immediately gave me a sense of tiredness and loneliness. The soot-covered train was limply heaving the last of its steam, and people were hurrying past me with their backs bent under the weight of their luggage. No one even glanced in my direction. Standing there in the chilly breeze, I became keenly aware of the fact that I was in a strange city now, hundreds of miles away from my family, and I was on my way to live in a village among peasants for the rest of my life. The thought of living in a poor village for the rest of my life depressed me.

I picked up the bags and shuffled toward the exit gate. The gate was still crowded with people who pushed one another to try to get out quickly. I could see my two friends, with bags on their shoulders, pushing hard through the crowd. Anxiously, I watched them fight their way toward the gate because I knew that it was crucial that they got out of the train station as soon as possible, in order to reach the ticket counter for the long-distance bus. The train ride to Xi'an was only half of our journey, the easy half. A bus ride of three hundred miles over rough country roads still lay ahead. Only three buses left each day and those who could not get bus tickets would have to spend a night or two at the crowded train station, sleeping on the hard benches. Few of us had the money to stay in a hotel.

As I was moving slowly and watching my friends, a peasant girl walked up to me.

"Would you like a boiled egg? Ten cents. Very fresh," she said with a thick accent and held an egg up to my face. Her other hand carried a wicker basket filled with boiled eggs and steamed bread.

"No," I said. I still had two or three boiled eggs in one of my bags, the remains of the food packed by my mother.

"How about a steamed bun? Two for ten cents. Just made today. Are you going to catch the bus to Shaanbei? It will take a whole day and there is no food on the bus." She put the egg into the basket and picked up two large steamed buns. I noticed that the hand holding the bread was grotesquely deformed, like an eagle's claw; her fingers could open barely enough to grasp the buns. Her hands must have been burned badly once.

I felt sorry for her; she was perhaps just my age. I put down the bags, took out a wrinkled ten-cent bill from my pocket, and bought the buns.

Twenty minutes later, I lugged my bags out the station gate and saw my two friends sitting triumphantly on their bedrolls in the sunshine in front of the bus station. They had already bought the bus tickets. Water Buffalo's brown shirt was opened at the collar and he was fanning his thick neck with a newspaper.

"If only I could have a bowl of *zhajiangmian* now," he said as he sniffed the air and looked longingly at the exhaust fan of a small restaurant on the corner of the station square. The wistful tone meant that his sentence would not be completed. Zhajiangmian was his favorite food; it consisted of noodles with fried soybean paste and shredded meat. Unfortunately, he had it only once a year, on the eve of the Spring Festival.

To show my gratitude, I handed him one of the steamed buns that I bought from the peasant girl. Water Buffalo took a big bite and chewed with an obvious expression of pleasure and gratitude.

Sitting beside Water Buffalo, Smoking Devil declined the steamed bun, and was practicing his "trade" again by drawing on a long pipe. He had already smoked so much in his life that all his fingers were the color of beef sticks, his lips the color of an eggplant, and half of his face the color of brown leather. He was the ultimate smoking connoisseur and could describe minute differences between each brand of cigarettes and pipe tobacco. There was nothing about smoking that he did not know. In his luggage, he had more than a dozen different pipes—clay, ceramic, porcelain, copper, steel, cherrywood, cottonwood, pinewood, and so on. Most of them he made himself. But what impressed me most about Smoking Devil was not his knowledge of tobacco, but his fantastic ways of smoking, like the "seven-hole puffing": he let a wreath of smoke slowly escape from his nostrils and mouth and swiveled his head slightly from side to side to weave the strands of smoke around his head, creating the illusion that the smoke actually came out of all seven holes in his head—his eyes, nostrils, mouth, and ears. He was so proud of his expertise that he nicknamed himself.

"Life is like a smoke," he often quoted his own aphorism. "You'd better enjoy it while it is there." At the moment, that was exactly what he was doing, amusing himself with his seven-hole puffing routine. I sat down beside him and took a bite of the steamed bun.

"Look at those people," said Smoking Devil, nodding to the crowd at the ticket window. "It's not going to be pretty when it's time to get on the bus."

I looked at the noisy mob apprehensively. "I hope we can get a seat on the bus," I said.

Taking a few quick puffs, Smoking Devil abruptly knocked the ashes out of his pipe and stood up. "Watch the luggage," he said to me. "I need to take a walk."

Half an hour later, he came back with a middle-aged man, wearing a greasy black overcoat, who looked like the bus driver. Smoking Devil beckoned to me and Water Buffalo to get up, and the three of us lugged our bags and followed the man to the back of the bus station. He walked to a Soviet antique of the '50s with mud and rusty patches all over its ancient body. Without a word, the man threw our luggage onto the luggage rack on top of the bus and opened the door to let us on. As I stepped on the bus, I noticed a brass pipe sticking out of the man's breast pocket.

Sitting comfortably in the seat just behind the driver's, Smoking Devil skillfully rolled a cigarette, lit it, took a deep draw, and blew out an almost perfect circle. "Smoking is the universal language," he said, turning and smiling to us proudly. "All smokers are brothers who help each other. The driver is a brother who will take care of us all the way to Shaanbei. It's a ten-hour ride. If you don't have a seat, God bless your legs. Now, close your windows. It will save us some trouble later." Although he was only three years older than I, Smoking Devil spoke like one of Plato's philosopher-kings. He sounded as if he had been through the toughest battles and had acquired, through those battles and deep reflection on everyday life, the divine wisdom we all seek. I was very proud to have a friend like him.

The driver came back half an hour later and started the engine. The ancient engine roared, and the bus shook some of the mud from its body and began to sway along the gravel path. Slowly, it turned around and rolled into the front of the station. A long line of people laden with bulky bags was waiting. Before the bus came to a stop, the queue disintegrated and people rushed the bus from all sides, attacking it like a school of piranha on a cow stranded in the Amazon River. I had seen people fighting to get on a bus in Beijing before, but never in my life had I seen as fierce a battle as the one unfolding before my eyes. As soon as the driver opened the door, it was promptly jammed by human bodies; no one wanted anyone else to get on first. Several young men stood on the shoulders of their friends and tried to climb in through the windows. Further away from the windows, people were throwing their luggage, which thumped and shook the bus as it landed on the rack. A bag thrown too far from one side sailed over the bus and landed on top of a girl on the other side. She let out a scream and fell to the ground. A few hands pulled her to the perimeter of the mayhem and lay her down by the curb. Behind me a young man climbed in headfirst through a window and dropped heavily to the floor of the bus. He immediately sprang up, rubbed his forehead, which had hit the steel leg of a seat, and turned to the window to pull in his friend.

A tall gaunt man in a sweat-streaked and wrinkled uniform pounded the metal hull and appealed to me to help pull him into the bus. His up-turned face was so close to mine that I could see giant soybeans of sweat on the man's hollow face and green luggage straps cutting deeply into his thin shoulders. "Please, young brother," he pleaded, a drop of sweat dripping into his mouth. "Please, little comrade. Little Brother, I will never forget your help if you—"

I thought of helping him to get at least his luggage in and I stood up to lift up the window.

"Don't do it!" Smoking Devil turned around and snarled at me. "Don't look at him. This is a help-yourself, dog-eat-dog world. You can't afford to help all the people who need help."

I obeyed, turning my head away from the window. From the scene all around the bus, I knew Smoking Devil was right. There was hardly any room in the bus already.

It was more than fifteen minutes before the battle ended, but the drama was far from over. All the seats were filled, most of them with one or two extra people, and the luggage racks overhead bulged with bags. But a few people were still trying to push their way into the bus; two of them had one foot on the step and hung halfway out of the bus. A loud female voice screamed from behind them.

"Get down! The two of you! Can't you see the bus is packed like a dung-beetle's ball?" The woman conductor grabbed the bags on the men's backs and pulled them backward. But the men stubbornly held on.

"Damn it! LET GO!" the driver suddenly roared. Till then, he had been quietly and patiently enjoying the whole drama. He stood up, craned his head over the people on the steps in the bus, and cursed again: "Damn it! If the conductor does not get on the bus, no one will leave. We are already half an hour late. GET THE HELL DOWN NOW! OR I'LL COME DOWN AND KICK YOU OFF!" He threw a ball of greasy rags at the face of the nearest man.

The two men finally let go of the door handles. The doors scraped heavily across the back of the conductor when the driver yanked on the lever that closed them. The bus started to roll away. But just as it was gaining speed, it suddenly lurched to a stop. The sudden stop caused a heavy bag to slid off the luggage rack and drop on someone's head.

"What the hell are you doing, Pickle Pot?" the woman conductor yelled at the driver, who in turn thrust his upper body out of the side window and yelled at a figure that blocked the bus: "Bastard! Do you want to go to hell right now?" Veins on his neck looked like ropes. "I should fucking crush you like a rotten egg—if I did, it wouldn't be my fault!"

I looked out the window and saw the person who blocked the bus. It was a young boy with a sickly yellow face. Running to the driver's side, he cupped his mouth with his hands and shouted: "My luggage is still on top of the bus. My luggage!"

"Shit! Why did you throw it up there if you can't get on the bus?" the driver said as much in exasperation as in anger. With a sigh, he then moved back into the bus, leaned back in his seat, and waited for the boy to climb up and get his bag.

The bus was quiet for a moment. The people who weren't lucky enough to get on the bus were returning to the shade under the veranda, to wait for the next bus, which would come in four hours. As people scattered, I noticed a young girl sitting on a bedroll on the veranda, quietly staring at the bus. She wore a light blue shirt and blue pants; her skin, in contrast to the people around her, was unusually white. Her very large eyes and sharply curved eyebrows all looked familiar, but I could not remember where I had seen her.

When the bus started moving again and we passed the girl, I was startled by the fiery look in those eyes. My heart began throbbing. The memory came back to me in a flash: two girls huddling with the mother as the Red Guards ransacked their home; Whiskers threatening to slap the younger girl, named Li Ling; and I holding the big picture book, walking past her as her eyes radiated hatred. I could never forget those eyes. The picture book with naked women was in my luggage with me. It was one of three books that I did not burn.

Obviously Li Ling did not recognize me when the bus rolled past her, which was a good thing. No doubt she'd have hated my guts if she recognized me as one of those Red Guards who killed her father. Still I felt that this ignominious episode—which I hated to remember—seemed to have created a special connection between her and me, and for a while I wondered if fate would allow me to see her again, even though I knew I probably would not have the courage to speak to her if I were to meet her again. Throughout the journey, as I dozed tiredly in the crowded bus, I could not put the image of her sitting quietly on her bedroll out of my mind and I thought from time to time what I would say to Li Ling if I saw her again.

## 9  The Beijing Kids

We arrived at the headquarters of the Dragon Gorge Commune the next morning. Uncle Cricket met our group in the commune's courtyard. He was the Party secretary of the Third Production Team, and was here to take us to his village. He was probably no more than fifty years of age but looked much older, his rough nut-brown face crisscrossed with deep wrinkles.

He dressed slightly differently from other peasants. Instead of a black homemade shirt stained with sweat, he wore a blue Mao jacket, although it was hard to tell whether it was blue or gray at first glance; the color, except under the armpits, was largely gone. Thirteen years of washing and sunshine will do that to a jacket. The reason I knew the exact age of the jacket was that he told us that it was bought to celebrate the birth of his last child, his only son—now thirteen years old—after suffering the humiliation of having five girls in a row. Considering its age, the jacket was still in good shape. The reason, we later found out, was that he wore it only on special occasions. And today was a special occasion.

Having loaded up our luggage onto two horse wagons, Uncle Cricket proudly drove off the lead wagon with nine of us "Beijing Kids" on board. From the very start, it was clear that he took the Great Leader's instruction very seriously, to "re-educate" the youths from the city. As the horse-drawn wagons swung along the rough country road, he gave us in his thick accent the first lengthy lecture on the revolution in the village. "You must keep your eyes wide open," he said slowly. The phrases seemed to jump out of his mouth in short spurts whenever the wagon hit a bump. "The enemies are everywhere. There is still a landlord's son in the village who we all know is a dangerous enemy. You must all watch out for him." We all smiled and nodded at his singsong accent. The novelty of riding a horse wagon with a peasant excited me and I forgot the fatigue of the long trip. Throughout the six-hour journey, I sang with others all the revolutionary songs we knew, especially our favorite song, "Harden

Our Hearts." It was a pleasant sunny morning and our young voices reverberated among the barren hills that seemed to share our innocent enthusiasm.

The Third Production Team included the entire village of Big Porcupine, with a population of eight hundred. The word "Big" distinguished it from two other porcupine villages, Black Porcupine, three miles to the east, and Small Porcupine, five miles to the southwest.

The two "cave-houses" that we settled in were halfway up a hill, just outside of the village. Like all the other cave-houses in that region, they were arched holes dug into the yellow clay hillside, about five or six steps wide and ten steps deep. The entrance was sealed by a dirt-brick wall with a door and a window whose panes were covered with rough straw paper. The inside of each cave-house was dominated by a large *kang*, a heated brick bed. The slightly larger cave-house on the left was for me and my five male comrades. The women's cave-house on the right, with a very large wood stove, also served as the communal kitchen for the group. There was no electricity, plumbing, or running water. The outhouse was on top of the hill up a steep footpath and was nothing more than four poles with a straw mat wrapped around them. A narrow footpath sloped down to the bottom of the ravine, through which ran a small stream bearing the grand name of "Dragon Gorge River." We would take turns fetching water to fill the two large vats we used for cooking and washing.

In the men's cave, beside me, Smoking Devil, and Water Buffalo, there were also my three new comrades, Green Olive, Mirror Wang, and Heart Attack.

Although a year older than I, Green Olive was nearly half a head shorter. He must have stopped growing when he was ten. The homemade, ill-fitting jacket he wore was at least two sizes too large and hung from his body as if from a scarecrow. Green Olive, however, was a very easygoing person and never seemed to notice any of these oddities.

In contrast to Green Olive's agreeable and mild outgoing nature, Mirror Wang was quiet and conscientious. He had thick glasses and came from a proper and intellectual family; both his father and mother had been instructors of Chinese literature at the Beijing Normal School. Unlike the rest of us with our short crew cuts, his hair was long and combed neatly to the left. He was so concerned about his hair that, whenever no one was looking (or so he thought), he would take out a little mirror that he carried in his pocket and check on its condition. When he talked, he would end each sentence with a quick sweep of the hand over his precious hair.

Heart Attack was a handsome young man of eighteen, with a square jaw and high cheekbones. He acquired his ominous name a week before my arrival, when he and some other Beijing Kids who came early were assembled at the headquarters of the Dragon Gorge Commune, waiting to be assigned to a village. During a meeting there, he fainted and was rushed to the county hospital where he stayed for two days. For a while, his heart raced so fast that the doctors thought he'd had a heart attack and sent an "imminent death notice" to his family in Beijing. But he miraculously recovered when his brother arrived two days later, and the doctors never could diagnose the problem. Since then, his name was Heart Attack to all the Beijing Kids, and strangely, he took it as a badge of honor and always cheerfully responded when someone shouted "Heart Attack."

Of the three girls in the cave-house next door, Ya Rong, at twenty-one, was not only the oldest of the entire group, but also the heaviest. Her large head sat directly and solidly on her round shoulders—no need for a neck. Dangling from the back of the massive head were two long, thin pigtails like two straw ropes. Of all the Beijing Kids, she was the one I liked the least, because she seemed genuinely eager to be re-educated by revolutionary peasants and she sat with a big and flattering smile by Uncle Cricket for the entire wagon ride. We called her Big Quilt because of her large, fleshy body and the big bedroll that she brought with her.

The two other girls, Yin Yin and Yang Yang, were twins, but seemed completely opposite persons with the same long and smooth face. Their parents somehow divined the temperament of each when they picked their names. Yin Yin—meaning cloudy—was always sullen and never smiled. Yang Yang—sunny—talked and laughed incessantly, as if she were trying to make up for her sister's deficiencies. For the first year, Yin Yin stayed home to make meals for the group, and Yang Yang sang in the field for us boys. Needless to say, we all liked Yang Yang the best.

Exhausted from the long journey, I slept soundly on the warm kang for nearly two days. On the third day, Uncle Cricket came and told us to get ready for work. "We have just embarked on a proud project: To 'Re-model the Globe,'" he said. "You probably have seen the big-letter posters throughout the village when you came. This is a project designed by the Great Leader himself, who has called on all the communes in China to remodel the earth, to build terraced fields on barren hills for better water conservation and a higher crop yield. Now, you came just in time for this most honorable project in our village."

At four o'clock the next morning, I was violently awakened by loud knocks on the door. Shivering, I quickly slipped into the padded winter jacket that my mother had remade for me out of an old army coat, and jumped to the ground. The cave-house was ice cold; the fire that heated the kang before we went to sleep had died during the night. I groped around in darkness, found the door, and opened it. It was still pitch black outside and a bitter draft rushed in. Along with the wind, the dark shadow of Uncle Cricket swept into the cave.

"The rooster *has* crowed!" he snarled in his thick singsong dialect. He seemed to be a completely different person now, sullen and impatient. He struck a match and lit the lamp. Finding all the other young men still in bed, he yelled: "Get up!" and roughly pulled up Green Olive's blanket, exposing a thin shivering body, like that of a plucked chicken. "All the villagers are already in the field. We are late. Hurry!"

"Isn't he like Skinner Zhou? It's only four o'clock!" Green Olive grumbled as soon as Uncle Cricket walked out to rouse the girls next door. Skinner Zhou was a rich landlord in a story who used to imitate the crow of roosters in the middle of the night and then drive his farmhands to work. But we were too busy to chuckle at the comparison. Smoking Devil rushed up the hill to occupy the outhouse while Water Buffalo sniffed around the room looking for leftovers to eat.

Ten minutes later, we set out to work. Except for a few dim flickering stars, the sky was dark and the pre-dawn gusts of wind cut our exposed skin like small razors. Behind Uncle Cricket, we stumbled along on the snowy road, carrying picks and shovels on our shoulders. The road was narrow and steep and sometimes I had to crawl on my hands and knees so that I would not fall down the slippery slope. "I wish I had the wisdom of Yin Yin," Smoking Devil muttered dolefully as his thin legs moved unsteadily on the scraggly path. Yin Yin was the only one who stayed behind and did not have to get up so early. I couldn't agree with Smoking Devil more.

Up one hill and down another—again and again—we seemed to have walked a long time and passed many shadowy hills, all looking the same.

We finally stopped on top of a large hill. The shirt inside my padded coat was already soaked through with sweat. Against the deep blue of the sky, I could see the silhouette of a large, round boulder peculiarly jutting out over the smooth snow-covered hill. Evidently, Uncle Cricket had chosen this hill for a particular purpose: to give us a lesson on the local history of the communist revolution. After assembling us under the boulder, he began the lecture: "This is the Red Army Hill. From where you stand right now, a Red Army General named Hu Tu directed a battle against the nationalist troops in 1946. During the battle, General Hu was struck by an enemy shell and died right on this spot. This land is soaked with a martyr's blood and has become a symbol of the revolution. Now we must carry on the Red Army's spirit and tame these barren hills. This is Chairman Mao's test of your revolutionary spirit."

For a semiliterate peasant, Uncle Cricket was surprisingly eloquent.

"You are the first to launch our campaign to 'Remodel the Globe,'" Uncle Cricket continued, sweeping his hand across the shadowy hills around us. "It is an honor that the Party has decided to bestow upon you, the Beijing Kids. Will you let the Party down? The Great Leader has said those who show a Red heart will be welcomed back to Beijing, and those who don't will spend the rest of their lives here. The village is watching you. The Party is watching you. The Great Leader is watching you. Now, before we start, let's recite the Great Leader's 'Harden Our Hearts.'"

Uncle Cricket's words filled my heart with apprehension: this was a test from the Great Leader and I could not afford to fail it. As soon as the work started, I threw myself energetically into the work, and being young and naïve, I did not question the sanity of what we were doing: eight young people trying to flatten a large hill with picks and shovels, and then carrying rocks up from the bottom of the ravine to protect the leveled patches of land from erosion. All I was thinking was to show Uncle Cricket my big Red heart so that he would allow me to return to Beijing some day.

The work was hard. The earth was frozen and each time my pick struck the ground, it sent a painful jolt like an electrical shock from my hands to my heart. But the result was only a pitiful white dent and a clump of dirt the size of a walnut. It took several swings to break through the layer of frost. The progress was painfully slow. And it was not long before I discovered several blisters on my hands.

Despite the frigid conditions and solid ground, we worked energetically for the first two hours; we even laughed sometimes and swung our picks at a feverish pace. Once in a while, Smoking Devil would urge Yang Yang to sing a song, and she would oblige with a song of the Great Leader's quotations. It seemed to me that this was a pleasant game designed for us by Chairman Mao and it would be over soon, so I wasn't too bothered by the pain in my hands.

The game singing and the laughter, however, did not last long. Hard as it was, leveling the ground turned out to be just a warm-up. After we had leveled a small strip of land, Uncle Cricket told us to switch to the next task—carrying rocks from the riverbank to the top of the hill. That soon silenced the songs and wiped the smiles off our young faces.

I had never carried a basket of rocks and did not know how heavy it would be. The first time I put a basket of rocks on my shoulders I nearly lost my balance and fell backward into the river. They weighed at least as much as I did. Each step up the hill was a struggle. I had to crawl on my hands and knees most of the time. It seemed a long time before I succeeded in crawling to the halfway point where Uncle Cricket was standing, and just as I passed him, I tripped and landed on my face. The basket rolled off my back. Lying on my stomach, I smelt the wet snow and could see a little drop of blood from my nose sinking a small crimson well in the white snow. I did not get up right away and thought of lying there for a while. But as soon as I saw Uncle Cricket turn around and watch me with a reproachful gaze, I scrambled up and collected my basket. I did not want him to think that I had failed the Great Leader's test, and I did not want to spend the rest of my life in the village. Again, I crawled slowly upward with the deadly weight on my back. The last fifty yards seemed like a journey through hell. Inch by inch, I dragged my legs up, my shoulders and my hands all hurting so much that I thought one part or another of my body might break off soon. And I had never known that lungs were capable of such pain. I did not moan, however, nor did I dare to stop.

Big Quilt was the first of us to reach the top with a basket of rocks. When I was scrambling up from my second fall, I heard her shout: "Long Live Chairman Mao!" and "Long Live the Revolutionary Spirit!" from the top of the hill. I started to develop a hatred for her. Her enthusiasm and success had made the rest of us look bad and had forced us to work faster.

By ten o'clock in the morning, time for breakfast, I had made a total of two trips and I felt I could not take another step. Besides the blisters and cuts on my hands—blood had made my gloves sticky—I felt I must have broken my collar bones, for my shoulders hurt so much that they involuntarily retracted even at the touch of my padded coat. Sitting against the round boulder, my shirt and coat completely soaked, I shivered in the harsh breeze as I munched on a cold *wotou* (cone-shaped steamed corn bread) and a pinch of salted turnip brought up by Yin Yin.

During the break, Uncle Cricket asked Big Quilt to read a few passages from the Great Leader's Little Red Book.

"We have made good progress," Uncle Cricket said after the reading. "As Chairman Mao has said, only sweat and blood can foster a true revolutionary spirit. This is just the beginning. The real test has yet to begin. No matter how hard it is, as long as you remember the Great Leader's words, you will have endless strength and you will conquer nature. Chairman Mao will give you strength. Before we start again, let's recite the Great Leader's famous 'Harden Our Hearts' once again." In his sing-song accent, he led off the passage:

"Harden our hearts, fear not sacrifices, overcome ten thousand obstacles, to achieve the ultimate victory . . . HARDEN OUR HEARTS, FEAR NOT SACRIFICES, OVERCOME TEN THOUSAND OBSTACLES, TO ACHIEVE THE ULTIMATE VICTORY!"

The endless incantation of the passage seemed to have worked wonders on the other members of my group. After the recitation, Big Quilt was the first to jump up, even before the break was over, and to rush down the hill to the riverbank. She was followed by Heart Attack and Yang Yang. They seemed full of energy once again. Even Smoking Devil appeared to have drawn sustenance from Mao's magical words, for he too was able to scramble up before me. That, of course, made me feel very bad about myself. When I strained to get up on my feet, my whole body was in such pain that I fell back to the comfort of the cold ground. The magical words of our great godlike leader had failed again to transform my battered body. The old question that had vexed me when I saw the Great Leader at Tiananmen Square returned to haunt me: Was there something wrong with me? Why wasn't I revivified like the others by the Great Leader's "magical words"? I tried to let Chairman God's words sink into my heart, but the excruciating pain in my body told me that nothing had changed.

Not long after the break, I fell again. This time, I felt relieved to see the basket and its stones roll down the slope and disappear into the icy water. As my knees hit the frozen ground, I did not even try to soften the impact with my hands. Nothing seemed to matter any more. All I craved was a moment's rest. But then, I saw Uncle Cricket strut toward me muttering some hateful reproach, and there was nothing else for me to do but to drag myself up with what seemed like my last drop of energy. I staggered slowly down the hill again to fish the basket out of the shallow river.

Just before dinner, Big Quilt fell too. (Served her right, I thought.) She was carrying a big basket of rocks and had almost reached the top when all of a sudden her legs gave out on her, and the basket emptied on her back, head, and torso. Her face hit a rock and a tooth fell out of her mouth. She looked as if she were dead when we gathered around her; blood was all over her face and for ten minutes, she lay motionless on the ground. I began to imagine the unpleasant task of having to carry her monstrous fleshy body back to the village. That would be worse than carrying a basket of rocks. But then her feet twitched a few times and she woke up. The amazing thing is, as soon as she opened her eyes, she wriggled in an effort to get up and to reach out to grab her basket again, just like a hero described in a revolutionary story would do. I had a suspicion that she faked the passing out in order to stage the heroic act, but Uncle Cricket was greatly impressed. (My hatred for her increased tenfold at that moment because that was exactly what I was thinking of doing—passing out heroically as I did at Tiananmen Square so that I would get to rest till the end of the day—and she took my game away.) That evening, at the assembly of the whole Third Production Team, Uncle Cricket extolled Big Quilt's determination and dedication and used her example to challenge the rest of the team: "If a fragile young city girl could work this hard for the Great Leader, how could the rest of us not follow her example?"

The first day of work did not end until it was dark. I don't remember how I carried myself back from the Red Army Hill that night. The warm kang in the cave house felt so welcome and comforting that I collapsed on it and slid into oblivion with my wet clothes still on.

The second and third days were harder still. Another spring snow had fallen on the second day, making the slope even more slippery and treacherous. The hard work soon took its toll on our young team. On the third day, Mirror Wang slipped at the riverbank and fell into the icy stream. He caught cold and was confined to bed for several days. At the end of the first week, Smoking Devil claimed that he had suffered a "crushed vertebra"—that was his term—and was permitted to stay home to help Yin Yin prepare meals. Water Buffalo sprained an ankle and had to stay home, too. By the end of the second week, only five people could work. I had a feeling that Uncle Cricket watched me especially closely and I did not dare to feign any injury or passing out.

In the next two weeks, I worked like a walking zombie; I was so tired that nothing mattered to me at night. My wet smelly clothes, the pain in my back and shoulders, Water Buffalo's snoring, Green Olive's talking in his sleep, Smoking Devil's noxious fumes—none of it disturbed me. The only thing still capable of bothering me was Uncle Cricket's violent knocking on the door early in the morning. Before the second week was over, I had already sworn to myself that I would leave the village at all costs. This was no place to spend my life. The Great Leader's order or no, I did not want to be a revolutionary peasant for another day.

The backbreaking work lasted three weeks. By the end of the third week, we had built several small strips of terraced land on top of Red Army Hill. From a distance, the strips looked like a few goose feathers, laying in a peculiar pattern on top of a barren hill. All told, we had salvaged no more than a quarter of an acre. Uncle Cricket named it the "Beijing Kids' Terraced Field" and proudly displayed it to the entire production team. Unfortunately, our achievement did not last long. Perhaps the Sea Dragon did not like us intruding on his sacred territory—I learned later from a folktale that peasants used to worship the Sea Dragon on this hill—and sent a torrential April rain that washed down most of the rocks we painstakingly carried up and made the hill once again a smooth baldhead. I was very thankful that the rain and the impending spring sowing ended our effort to "remodel the globe." It was a crazy project that was more for political propaganda than for any agricultural purpose.

"We will be back next spring!" Uncle Cricket vowed at the weekly Sunday rally of the Third Production Team shortly after the devastating storm. I shuddered at his words. I doubted I could survive another three weeks of such work. "We revolutionary peasants will never surrender to nature," Uncle Cricket continued. "As long as we have Chairman Mao's guidance and the Red Army spirit, we will conquer Red Army Hill. As the Great Leader said, 'Man will conquer the sky!' Long Live the Great Leader!"

He sounded more and more like a clown to me. But I had to win his favor if I wanted to get out of the mountain village some day, so I shouted loudly with him: "Man will conquer the sky! Long Live the Great Leader!"

## IO "Be a *Revolutionary* Peasant!"

My wish to escape the village did not come to pass quickly, but I soon learned to ease the harsh labor and to make my existence in the village more tolerable. For this I owe infinite gratitude to Smoking Devil, who had emerged as the spiritual leader of our group and had taught us various ways to live and work at a leisurely pace like those "revolutionary" peasants.

"The Great Leader sent us here to learn from revolutionary peasants, and we must follow His Excellency's words to the letter," Smoking Devil told us one morning when we arrived at our allotted field. This was in late spring, after we had abandoned building the terraced field and had begun the spring planting. Pointing to the peasants who were lying in the bean field and gossiping about women, sage Smoking Devil said: "Look at the real peasants and listen to them. To be a true revolutionary peasant, we must learn to talk like them, dress like them, smoke like them, and work like them!" We all laughed. Uncle Cricket would have appreciated his pep talk and surely would have missed the sarcastic double-talk that brought smiles to our faces.

True to his words, Smoking Devil led the way in "the revolution to become real peasants." The day after the pep talk, he went to the field in a pair of homemade large-crotched pants, which he had acquired from a peasant by trading his khaki pants. Like a peasant, he wore them without underwear. "They're the most sanitary and economical pants under the circumstances," he said, showing off a large crotch wide enough to hide a pig. "When you are washed only twice in your life—the time you are born and the time you are buried—you've got to wear this to keep yourself clean. With no underwear you leave no place for lice and fleas to hide, and the large crotch gives you good ventilation in hot weather. Besides, you save money. There is no need for underwear." He was a good salesman. The next day, Water Buffalo, Green Olive, and Heart Attack all showed up with black large-crotched pants, complete with chalky lines of sweat around the waist. I too acquired a pair from a peasant, but I did not like the smell of them. I wore them nevertheless, for by wearing the peasant attire I blended in well with other peasants when we slept in the field and Uncle Cricket could not single me out from a distance.

"The next thing to learn," lectured Professor Smoking Devil a few days later, "is to smoke hemp like the peasants." Purple-stemmed hemp was the major cash crop of the Third Production Team. Besides firewood and cooking oil, it provided the only recreation for everybody in the village. Men, women, and children all smoked it with water pipes. "Shaanbei hemp is the best in the world," Smoking Devil declared. "It is the most potent marijuana there is—so powerful that it can knock your pants off and let you see the Devil himself. But if you smoke it with a water pipe, as the peasants do, it is a smooth, easy smoke. With just one drag, you feel like sleeping in the South China Sea with the goddess Guanyin herself." Over the course of the next few weeks, every Beijing Kid got himself a water pipe. Even Mirror Wang and I, who did not smoke, got pipes for ourselves, to show solidarity with our smoking comrades. Seeing us with water pipes, other peasants began to treat us as their own and always warned us when Uncle Cricket approached our field.

"But the most important thing is, you are not a true revolutionary peasant if you do not work like a revolutionary peasant," Professor Smoking Devil taught us again one day. "Work is not just work; it is an art. You must learn to appreciate the artistry of work. Just watch how the revolutionary peasants work and follow their example." Every Beijing Kid, I especially, was immensely grateful for this insightful teaching. We watched the peasants in the field and followed suit. We got up as usual when Uncle Cricket roused us before dawn, and were in the field while it was still dark. But as soon as Uncle Cricket headed back to village for meetings, we all lay down in the field and slept till the sun warmed our behinds and breakfast arrived. After lunch, we took another long nap and got up just before dinner. In between the naps, we hoed beans or corn or hemp, not in any rush, as we did when building the terraced field, but at a slow, deliberate pace. When we reached the end of each row, we sat down with the other peasants and smoked a pipe. After that, it was story time. It was during those smoking breaks that we learned all the colorful stories that the peasants told about each other's wives and the women in the village.

Smoking Devil had a knack for dialects. Scarcely three months had passed before he spoke the Shaanbei dialect perfectly, with all its idioms and even its singsong tone. Empowered by his newly acquired dialect, he conversed freely with the peasants and learned all the juicy gossip in the village, past and present, which he then passed on to his less linguistically gifted friends. Among other things, he told us the original story of Red Army Hill and the Sea Dragon, a story that explained why attempting to remodel Red Army Hill was such a bad idea.

Smoking Devil told us that before the Cultural Revolution changed its name, Red Army Hill was called Nipple Hill. The name came from a legend a thousand years old. "Many, many years ago," Smoking Devil began the story over his water pipe:

"A catastrophic drought struck the region. There had been very little rain in the previous two years, but this year there was not a single drop. First, the crops and grass died. Then the trees and animals died. And finally, people started to die. Every day, people gathered at the Temple of Sea Dragon on the top of the hill, to pray for water. One night, when villagers were praying at the temple, thunder struck the temple and a voice spoke from its center. 'A young mother from the village must make a sacrifice alone in the temple before the rain returns.'

"When a young mother by the name of Sweet Yucca heard the news, she resolved that she would save the village. That night, she said goodbye to her husband and infant son, and went to the temple alone. The temple was dark when Sweet Yucca entered. On the altar, the small flame from the single candle flickered in the hot dry breeze. The shadow of the statue of the fierce-looking Sea Dragon, projected by the wavering light, became a towering giant on the wall, as if preparing to jump off the ceiling and snatch away the young woman. Sweet Yucca knelt down before the statue, closed her eyes, and started to pray. Presently, she felt something nudge her feet. Opening her eyes, she saw a large black porcupine. It was a very old and ugly porcupine. His opaque brown eyes were half closed and many of the foot-long spikes on his back were broken. He must have been a thousand years old. He was weak, limp, and dying of thirst.

" 'Could you give me something to drink?' The old porcupine murmured, his head resting on the dusty ground. But there was no water to be had. Sweet Yucca took pity on the old porcupine and picked up the beast, raised her blouse, and put him to her breast. Sweet milk flowed into the mouth of the dying animal. The porcupine's spikes pricked her hands and chest, but she held on. Finally, the porcupine was revived.

" 'Thank you,' he said, as Sweet Yucca laid him on the ground. Tears sparkled in the old porcupine's eyes as he slowly crawled toward the door. As he disappeared in the darkness, lightning tore apart the sky and rain poured on the earth. For three days it rained. When the sun finally came out, people saw a giant round boulder where the Temple of the Sea Dragon formerly stood. The round boulder was shaped like a nipple. The villagers named it 'Nipple Hill,' to commemorate Sweet Yucca, who, the villagers said, had turned into the boulder."

"Now I know," I said as Smoking Devil finished his story and filled another pipe, "Why in April we had such an unusual storm that washed down our terraced field. It's the Sea Dragon's territory."

"No doubt about it," said Smoking Devil. "Perhaps Uncle Cricket is the only one around here who does not believe in the Sea Dragon. Speaking of Uncle Cricket, do you want to hear some stories about our famous Party secretary?" Seeing uniformly eager nodding from us, he proceeded to relate the latest tales about Uncle Cricket, which were just as good as the Nipple Hill story. Smoking Devil was a good storyteller. Adding the raconteur's equivalent of soy sauce, vinegar, and spices, he could make any story colorful and tasty, especially erotic ones. I often admired his astounding knowledge of what went on between men and women, knowledge that was beyond that of a normal seventeen-year-old.

Uncle Cricket, said Smoking Devil, was actually revered by the fellow peasants not for his piety for the Great Leader, but for the almost supernatural prowess of his crotch. By one account (Smoking Devil would not reveal the source), Uncle Cricket had slept with half the women in the village. Some said that he had eighteen children, even though only six were legitimate. Even now, he told us, one of the Beijing girls was sleeping with him.

The news shocked me, but it did not take me long to figure it out. "It must be Big Quilt," I said and Smoking Devil smiled. On most of the evenings since we had arrived in the village, Uncle Cricket came after supper and called for Big Quilt to go with him to the headquarters of the Party to study the Great Leader's works. "She's a good youth, but needs extra guidance to become a true revolutionary," I remembered Uncle Cricket telling us.

A few months after we heard Smoking Devil's story, the result of Big Quilt's intensive study with Uncle Cricket became obvious to everybody: her belly was getting bigger every day. One night, she did not return from Uncle Cricket's study. The next day, he came to her cave-house to collect her things and to tell us the good news: "Thanks to Big Quilt's progress in studying Chairman Mao's works and learning the revolutionary spirit from the peasants, she has been chosen by the Party to study at a nursing school in Yan'an. All the rest of you," Uncle Cricket added, emphatically eyeing Yin Yin and Yang Yang, "if you also study hard and earnestly accept the re-education from revolutionary peasants, you will also graduate from here soon. She has set a good example for all of you. Remember why the Great Leader sent you here: To learn from the revolutionary peasants."

"Learn from revolutionary peasants!" everybody shouted jokingly, Smoking Devil and I the loudest.

Later, I learned that Big Quilt had an abortion and was happy to have escaped the hard labor of Big Porcupine village. Although her method of escape was distasteful to me, it had given me a useful lesson on dealing with Uncle Cricket, which would serve me well in the future.

"We have all become revolutionary peasants now, but there is still more to do," Smoking Devil declared one afternoon with a broad smile on his face. Stretching his arms after his nap he surveyed the field of sleeping bodies that were waking up around him in the warm autumn sun. This was the beginning of the wheat harvest season in late July. "We must thank the Great Leader for sending us here, and we do His Excellent Excellency great injustice if we do not take advantage of all the revolutionary opportunities that he provides us," said our philosopher. He was referring to an ingenious plan that he had just hatched. The plan was to take advantage of the fact that the government had mandated that production teams must provide each Beijing Kid with two hundred kilograms of grain a year, regardless how much work he had done.

In October after the fall harvest, Smoking Devil and Water Buffalo collected their share of the newly harvested crop and proceeded to execute an ingenious scheme. As soon as snow had fallen, they started to develop illnesses, or rather, their chronic illnesses reemerged. Smoking Devil's "crushed vertebra" returned and so did Water Buffalo's back pains, and they needed to see doctors in Beijing. After obtaining permission from Uncle Cricket, they sold their allotments of grain, which provided them with money for train tickets, and went home in January—just in time to catch the Spring Festival. For the next six months, they recuperated in Beijing, and in the late summer, when most of the hard work in the village was done, they came back to do some token work, then collected their allotment of grain and got ready to sell it and go home again.

It was a smart game for them. "I love being *re-educated* by revolutionary peasants," Smoking Devil said solemnly to Uncle Cricket when asking for permission to see doctors in Beijing again. "No matter how many broken vertebrae I have, I will always return here as soon as possible to continue my education. We must live up to the Great Leader's expectations." This time, Heart Attack had also developed a medical problem—chronic heart attack—and got permission to go back to Beijing for treatment too. The three imposters even had the audacity to travel together on the same train.

I could not benefit from such an ingenious plan, however. Since my parents were still in trouble, I could not go home to celebrate the Spring Festival in Beijing. I would cause more problems for my parents if Duck Egg found out that I did not remain in the countryside, and my parents would certainly be mad at me.

In April, after Smoking Devil and Water Buffalo had gone home, I received a letter from my friend Baby Dragon, who had joined the army a year earlier. Lately, Baby Dragon family's fortunes had flourished, thanks to a new friendship between his father and Marshal Ye Jianying, the new defense minister. His father, Baby Dragon proudly wrote, had been promoted to deputy defense minister, and the family had moved out of the Big Courtyard and into an exquisite fourteen-room mansion in downtown Beijing. He got special permission to come back from the army to help his family move. But the strange thing was that his new family home was right next door to the house that we once ransacked at the beginning of the Cultural Revolution. "It still gives me the creeps when I think of the dead doctor with his belly full of soy sauce," he said in his letter.

Baby Dragon's fortune did not cheer me up, but only made me more aware of my bleak situation as I sat in the dark cave-house and read his letter by the dim oil lamp, and it again strengthened my desire to escape the village. That night I did not sleep much, and thought long and hard about how to get permission from Uncle Cricket to leave.

## *11* **The Great Mountain Flood**

The day after I received Baby Dragon's letter, I went to see Uncle Cricket in the village office after work. "Uncle Cricket," I said with a big smile. "You have taught me many great revolutionary ideas and I certainly would like to learn more, like Big Quilt has done with you. Would you take me up as your special student and teach me more of the Great Leader's ideas? And by the way, if there's another chance for one of us to go to school, would you please consider me?"

"Well, Fan Shen," said the Party secretary, looking at me without much interest. "Your enthusiasm is good, but you must remember that learning from revolutionary peasants is a long process, and you have just started. You will certainly learn more working in the fields than in school, as the Great Leader says. I'm too busy to take a special student now, but I will pay more attention to your progress. When you are ready, I will bring the matter up to the Party Committee and we will discuss it." From his official tone, I knew perfectly well that he had no intention of helping me at all, and to get him to help me, I needed something more substantial than words. I needed a chance to do him a favor big enough that he would help me get out of the village.

Fortunately, beginning in the second year of our settlement in Big Porcupine, a drought began to develop in the region, which eventually brought me the chance I needed.

It was an extremely hot year. In early January, a villager by the name of Broken Shoe claimed that he had seen a wild red goat on Nipple Hill. "That's a bad omen," everybody said. "A red goat in winter, a scorched earth in summer." It meant that a terrible drought was coming. Even Uncle Cricket appeared apprehensive, although he denounced the prophetic vision as superstition at the village meeting. But the superstitious peasants were right.

There was hardly a drop of rain after we plowed the fields in March. It was so dry that by May, the Dragon Gorge River below our cave-houses had dried up and two of the three wells in the village had become muddy wallows infested with knots of black toads. The third was reduced to a yield of one small bucket of water an hour, barely enough for the residents to drink. Each day, two of us had to stand in line to get water from the well, and it took two or three hours to collect the water we needed. In June, the water from the well trickled out so slowly that it had to be rationed: a half bucket per household per day. Horses, cows, pigs, and goats, getting little water, started to wither and die. Some people began secretly praying to the Sea Dragon on old Nipple Hill for rain. The practice was repeatedly denounced by the Communist Party Committee, and Uncle Cricket threatened to take action against the offenders.

To counter the superstition, he called an emergency meeting of the Party Committee of the Third Production Team in June and they decided to dig a new well. Sinking a water well is an important event for a Shaanbei village. Traditionally, the site for the well is divined by a feng shui master—a master of Wind and Water—who chooses the location according to the *qi,* the "vital energy," of the village. Those masters had all been banished or killed off during the revolutionary years, however; and the government had declared the practice of feng shui a relic of feudal society.

So Uncle Cricket took it upon himself to find a suitable site. No one knew exactly how he came up with the spot, but it was certainly an odd location for a new well, right in the backyard of Broken Shoe, with whose wife Uncle Cricket was rumored to be having an affair. To compensate for the loss of the backyard, Uncle Cricket offered Broken Shoe the lucrative job of tractor driver, the principal duty of which is to drive "the Pomp-Pomp," the single-cylindered tractor, to transport goods between the village and the county. Broken Shoe was overjoyed by the offer. His frequent absences would, of course, make other people happy as well.

Work on the new well started immediately. Digging around the clock, we and the villagers made good progress on the well. On the third day, the well was twenty-two yards deep; on the fourth day, thirty-eight yards—five yards deeper than the deepest existing well. But there was still no sign of water. Insisting that the location was right, Uncle Cricket diligently supervised the project, sometimes lowering himself down the shaft to inspect the progress. People had been murmuring that we should try another site, but no one dared to mention such a suggestion to Uncle Cricket.

On the fifth day, after dinner, Green Olive and I sat down by the well, and he pulled out and packed a water pipe. A kerosene lamp hanging on the windlass shed a ghastly bluish light on the giant pile of dirt from the well in the yard. Everybody was taking a break except Uncle Cricket, who was checking progress in the well.

"I hate to waste my time here," I said, looking at the amount of dirt that threatened to swallow Broken Shoe's house. Green Olive nodded his head and continued to smoke. He had learned the trick of "the seven-hole puff" from Smoking Devil and was diligently practicing it.

"What is Uncle Cricket doing in the well now?" I continued. "Reading the Great Leader's Little Red Book? Somebody ought to let him know that there won't be water in this well." My butt was sore again, and sure enough, from my sore butt a small "wicked" thought grew and rose to my brain. I jumped up immediately.

Grabbing a pair of gunnysacks which we had used to hoist the dirt, I walked to the opening of the well and shouted in:

"Comrades, let's start working now. It's getting late." Pretending that I did not know Uncle Cricket was in the well, I dropped the gunnysacks into the dark hole. Wet and heavy, they swept down the deep shaft as if sucked in by a hungry dragon.

A few seconds later there was a muffled thud. Peeping into the well, I smiled with satisfaction. The heavy sacks struck Uncle Cricket on the head and knocked him head first into the mud.

More than a minute later, we heard a faint savage curse drift out of the dark hole: "Which . . . which fucking bastard dropped . . . dropped the gunnysacks on me? WHO'S TRYING TO MURDER THE PARTY SECRETARY?" Hearing that, we both laughed silently. It was perhaps the happiest moment I'd had since I came to the village.

When we hoisted Uncle Cricket up in the basket of the windlass, he was completely covered with mud. His gray hair was plastered together with mud, forming a warped broken horn that dangled sideways on his temple, and he was using a stick to pry dirt out of his nostrils. Several other peasants, coming back for their evening shift, could hardly contain their laughter.

"I am going to catch the bastard. This must be an anti-revolutionary revenge," muttered Uncle Cricket, blobs of mud dropping from his mouth and nose as he shook with rage.

With a pretended sincerity, I rushed forward to help him out of the basket and wiped his face with a dirty rag. "Oh, it was you, Uncle Cricket! Oh Secretary, how stupid I was! I did not know. We were so eager to get started, you know. We thought this was the best time to test our revolutionary determination, and we wanted to prove to people that the Party could not go wrong under your leadership. Green Olive and I were just thinking of the Great Leader's saying . . ."

Green Olive had to turn around to conceal his grin.

Uncle Cricket's face was like a painted mask in Beijing Opera, distorted, with stripes of mud and straw; he did not know if he should continue to be angry or if he should praise me for my revolutionary enthusiasm. Muttering incomprehensibly, he tottered toward Broken Shoe's house and did not return for two days.

Long before the wheat harvest season began in late July, it was obvious that there would be little to reap. The well, whose depth had reached a record forty-eight yards, was bone dry and was finally abandoned. Uncle Cricket, however, was not discouraged. At the mass rally after the symbolic summer harvest, which did not yield even a full sack of wheat from 150 acres, he declared hollowly: "We revolutionary peasants will never surrender to natural disasters. The enemies of the revolution are watching us, waiting for us to crawl to them to beg for food. The Soviet revisionists are watching, the American imperialists are watching, the Nationalist reactionaries in Taiwan are watching. But we will never give them the pleasure of laughing at us. As long as we persevere in our revolutionary spirit, we will find a way to conquer drought and hunger. The Third Production Team will set a good example for the rest of the commune. This year, despite the loss, we will give our allocated grain to the state just as we have every other year. As the Great Leader said: 'The revolutionary spirit will conquer the sky.'"

Weakly we echoed his slogan at the end of the rally. As two teams of horses carried the grain from the last year's reserves to the state granary, Uncle Cricket again led the Party members to shout: "Long Live Chairman Mao! Long Live the Great Proletariat Cultural Revolution! Long Live the People's Commune!" To this day, I cannot understand how sometimes people could be so stupid and write their own death sentences with such enthusiasm.

The next day, the Third Production Team opened up its grain warehouse and distributed what was left of the last year's harvest. Each person, except for the Beijing Kids, received twelve kilograms of millet and sorghum, less than one-tenth of what they would normally receive for the summer harvest. The Dragon Gorge Commune sent some grain for the Beijing Kids, so we each received thirty kilograms. With so little to eat and virtually nothing to sell, Smoking Devil and Water Buffalo sold some of their belongings—a pair of shoes, an old pocket watch, etc.—

and scraped together just enough money for train tickets. They left the village immediately after the "summer harvest." Heart Attack did not have enough money to buy a train ticket so he stayed that year.

Like its summer cousin, the autumn crop yielded nothing. The terrible drought continued into the next year. Long before the spring of 1970 arrived, most peasants had exhausted their food supply and were surviving on tree bark boiled in thin millet porridge. Every day at mealtime, more than a dozen hungry children would gather around our cave-house, looking quietly as we prepared our meal. We could not bear to eat in front of hungry children, so we gave each of them a piece of bread and sent them on their way. Then one day, after supper, Yin Yin, our cook, said to us: "Our supply of grain is getting very low now. Starting tomorrow, we can eat corn bread only for lunch. For breakfast and supper we will have to eat porridge. But even with these measures, I doubt our food will last until May." But our food supply dwindled much faster than she had estimated. By April, my comrades and I were eating only two meals a day: thin millet porridge mixed with leaves that we gathered from elm and mulberry trees around the village. But soon the edible leaves from these trees were plucked clean. Spring came and passed and we did not plant anything that year, for there was no point. The earth was so dry and hard that it cracked everywhere like the carapace of a turtle, and any way there were hardly any seeds left to sow.

After the Spring Festival, beggars started to trickle into the village, telling tales of mass starvation and death in the northern counties. When summer began, the trickle became a flood. In groups of ten or fifteen, haggard men, women, and children, pushing carts and carrying babies on their backs, staggered through the village every day, traveling south in search of food and water. Once, an old man and a child who were passing through the village died before food could be brought to them. The villagers were sympathetic, but few could offer anything more than a bowl of thin millet porridge. Some of the villagers, in fact, joined the beggars and migrated south when their food ran out.

My friends and I had started to feel the hunger, too. Having exhausted our ration of grain, we sold most of our belongings, including our only transistor radio and some clothes and shoes, in exchange for food. Heart Attack's radio, which was worth a hundred kilograms of wheat flour during normal times, fetched only one kilogram of corn flour and a half-dozen eggs, not even enough for a full meal for us. Day by day, I could see the change in myself and my comrades. My legs became puffy and my flesh, when pressed, was slow to return to its normal shape. Green Olive had shriveled another size from his already bird-like stature. Heart Attack spent most of his time on the kang now, too weak to play cards. Mirror Wang, his cheeks sunken and his large eyes bulging from their sockets, had not touched his mirror for months. If not for an occasional package of food from Mirror Wang's parents in Beijing, we would have fared much worse.

Day and night, the loudspeakers in the village broadcast revolutionary marches, especially the famous song based on the Great Leader's "Harden Our Hearts," intermingled with Uncle Cricket's speeches, rallying people to fight hunger with revolutionary spirit. But such revolutionary rhetoric sounded more ridiculous than ever on our empty stomachs. Many evenings after the scorching sun was down, I observed a handful of villagers slowly drag themselves up Nipple Hill, to burn fake money and to pray to the Sea Dragon for rain. Uncle Cricket tried to guard the road himself to stop the feudal superstitious practice but people got around him at night and continued to go up the hill.

On the night of July 23, 1970, it finally rained. And then it continued raining and raining and raining. At first, we all cheered and danced in the downpour. But after hours and hours of continuous rain, people started to grow afraid. Water leaked through the mud-and-straw roofs of most houses and turned dry streets into muddy streams. A number of older cave-houses were partially dissolved and began to crumble.

"It is my fault," Broken Shoe confessed to me on the second day of the downpour. He was on his way to Nipple Hill again to pray. "I probably prayed too hard on Nipple Hill last week. I even promised that I would give my wife to the Sea Dragon if he would bring rain. If only I had known He would bring us this much rain, I would have offered only half of my wife."

On and off the sky poured down on us for nearly four days and nights. Starting on the third day, more and more terrified peasants began trudging up in the direction of Nipple Hill again. They wanted to thank the Sea Dragon and to pray for Him to stop the rain. On the morning of the fourth day, as the torrential rain tapered into a drizzle, I saw Broken Shoe and a few others come over on their way to Nipple Hill. And then suddenly, Broken Shoe crouched on the ground and listened. When he straightened up, he appeared both excited and frightened and pointed to the deep gorge in the north. I was standing in front of my cave-room and I soon heard the strange sound, too, but I could not make out why the sound made him so anxious.

It was like a low-pitched hum, hardly discernable at first. Then it became a little louder and the air seemed to vibrate. Along with the sound, a dark chilly breeze, along with a foul, rotten smell, swept over the hill, as if it were the prelude to the appearance of some ghost. The villagers passed hurriedly before my cave-house and pointed to a brownish spot in the distant Dragon Gorge, which was growing rapidly larger. Finally I figured out what was making them so excited.

"LOOK! THE MOUNTAIN FLOOD!" Broken Shoe let out an excited and hysterical howl.

Within seconds, a vertical wall of water the color of sepia crashed through the gorge below me. The ground vibrated slightly as if it were a small earthquake. A powerful chilly gust of wind smacked me in the face. I was more fascinated, however, than frightened, seeing the torrent pick up some of the houses on the lower edge of the village and toss them like dried cow patties into the stupendous roaring rush. In no time, the narrow deep gorge in front of our cave-house became a sizable lake. Millions of objects, washed down by the terrible deluge, floated on the lake. Trees, planks, furniture, and dead farm animals bobbed up and down like shredded cabbage and beans in a boiling cauldron.

As I watched in amazement, someone tolled the village bell. Scores of hungry villagers ran toward our cave house, which was just above the bank of the new lake. As soon as they arrived, they wasted no time in taking advantage of the windfall and immediately began fishing for floating booty. Goatee Li, the Production Team's accountant, was the first to make a catch; he snagged a drowned, bloated goat. His wife butchered the animal on the spot. She plunged a knife into its belly and a small geyser of yellowish-green water spurted from its guts and spilled onto the muddy bank of the new lake. The goat must have been in the water for some time; the woman peeled off its skin as if it were a pillowcase.

Another villager, One-Ear Jiang, hooked a large wooden chest with his rake, but the swift current prevented him from pulling it ashore. He was locked in a futile battle with the current and was yelling for help. But no one came to his aid; everybody was busy searching and trying to snag his own goodies. Before long, everyone in the village who could move was at the shore, which was barely ten yards from the door of our cave-house. Most of the floating treasure was too distant to be reached, and with each animal or a piece of furniture passing by, people sighed in disappointment. Two teenagers had hooked a piglet but, pulling in different directions, they tore the animal apart in the water. Then a cow, tangled in the branches of a large tree, floated by, not far from the shore, and people's eyes lit up in anticipation.

Like Admiral Nelson spotting the French fleet at Trafalgar, Uncle Cricket immediately gave the battle order: "Comrades, DON'T let it pass!" which was completely unnecessary. People had already lined up and were pitching hooks frantically at the carcass. But the cow was too far from the shore to be reached by rakes or hooks. Several young men quickly tied ropes around their waists and jumped into the water, trying to swim to the cow. But the current was too swift and none could swim more than a few yards. One was even swept downstream when he ventured into the main torrent, and it took several people half an hour to pull him back to shore.

Closer to shore, a human corpse floated face down past the cow. No one paid any attention. I could not tell whether it was a man or a woman. The gray skin on its neck had been gnawed open and something was eating its way out of the dark wound.

"What are you standing here for?" Broken Shoe said to me as he rushed along the shore, chasing a wooden table. "This kind of fortune comes once every hundred years. Good Old Heaven has sent us food!" He seemed as happy as a summer grasshopper on an ear of corn and he hummed Chairman Mao's song "Harden Our Hearts" as he ran along. It was perhaps the only song he knew.

He was not the only one who was in such an elated mood. The whole lake bank was bubbled with excitement, for the bank was littered with valuable booty: planks, old furniture, and dead animals. Everything was closely guarded by the women and children. It was a heroic moment for the men.

"Take this," Green Olive said, handing me a rake tied to a rope. "You can throw better than I can. We'd better start working. Can't go home empty-handed today."

And as luck would have it, my first pitch hooked a big prize, a bloated pig, to the envy of Uncle Cricket and all the peasants nearby. The pig was so big that it took the three of us, Green Olive, Heart Attack, and me, to pull it ashore. It was white and, with its bellyful of water and the layer of mud on its back, must have weighed five hundred pounds.

"We'll have a feast tonight," Heart Attack said, looking at the mount of flesh hungrily. "I am going to get Yin Yin to start boiling water now."

"I don't think I can eat this," I said, feeling queasy just looking at the dark muddy water oozing from the pig's mouth.

"Say that again when you smell the roast ribs tonight," said Heart Attack.

Heart Attack was right. The smell of the roast pig was too strong a temptation for my empty stomach. I ate my share of ribs, though I had to make an effort not to think of the half-rotten intestines that I had helped to clean out. After months of hunger, the meat tasted very, very good. Heart Attack ate so much that he moaned all night, claiming that he was about to have another heart attack. Green Olive was completely silent, curled up on the kang, too full and too weak to even speak. After dinner, when he thought we were not looking, Mirror Wang took out his mirror and groomed his hair again, the first time he had done so in many months.

The village had a joyous celebration that night. The mood was merrier than that of any Spring Festival. Throughout the night we could hear people laughing and singing in the village. Some people even set off firecrackers and tolled the village bell. All night long the loudspeakers broadcast "Socialism Is Good" and "Only the Communist Party Can Save China," two songs we all knew well.

My friends and I kept half of the pig, which we salted and dried and hung up in the women's cave-house. Representing the Beijing Kids, I presented a quarter of the pig to Uncle Cricket, who was so clumsy that, other than a rotten chicken, he did not catch anything worthwhile during the flood. After a few minutes of ceremonial hesitation, he graciously accepted my gift. At the next meeting, he praised me and my friends for our heroic actions during the flood and for our thoughtfulness to senior revolutionary peasants. Although I hated most of Uncle Cricket's meetings, this was one meeting that I enjoyed.

"Our revolutionary spirit," declared Uncle Cricket at the Sunday assembly of the Third Production Team, "has finally conquered the worst drought and famine in eighty years. This harvest is a great victory for the Cultural Revolution and a great victory for Chairman Mao, thanks to the leadership of the village Party Committee, to Fan Shen, and to the courageous actions of the Beijing Kids. The Party Committee has decided to name Fan Shen 'Model Revolutionary Peasant of the Year!'"

The pig had worked. My chance to get out of the village had finally come.

## *12* **The Barefoot Doctor**

The water eventually receded, but my fortune began to rise. Three weeks after the great mountain flood, Uncle Cricket rewarded me for my pig-catching effort and nominated me to be the village "barefoot doctor." Armed with a letter from Uncle Cricket, I left for the headquarters of the commune for a three-month training session. I was overjoyed. At least, this was a small step toward my goal of escaping the village.

The barefoot doctor program was the latest political movement. The Great Leader had decreed that each village should have a barefoot doctor, who would work barefoot like the rest of the peasants during the day and treat patients in the evening or during breaks in the fields.

The training class at the headquarters of the Dragon Gorge Commune moved along at a rapid pace but we did not learn anything related to medicine for the first month. We spent the whole month studying the Great Leader's works on serving the people. The Party secretary of the Commune, Sha Gua, taught most of these classes. "You must remember Chairman Mao's teaching," he said at the opening class. "We would rather have a doctor with a Red heart and little skill than a doctor with a White heart and better medical skills. A Red heart will take care of everything else. You must be revolutionaries first, doctors second. You must never forget this."

His words did not register in me at all. I simply did not believe that one could be a good doctor without a good knowledge of medicine and I wanted to be a good doctor—Red heart or White heart, I didn't care. In the second month, when classes on basic medicine began, I took my studies very seriously and studied hard. With the little money I had brought with me, I bought several weighty volumes, *Handbook for Barefoot Doctors*, *An Introduction to Herbal Medicine* (I was expected to prepare most of the medicines myself), *An Introduction to Human Anatomy*, and *General Surgery*—in fact, all the books on medicine in the tiny bookstore in town. I knew I had a great deal to learn in a very short time, and I used every minute of it, sleeping only three or four hours a night. But when the three months were over I still felt empty and ignorant. I worried that the villagers would not trust me, who had so little knowledge and experience in medicine, to be their doctor.

But when I returned to my village I promptly discovered that my worries were unwarranted and that I had actually acquired the status of a demigod, thanks largely to the white wooden medicine box with a red cross on its lid that I carried back from the commune headquarters. All there was in the box was a roll of bandages, a box of acupuncture needles, a small set of surgical tools that I had bought myself, and some herbal medicines for colds and coughs. But the box immediately evoked awe and respect from all the villagers, including Uncle Cricket. Since it was an entire day's journey from the village to the nearest town with a clinic, most of the peasants had never seen a doctor, and many never would have gone to a clinic anyway, for few could afford the expense. Now that I had the magic box, I was expected to treat every illness that a big hospital would treat. Everybody in the village, even the eighty-year-old village patriarchs, called me Doctor Shen with the same piety and reverence that they had reserved for the Sea Dragon a few months before.

Their trust in me was complete and profound. For the first three days, my cave-house became the center of a "Festival of Illnesses": nearly everybody in the village came down with something—illnesses they never knew they had before—and they all happily walked over to try out my magic box. The whole village congregated inside and outside my cave-house, chatting, joking, laughing, waiting to receive my divine ministrations. Men's illnesses ranged from skin rashes to back pain; most women's had to do with their menstrual cycles. No matter what the illness, I maintained a strict equality among my patients, an equality that even the most democratic of nations would envy: all patients received an acupuncture needle and a cough drop, and all went away cured and grateful.

On the fourth day after my return, however, I received my first serious case and my fears returned. This case was not one that I could dismiss with cough drops. A young mother brought to my cave-house her three-year-old son, who was naked except for a dirty rag wrapped around his left arm. She said the boy had been stung by a wasp three weeks earlier and the wound had not healed. The boy was pale and limp, barely moving, and could manage only squeaky cries in response to my probing.

The mother herself could not have been more than sixteen. As she sat down, she bared one of her breasts and started to suckle another baby in her arms.

Laying the boy on the kang, I carefully unwrapped the dirty rag that was half stuck to the wound, and the boy moaned weakly. A pungent odor of spoiled eggs rushed to my nostrils. The wound was below the elbow, a deep open sore the size of a five-cent piece, so deep that I could see the white bone below. The boy's dark purple hand was the size of a freshly baked loaf of bread, and he was running a high fever. Judging by the wound, I thought that gangrene would probably kill him in a day or two. I had never performed surgery before, but I knew I had no choice.

"I will have to amputate your son's arm if you want to save his life," I said to the young mother. She looked up from her baby, but did not seem to comprehend my words at first.

When she finally did understand, she bawled hysterically. "I can't let you cut off my boy's arm! I have to take him home. His dad will be home after work. He won't allow it!" she cried, grabbing the boy's arm. The baby in her arms started to whine hysterically too, having lost the nipple.

It was no use trying to explain anything to the hysterical woman. The boy would probably go into shock soon and I did not have any antibiotics to give him. I asked Heart Attack to fetch Uncle Cricket and the boy's father.

An hour later, both arrived. Patiently, I explained the situation and finally, Uncle Cricket gave the order, which the boy's father reluctantly obeyed.

As I was preparing the operation, laying out the scalpel and scissors, my hands were shaking with fear. I had a good reason to be nervous: I had previously only observed a few cases of surgery at the commune's hospital—an appendectomy, a couple of cases of broken bones, and a tonsillectomy—and I was barely seventeen and had never even taken a knife to a live chicken. To calm down my nerves, I quickly consulted the *Handbook for Barefoot Doctors*. Then I asked the father and Heart Attack to hold the boy. Hardening my heart, I cleaned the wound, and tied up the boy's arm with a flaxen string to cut off the blood supply.

Everybody averted his eyes when I put the knife to the boy's arm. It was strange that once the sharp instrument sliced into flesh, I became calmer and my hand was no longer shaking. The boy whimpered and his legs twitched a little. I wiped off the blood with cotton swabs and cut deeper. As I was working, I could hear a voice in my mind loudly reminding me of the procedure described in the book.

An hour and a half later, exhausted, I wrapped up the boy's arm and sent him home. Truth be told, I do not remember how I completed the operation. For the next few weeks, I visited the boy every day and changed his bandage, which was always soaked with herbal medicine. It seemed a miracle that there were no major complications and the boy recovered in three weeks. I am sure that it was simply dumb luck on my part. But the boy's parents thought I was a magic doctor.

Every year since then, a few days before the Spring Festival I received a basket of eggs from the grateful parents. After I left the village and sending eggs became impractical, they sent a small box of homemade moon cakes.

A month after I amputated the boy's arm, I was summoned home to treat a Beijing girl from the village of Black Porcupine. It turned out to be another terrifying experience for me as a barefoot doctor. The girl had been working with the group of Beijing Kids building terraced fields. She was piling up stones on a lower terrace when a boy, swinging a pick on a higher terrace, lost the grip on his pick. Its sharp tip grazed the girl's forehead and gouged out her right eye. When I saw the bloody bulb dangling out of her eye socket, my stomach turned. I had seen injuries before, but not the mutilation of a pretty girl's face. The injured girl would probably have wanted to die if she had known the full extent of her terrible injury.

Feeling nauseous and weak, I started to clean the wound to determine what to do next. The anxious eyes of all seven of the Beijing Kids, who had carried her to my cave-house from Black Porcupine, were fixed on my hands. I could feel the weight of their gaze. The air in the cave-house became heavy and stifling too. I bit my lips and worked as carefully as I could with cotton swabs. But I was so nervous that my spine felt like a frozen snake.

After cleaning the wound, I was certain that there was no way I could save her eye and all I could do was to remove the eyeball to prevent infection. I ordered all the people out of the room because I could no longer bear their anxious gazes. As soon as they left, I picked up a pair of scissors and quickly and cleanly cut off the dangling tissue that connected the eyeball. To wait a moment longer would sap all the courage I had. I had no anesthetics and simply hoped that the pain was not severe. The girl let out a faint groan and passed out. I cleaned the wound and dressed it with some herbs.

While I was addressing the wound, I could hear someone sobbing outside the cave door. I found out later that it was the young man who had gouged out the girl's eye by accident. A meeting of the seven Beijing Kids from the village of Black Porcupine had been held while I was attending to the girl. Since she had been permanently maimed and was not likely to find a husband, the group thought that it was the young man's duty to marry her. Beside himself and sobbing, he accepted his responsibility.

The next day, riding seven hours in a borrowed horse cart, the young man and I accompanied the girl to the county hospital, where the doctor praised me and told me that I probably had saved the girl's life. I was very relieved that I did not bungle this one.

The wedding took place two months later, in a cave-house similar to mine. It was the first wedding among the Beijing Kids in the area. I was the guest of honor and was presented the first cup of liquor of the day. Despite the black patch over her eye, the bride looked beautiful in a red silk blouse and blue pants. After bowing to the picture of the Great Leader three times, the newly wedded couple sang "Red is the East" together, and then all the guests joined in. It was a typical revolutionary wedding, fashionable in those times. Even though I thought it kind of stupid to bow to the Great Leader at a wedding, I nevertheless enjoyed the ceremony and was happy with my accomplishments as a barefoot doctor.

Over the next two years I gradually acquired a little fame, and peasants from villages as far as thirty miles away would send their sick patients to me. Relying on instinct more than experience and equipment, I performed dozens of operations, often for work-related injuries. Not all of the operations were successful. Two patients—a young man who fell down a ravine and broke his neck and one older man who was run over by a tractor—died while my hands were on them. But whatever the consequences, I knew I could never turn down a case. I was their last hope.

Not infrequently, for lack of equipment and medicine, I had to improvise in ways that I still shudder to think about years later. One such operation, however, helped to clinch my fame in the minds of peasants and saved the life of a woman. I will never forget that day. It was my eighteenth birthday. Shortly after midnight I was called to a farmhouse in the village of Little Porcupine. The midwife informed me that the woman on the kang had just given birth to a baby, but her bleeding would not stop.

The woman was bloated and nearly unconscious. The bleeding was internal, in her abdomen. Her face was completely white and her pulse was barely discernable. I knew that she would die if I did not stop the bleeding quickly. Closing off or repairing the broken artery alone, however, would not save her life, for she needed a blood transfusion immediately. But that was impossible, for I had no means of identifying her blood type or that of any potential donor, even if a donor could be found at this hour. Then a wild idea, born of desperation, struck me. Without hesitation I cut open the woman's abdomen and drew several large syringes of the blood that had accumulated. Having cleared away the blood, I found the broken artery and closed it off. I then injected syringe after syringe of blood into the veins of her arm. I did not worry about contamination, for the woman was already as good as dead. When I finished, her pulse was no longer detectable and her breathing had all but stopped.

The crude blood transfusion appeared to be a failure. The woman showed no sign of life and her husband crouched under the kang crying. For what seemed a long time, I sat on a stool and leaned against a brick stove, too tired and confused to know what to do next. Eventually I drifted into sleep. When I opened my eyes again, I noticed that the man had stopped crying and was holding his wife's hand. The woman had begun to breathe again. Somehow I had saved her life.

A month after the desperate operation, I returned to see how well the woman had recovered and was surprised to see her hoeing a vegetable garden alongside her house. A baby was in a willow cradle by the garden and two young girls were playing with the infant. Her husband came running to greet me.

"Dr. Shen, see how strong she is," he said, proudly pointing to his wife. "I knew she would not die. She was born in the Year of the Horse, and she is as tough as a horse. That's my oldest daughter, the one holding the baby. She will be fourteen next year, and was also born in the Year of the Horse. As strong as her mother, Dr. Shen. If you don't despise us peasants, I will be glad to give her to you as your wife. Just let me know if you want her."

I smiled. Turning to the girl with the baby, the husband shouted, "Juhua, catch a chicken and light the fire. Dr. Shen will have lunch with us." The girl scampered toward the back of the house. The man followed the girl's movement with satisfaction. "She's a good cook. She already had a marriage proposal earlier this year, but I want to wait a little." It was another of those moments when I felt very proud of myself.

## 13  Moon Face

The winter after the great mountain flood was especially long and harsh. With Smoking Devil and Water Buffalo gone and knee-deep snow and ice having closed off the roads, life in our small crowded cave-room was slow and sometimes boring. There was little to do and few patients to see. Green Olive, Heart Attack and the twin girls, Yin Yin and Yang Yang, played "driving the pig," an old card game, all day long. Mirror Wang sat in a corner, quietly grooming his hair while pretending to watch the game. On those days, I often felt listless and lonely and wished I had some books to read or someone to talk to. Eventually I did find someone very interesting to talk to, even though he was considered the most dangerous person in the village.

His name was Ni Keming, but no one ever called him that. Everybody called him "Moon Face," after his very large, flat, pale face. It was not exactly a complimentary name, for it sounded too feminine. Moon Face was the most "dangerous" person in the village: he was the son of a landlord who had owned nearly every inch of the land in the Three Porcupine area. In 1951, the first year of land reform after the founding of the People's Republic of China, his father was summarily shot at a mass rally and his land was distributed among his former tenants.

The very first week we were in the village, Uncle Cricket had warned us about the only enemy in the village, and cautioned us to stay away from him.

"He is an unreformed landlord's son, despite all the revolutionary education he has received," Uncle Cricket said. "There are still many unclean ideas in his head, and he is living proof of the Great Leader's words: class struggle will never end."

Moon Face was ten when his father was executed. Since then, he had taken his father's place and repeatedly served as the living enemy of every political movement. In 1958, at the height of the national movement to establish communes in rural areas, he was charged with viciously desecrating a portrait of Chairman Mao after someone found a picture of the Great Leader lying on the floor of his room. No one believed his claim that the picture had been on the wall when he left for work in the morning, and he was sentenced to three years of hard labor. In 1966, the first year of the Cultural Revolution, he was one of the first to be arrested by the Red Guards, and he was paraded at endless political rallies in every village in the Dragon Gorge Commune. At a rally in Black Porcupine, he was hoisted to the top of a column of stacked benches, and when a Red Guard kicked away the lowest bench, he fell down and broke a leg and three ribs. The leg never healed properly and since then he walked with a limp. Although just over thirty, he bore all the signs of premature aging: his hair was thinning, his back was stooped, and his thin frame constantly shook from a violent cough.

He was a complete social outcast. Despised by everybody, he lived on the outskirts of the village, in an abandoned cave-room whose door was so rotten that several holes the size of grapefruits could be found on all four corners. He plugged them with rags, but rags were no match for the winter winds. That's probably why his cough never went away.

I had heard many stories about the dangerous enemy in our midst during my first few months in the village, some of them so ridiculous that it was hard to keep a straight face. I had little contact with Moon Face during my first two years there, for Uncle Cricket was always careful to assign him to the farthest field, away from everyone else, so that he would not have the opportunity to contaminate the younger people, especially the Beijing Kids. It was a few months after I became a barefoot doctor that I finally got to know him.

When his cough or the pain in his leg became really bad that winter, Moon Face began to come to my cave-room for a little herbal medicine. His visits were always at night, and at first he was very timid. Although my limited herbal medicine could do little for his cough or leg, which I suspected had developed rheumatoid arthritis, we somehow broached the subject of literature, and I was astonished to discover that Moon Face had read practically all the Chinese classics. *The Romance of the Three Kingdoms*, *The Dream of the Red Chamber*, *Journey to the West*, and others were all familiar to him, and he also knew the works of many foreign authors such as Charles Dickens and Honoré de Balzac. He was especially fond of Russian writers, though, and had read all the works by Tolstoy, Turgenev, Dostoyevsky, and Gorky that had been translated, for they had been available in the county library. In his solitary years before the Cultural Revolution, he told me, he would get up at two o'clock in the morning on Sundays, walk ten hours to the county library, borrow two books (the maximum allowed), and come home after midnight.

I had never had more fun talking about books with someone than I did with Moon Face. He had a good memory and could remember almost everything he had read. He told me that he took detailed notes on many books, which filled a dozen notebooks. But, he added with a dry smile and resignation, he was no longer in possession of the notebooks; they had been confiscated and burned by the Red Guards.

"I still have them here, though," he said, pointing to his head. "I will never lose them." I blushed a little as I remembered the bonfire in the Big Courtyard and all the books my friends and I burned.

Moon Face was a talented storyteller. Night after night, he told me stories that he had read in books. What amazed me most was his ability to pronounce those complicated bookish words and long foreign names so exactly and smoothly that it was as if he were reading them from a book. His voice was dramatic, sometimes slow and quiet, sometimes quick and tense, and we were captivated by his stories from start to finish. I say "we," for I was not the only one listening on many occasions. My remaining roommates, Heart Attack, Green Olive, and the twin girls, when they tired of playing "driving the pig," frequently sat on the kang with me to listen. Even Mirror Wang would crawl closer and listen while stealthily continuing to preen. From Moon Face I learned a great deal about the art of storytelling, which would save my life one day. In addition to the stories, Moon Face could sing many passages from the old Beijing operas, including *Farewell My Concubine*, *The White Snake*, and *The Romance of the Western Chamber*. My friends and I were amused but also impressed by his feminine voice; and sometimes we could see tears twinkling in his large eyes as he put his soul into those romantic melodies.

The big warm kang was the only place of comfort on cold winter nights, especially for Moon Face, who often could not afford to heat his own kang. Thanks to a government ordinance, we enjoyed a luxurious supply of coal, while most peasants heated their kangs with crop stalks. Moon Face was a gentleman and openly expressed his gratitude for being allowed to share the warm kang in our cave-room during those harsh winter nights.

My friends and I rarely mentioned Moon Face's visits to any peasants, but despite our caution, word eventually reached Uncle Cricket. He was greatly alarmed by "the new signs of class struggle at Big Porcupine," and immediately convened a special meeting for Party members and Beijing

Kids. At the meeting, the Party members unanimously decided that Moon Face must be kept away from the Beijing Kids. Before the meeting adjourned, Uncle Cricket asked me to read the entire section of the Great Leader's Little Red Book on class struggle. "It is for the benefit of all of you," he said. "Remember, Fan Shen," he added gravely after my reading, "Class struggle will never end. Chairman Mao has taught us that the enemy's most evil and insidious scheme is to corrupt our children. The counter-revolutionaries pin their hopes on young people like you. I think you would have been fooled by Moon Face if not for my quick intervention. This was not just storytelling; he was using the occasions to ingratiate himself so that he could spread his bourgeois venom. I heard that he was telling stories by bourgeois foreign authors."

I knew perfectly well what Uncle Cricket said about Moon Face was nonsense but I did not contradict Uncle Cricket. I said nothing to protect Moon Face during the meeting. By nature, I was timid and did not like direct confrontation with authorities and I knew that protests would be futile and detrimental to my standing in the community. Worse than that, I knew how dangerous it was to be found in sympathy with an anti-revolutionary. I merely nodded politely as Uncle Cricket rambled on.

To make sure that Moon Face would not get another chance to "corrupt" me, Uncle Cricket sent him to a reservoir construction site forty miles away and requested that the team leader there keep a close eye on him.

I felt sorry for my friend and the night before he left I paid him a secret visit. "Take this," I said, handing him my sweater, the only one I had. "This will help with your cough."

"I can't take it," he said, pushing it back weakly. "You need it, too."

"I won't need it," I said and threw the sweater to the corner of his kang. "I won't go out much this winter. I will come and see you some day." I turned and left before he could give the sweater back to me.

## *14* Smoking Devil's Wedding

Toward the end of the fourth year, the Beijing Kids began to leave the villages. Some were sent to vocational schools; others were recruited by local factories. Anything was better than the harsh life in the villages, and everybody was glad when his chance to leave came. Several people from Big Porcupine's Third Production Team had already left. Besides Big Quilt, who had been sent to a nursing school after studying under Uncle Cricket, Mirror Wang was recruited to work as a coal miner in Tongchuan. Yin Yin was sent by Uncle Cricket to the Yan'an College of Agriculture to study agricultural science. It was not her field of choice—she would have preferred to study political science or history—but it was better than cooking meals for eight or nine people everyday. Her twin sister Yang Yang, with Uncle Cricket's recommendation, went to work at the Big Leap Forward Pickle Factory at the Dragon Gorge Commune. Not long after that, Heart Attack got lucky, too. Uncle Cricket recommended him to the recruiters of the Yan'an Brick and Tile Factory.

The biggest surprise came in May, when Water Buffalo announced that he was not only leaving the village, but was going back to Beijing—the first Beijing Kid to return home. The official reason was that he suffered from serious back problems, problems that permanently disabled him and required medical treatment available only in Beijing. The real reason, we all knew, was that his father had decided to retire early so that Water Buffalo could inherit his job in a meat-packing plant. It took more than a few serious bribes to secure all the needed approvals: Uncle Cricket received three roasted Peking ducks, according to a rumor, but that was peanuts compared to the money his family spent on officials in Beijing.

As more and more of my comrades were leaving, I became more anxious and lonely, and wanted desperately to leave the village, but I was still hampered by my "family problem"—the fact that my father was still in a labor camp was prominently stated in my political file. I was thus invariably passed over by factory and school recruiters. Short of a strong recommendation from the Communist Party, I knew, I would never get out of the village.

Encouraged by Water Buffalo's success, Smoking Devil had been working on a scheme of his own to return to Beijing too: he announced that his "crushed vertebra" had been injured again and he was going to be crippled for life unless he went to Beijing for treatment. For weeks, Smoking Devil diligently executed his plan: he delivered several Peking ducks to Uncle Cricket and his parents paid the bribes necessary to obtain papers in Beijing. On the verge of a resounding success, however, his plan was torpedoed by an unexpected turn of events.

In his leisure days, which were many, as he always had some kind of pain in his body, Smoking Devil lounged around the village. Just when and how he began flirting with the youngest daughter of Uncle Cricket is unclear. Her name was Caihong, which means rainbow. At fifteen, Rainbow was the prettiest girl in the village. No one knew exactly what happened between Rainbow and Smoking Devil, not even Smoking Devil himself, if you believe his version of the story. Obviously, they did some quick flirting without Uncle Cricket's permission, and there was some hanky-panky in the bushes. And now, just as Smoking Devil was getting his papers ready to leave, the girl told her father that she was pregnant.

Despite Uncle Cricket's best efforts to keep it quiet, the scandalous news spread throughout the entire village literally overnight. The next day, a mad-as-hell Uncle Cricket and his eldest son-in-law, who was the commander of the village militia, stormed our cave-house and ordered Smoking Devil to go with them. I found out later that Smoking Devil was given two choices in Uncle Cricket's office: marry the girl and stay in the village, or be taken to the county jail for raping the girl. A conviction for rape was virtually assured—Uncle Cricket made it clear that he would have no trouble producing witnesses—and the crime was a capital offense. Being a smart man, Smoking Devil knew what to do and I don't blame him for his choice. He stood up and called Uncle Cricket "Dad."

Smoking Devil's wedding was a simple one, although the whole village was invited. It centered around the traditional meal of "haha-soup," which was made only on such special occasions. When the noodles were cooked, they were scooped into large bowls along with the soup and carried by the younger women to guests. But unlike ordinary meals, only a small number of noodles was ladled into each bowl, and the soup had to be saved for later, not drunk. After the noodles were eaten, the soup was poured back into the cauldron. The haha-soup—the saliva from the mouths of the whole village—then commingled to make a soup that seemed to the peasants to acquire a special delicate flavor. Since each bowl contained only a mouthful of noodles, every guest had to be served two dozen or more bowls to be satisfied. Only at the end of the meal were the guests allowed to drink the haha-soup and even then, each person was allotted only a single bowl. Truth be told, I did not detect any special flavor from the sacred soup.

"You know what I dread?" He asked me after we had finished the noodles. "I am afraid that this silly father-in-law of mine will make me study Chairman Mao's works every night when I want to make love to his daughter. I envy you guys now. From now on, I am like a man in a trap. I have no freedom." But typical of Smoking Devil, who was a perpetual optimist, the mood did not last. "Ah, don't worry about me. I will have fun. I will let you guys see that Smoking Devil is not a buried eel yet. He is still a little dragon." He need not have reassured me of that. If anyone could make a disaster into a triumph, it was Smoking Devil.

Still, the wedding itself was a sad event for me, for I had counted on Smoking Devil to help me get out the village once he got out. Now that he was staying, I had to find a way to get out myself.

**The Death of Uncle Cricket**

Shortly after Smoking Devil's wedding, Uncle Cricket sent me to the construction site at the Three Red Flag Reservoir. I had been assigned to a six-month tour of duty as a barefoot doctor there, and I was glad for the change. In additional to the benefit of escaping Uncle Cricket's boring lectures every week, I now could see Moon Face again and resume our conversations about literature, which always brought me much pleasure.

The work was backbreaking. Three thousand peasants and Beijing Kids had been working on the project for more than two years, and it was barely halfway complete. Like the terraced fields, it was another of those revolutionary projects that were ill designed and doomed to fail. There was no heavy construction equipment. The only bulldozer, an American-made machine said to have been captured during the Korean War, had broken down a year earlier and remained immobile at the foot of one of the dams. Wheelbarrows and shoulder poles were used to move dirt to the dam, and hand-tampers to pack it down. Progress was slow and injuries numerous, which kept me busy.

My clinic was set up in a tent by the broken bulldozer, which had become a landmark that could be seen from any position in the construction site. Most of the injuries were accidents—gashes on the arms or legs, sprained ankles, or the occasional broken leg. I could handle the minor injuries without much trouble, but I would send those with broken bones to the county hospital, after stabilizing their condition. As it was late fall, there were also a number of flu cases and, once, an outbreak of food poisoning from spoiled goat meat.

Although I was busy and overworked from the moment I arrived, I was quite happy because I could now talk freely with Moon Face without the fear of being discovered by Uncle Cricket. Every evening after dinner, the two of us would climb to the top of the hill overlooking the construction camp and, in the bracing autumn breeze, talk about books for hours.

On an afternoon in my third month at the site, I received an unusual patient. Two men carried a young woman in on a stretcher. Her face was as white as bleached sheepskin. But even in pain and with mud on her face, she was still beautiful. I recognized her immediately—the singularly large eyes and the sharply upturned eyebrows could not be mistaken, even though she had obviously grown to maturity in the four years since I had last seen her at the Xi'an bus station. Li Ling, of course, did not recognize me.

One of the young men explained that Li Ling was carrying dirt with a shoulder pole when she tripped and rolled down the entire face of the dam. After a quick examination, it was evident that the injury to her back was serious. I pinched her toes, but there was no response. Neither did she appear to have any sensation in her legs. Her arms were numb but still responsive. Although I did not say anything, I feared the worst: her spinal cord could be broken and she might be permanently paralyzed. With the help of the young men, I carefully rolled her on her side, gently lifted her blouse, and examined her spine and neck. As I touched her white skin, a strange sensation I had never experienced before shot through my body. I lowered my head immediately because I knew my cheeks were burning. There was no swelling or red patch on her back. That was good, but it was still too early to tell what the exact extent of her injuries was.

At the moment, the only thing that might be helpful was to try acupuncture, in order to alleviate the pain and to stimulate the return of sensation. I chose several acupuncture points on Li Ling's hands and feet, inserted the needles, and slowly twisted each needle to maximize the effect. Her eyes were closed, but she seemed calmer, as if she had fallen asleep.

The acupuncture treatment took half an hour. Shortly afterwards, a truck going to the county to bring provisions for the camp passed by on its appointed schedule, and I flagged it down and explained the situation to the driver. He helped me carry Li Ling aboard, and I escorted her to the county hospital.

That evening, I returned to the construction site with the food truck, leaving Li Ling at the hospital. She was in stable condition when I left her. I was quite relieved that her injury, though serious, did not paralyze her and she had largely regained sensation in her legs. The doctor warned, however, that she would probably be haunted by back pain for the rest of her life and recommended that I continue acupuncture treatments after she was discharged.

I sneaked into my tent around ten o'clock, ready to hit the bed, but I found an urgent telephone message from the headquarters of the Dragon Gorge Commune awaiting me on my bed. It was from Smoking Devil. "Fan Shen," the note said, "Come back to Big Porcupine immediately. Uncle Cricket is seriously ill. Hurry!"

I hitchhiked on a truck and went back to the village that night. It was after three o'clock when I arrived in Big Porcupine. The village was dark and quiet. Carrying my medicine bag, I walked directly to Uncle Cricket's house at the center of the village.

Uncle Cricket did not look good. I was surprised at how much weight he had lost since I had last seen him. His swarthy face looked waxy and sunken, like a cucumber that had hung on its stalk long after the first frost. "He has been suffering from severe diarrhea for several days but refused to go to the county hospital," Smoking Devil informed me. Hearing our voice, the old man acknowledged my presence by blinking his eyes, and then seemed to drift into a deep slumber. His pulse was weak and his breathing heavy and uneven.

After examining him, I stepped into the outer room, which was connected to the kitchen. Smoking Devil had awakened his wife Rainbow, a few months pregnant, to cook a bowl of noodles for me.

"It's so good to see you," Smoking Devil said as he lit a pipe. As usual, he did most of the talking. "It is so damned stressful to live in the house of the Party secretary, you know. The first three months almost killed me. We had to thank the Great Leader and read a passage from his works at least five times a day—three times at meals, right after getting up in the morning, and before going to bed at night. I have never met a Party member who's more devoted to the Great Leader. You know what . . . ." he paused for a moment and watched the rhythmic movement of the knife in his wife's hand cutting the noodles in the kitchen. Sure that she was not listening, he continued, "You know how the old fool got sick? He ate practically a whole moldy duck by himself. It was a gift from Green Olive when he returned from Beijing. Green Olive was following Water Buffalo's example and wanted to make sure he would be the next to get a city job. We all told the old man that the duck was no good—it was cooked in Beijing more than ten days ago—but he had starved so many times in his life that he would never throw away anything edible, least of all meat. So he cut off the green mold and ate the whole thing himself. He started vomiting and had bloody diarrhea that same night. We told him that it was food poisoning, but he would not admit it. He said it was just an upset stomach and it would go away after a good sleep."

"We have to get him to a hospital right away," I said. "There's no question this is food poisoning. It does not look good."

"The old fool will kill you if you try to send him to a hospital if there is any strength left in him. Believe me, we've tried—"

"The noodles are not very good," Rainbow said, setting down a big bowl of steaming noodles on the table. Following Chinese tradition, she apologized as she proudly presented her achievement. "I am not a very good cook. Please be kind and tolerant and try to have a bit of it." Minced hot chili and a big white piece of fatty pork floated in the soup, and the aroma of homemade vinegar rose from the bowl and filled the room. I felt hungry.

Smoking Devil waved her away, giving her an affectionate pinch on the hip as she walked passed him. The noodles were delicious. I devoured them in no time. Rainbow was an excellent cook.

I checked on Uncle Cricket again. He seemed to be sleeping better now, his breathing deeper and smoother. Since it was past three o'clock, Smoking Devil and I decided to borrow the team of horses at daybreak and transport Uncle Cricket to the county hospital, whether he liked it or not. Now dog-tired, I went back to my old cave-house to catch two hours of sleep. It is a decision that I still regret to this day.

I went back to Smoking Devil's place before dawn. When Smoking Devil and I carried Uncle Cricket to the horse wagon outside, we were surprised that he made no trouble at all. He merely moaned once or twice and went back to sleep. We started the journey at sunrise and expected to reach the county hospital by early evening. But less than two hours into our journey, as we were passing Nipple Hill, I checked Uncle Cricket's pulse and was startled that I could hardly detect any pulse. "Run the horse as fast as you can," I yelled to Smoking Devil, who was driving the horse at the front. "Uncle Cricket does not look good right now."

Smoking Devil flipped his whip and let loose the horse. But as the wagon bumped noisily I had a feeling that it was probably too late. Around noon, Smoking Devil stopped the horse to take a break, and I checked on Uncle Cricket again but found no breathing at all. For half an hour I tried to revive him with water and acupuncture, but I knew I was working on a dead man. He had been dead for some time. Finally, I told Smoking Devil the truth and asked him to turn back. Seeing his father-in-law dead, Smoking Devil suddenly cried as he slowly turned the horse around. It was the only time I ever saw him cry. Even though I never liked Uncle Cricket's pompous revolutionary lectures, it pained my heart that I did not save his life.

Three days later, Uncle Cricket was buried at the foot of Nipple Hill, near the place where we once built the "Beijing Kids' Terraced Field." Strangely, his death was the beginning of my final escape from the village.

A month after Uncle Cricket's death, two events suddenly sent my life in a new direction. The first event was that my father was abruptly "liberated." After working in a labor camp on and off for several years, he was reinstated at his former rank and appointed deputy director of the army's Strategic Research Institute. My mother's political problem was subsequently solved in the same mysterious manner, and she was even promoted to the position of party secretary at the Beijing Museum of Natural History. With their improved political fortunes, they moved to a bigger apartment in the Big Courtyard. I did not know what prompted their sudden "liberation," but I was certainly glad that the dark political cloud on my head had lifted and I was now eligible for recruitment. What I needed now was a recommendation from the local Communist Party.

The second event, which happened at the same time, was that my good friend, Moon Face, finally had a turn of good luck himself. The party secretary of the county had recently visited the Three Red Flag Reservoir construction site, and upon seeing a number of elegant big-letter posters around the camp, inquired about the calligrapher. It was Moon Face who did all the calligraphy and painting for the camp. After a chat with him, the party secretary was so impressed that he ordered Moon Face transferred to the county to serve as his personal assistant. It was only years later that rumors reached me that the party secretary and Moon Face became lovers shortly after that.

In February 1972, just after the Spring Festival, I sent a letter, along with a roast Peking duck, to Moon Face, to see if he could get the party secretary to find a position for me. Moon Face's reply soon came back. He told me that he had delivered the duck to the secretary and it just so happened that the director of the East Wind Aircraft Factory had come to recruit workers, so the secretary recommended me. "This factory is an elite military installation," he wrote. "The secretary's own son will go there, too. You should receive your papers soon."

A week later, a thick letter came by registered mail, notifying me that I had been hired by the factory and was to report immediately to the director in Yan'an for my physical examination. I could not believe my good fortune.

The day I left the village of Big Porcupine went like a dream. For more than four years, I had dreamed of getting out of the place where as far as the eye could see there was nothing but barren yellow hills. I knew on such an occasion I should laugh madly like some movie actor, but I decided not to give in to my emotions, for I had to be sensitive to Green Olive's feelings; he would be the only one left in our once crowded cave-houses after I left. So I went about my packing as quietly as possible. My parting gift to Green Olive was my medicine box and books. He would be the new barefoot doctor.

On the afternoon of my departure, the sky was bright, the air cool, and the mountain roads muddy—the ground was just beginning to thaw after a harsh winter. Green Olive and Smoking Devil drove me by wagon to the bus station in the county. As the horse-drawn wagon turned and slowly drew past Nipple Hill and Uncle Cricket's grave, I looked up at what was left of the "Beijing Kids' Terraced Field" and thought of the day the nine of us arrived, our bedrolls piled high and Uncle Cricket yelling at the horses. Our songs reverberated through the hills that day. I also thought of the chilly morning when Big Quilt fainted on the hill, the great feast after the mountain flood, the joyous haha-soup banquet at Smoking Devil's wedding and many other incidents of lesser importance. The thought that all the hard labor, the pain, the famine, and the fear were now behind me finally sunk in, and all of a sudden I could not control my emotions anymore. I began to sing loudly a familiar song that I had sung many times before:

Harden our hearts,
Fear not sacrifices,
Overcome ten thousand obstacles,
To achieve the ultimate victory!

I listened to the echoes of my words bouncing back from the hills. The Great Leader's words had never sounded so sweet to my ear before. I had won my first battle against the Great Leader, and it was won by following his own instructions. I sang the whole journey till my voice was gone.

During the entire journey, Smoking Devil smoked a lot and hardly said anything. Nor did he speak when we unloaded my luggage at the station and waited for the bus to Yan'an. It was very sad as the three of us sat silently outside the bus station, looking at the setting sun, and I was relieved when the bus finally came. I waited till the last moment to get on. As it pulled out of the station, I extended my hand out the window to grasp my friends' hands for the last time. But Smoking Devil had one last trick to play. He thrust a hard white object into my hand and quickly blurted out: "Take care of this for me, will you?" His voice was raspy and he turned his back quickly, but I still saw a flicker of tears in his eyes. The hard white object was his favorite porcelain pipe.

In a small dirty restaurant in Yan'an, I met Moon Face. He was there on business; I was there to leave for the East Wind Aircraft Factory the next day. Moon Face had visibly changed in the few months since he had become the personal assistant to the party secretary. He had gained weight, his pale face was fuller, and there was a tincture of red in his cheeks. He told me that he had accompanied the secretary to many communes in the county, and that they were treated to sumptuous official banquets everywhere they went.

"I have never had so much to eat in my life," he said with a lopsided smile. "The next time you see me, I am afraid I will be a fat pig." He laughed awkwardly, and I realized that I had never seen Moon Face laugh with such relaxed pleasure before.

"I am glad that you are leaving this place," he said in a more serious tone, after downing his third glass of liquor. "Fan Shen, you have been my best friend for years and I don't know how to thank you. I had never trusted anyone before in my life . . . never had a close friend, or even a friend, for that matter. But I feel that I have changed—since I got to know you. I know I can trust you. My dream has been to live an ordinary life, and grow to be an old peaceful peasant in my own house. I don't know how long my present luck will last, but I will always remember that I have a friend. Unlike me, you are from a revolutionary family and will have a bright future."

I was touched but felt uneasy. Perhaps it is my temperament or perhaps it is my upbringing, but I have always felt awkward when people become sentimental, even though I am a person of strong feelings myself and am given to sentimentality. In any case, I reached for the liquor bottle, filled up our cups, and pushed one across the table to Moon Face.

"Today is a good day for both of us," I said, trying to lighten the mood. "Let's not talk about sad things. We may not see each other for a while, so let's get drunk while we are together." I felt as if Smoking Devil were speaking through me.

We again brought our cups together, toasted each other, and gulped down the liquor. I could instantly feel a burning sensation in my stomach.

"Before I forget," I said, "I have a gift for you." I reached down, took a heavy parcel out my satchel, and placed it in front of Moon Face. The wrapping paper was an old copy of *The Communist Youth*, one of the few newspapers we were allowed to read. Moon Face opened the parcel carefully and looked down dumbfounded at the brand new green cover of an eighteenth-century Chinese classic, *The Dream of the Red Chamber*. It was a set of four volumes. "I know you love the Chinese classics. As they say, 'You are not a true Chinese if you have not read *The Dream of the Red Chamber*.' This is the first printing of the book since the beginning of the Cultural Revolution. Just came out."

Slightly gliding his fingers over the smooth cover of the book, flipping the pages and lingering three or four seconds at the beginning of a few select chapters, Moon Face was obviously deeply pleased. "I have already read the book three times, always surreptitiously. Now I am going to read it openly another half-dozen times."

As we were leaving the restaurant, I noticed an old beggar, a crippled man sitting on the damp brick floor. His stubs of legs were tucked under his body, which seemed weighted down by an enormous head with a large crop of dirty hair. In front of him on the floor was a white cloth. I walked over and read the words on the cloth: "I was one of Chairman Mao's Red Guards and lost my legs serving his revolution. Please help." He reminded me of Chunky, who was crippled for life in prison. On a moment like this, there was nothing else for me to do but dig all the money out of my pocket and place everything in his basket. The old Red Guard also did what he had to do. He nodded his head silently, flashed something on his scarred face that remotely resembled a smile, and took out a small pin of the Great Leader from his pocket. He held his hand out. I took the pin and put it on my jacket above my breast pocket. I did it only to show sympathy to the old Red Guard, and not out of any respect for the Great Saint. Having been re-educated by his so-called revolutionary peasants, I had no more illusions about his revolution. It was all a sham. If only the old Red Guard knew how he had fought for the Great Leader who could care less about him.

A huge cloud that looked like the aftermath of an atomic explosion towered over me as I walked back to the county administrative building, where fifty other new recruits and I were staying for the night. I took a shortcut across a cornfield that had just been harvested. A strong breeze swept up from the Yan River. I walked at a deliberate pace against the

wind, and made sure I was not moving too fast, so I could feel the sooth-
ing wind gently pressing my chest. I felt a lightness that I had never felt
before, perhaps partly because I was finally leaving the countryside and
did not have a cent to my name. And I could not help chuckling to myself as I remembered "The Song of Gold and Fold" in *The Dream of the
Red Chamber:*

> Men think it's good to be God,
> But will never forget their gold,
> They hoard and hoard till they are old,
> And where is the gold when they fold?

But like everything else, the reverie had to end. The ground was dry,
and I walked slowly and carefully between the corn stalks and began
contemplating my life in the aircraft factory. When I was small, my
mother often said that I had a good mechanical mind and should become an engineer like my father when I grew up. Now fate seemed indeed to have given me another chance to follow in my father's footsteps:
even though I had failed to follow him as a revolutionary, I could now
follow him as an engineer.

We are all in a gutter, but some of us are looking at the stars.

*Oscar Wilde*

# *3* **Metal**

The No. 8 Workshop of the East Wind Aircraft Factory to which I was assigned was a large concrete building, the size of a soccer field, where jet engines for MiG-19 fighters were assembled.

More than anything else, the workshop reminded me of a hospital: it was clean, quiet, and white. All workers wore white uniforms and white shoes, and the entire assembly line was painted white. The first time I walked into the building, I was mesmerized by the white cranes that moved smoothly on rails attached to the ceiling, and by the white steel cabinets that housed spotlessly clean tools. The ghostlike battery-operated car that noiselessly pulled the assembled engines into and out of the building was also white, and the gargantuan doors it pulled them through were white as well. Although the sterile atmosphere gave me a slightly uneasy feeling and the gasoline fumes made me queasy, my excitement and eagerness to explore the wonderful technology and organized efficiency of modern industry more than made up for any negative feelings. All day long, I listened to the faint clinking sound of metal on metal coming from different directions in the workshop and enjoyed it as much as I would have enjoyed a harmonious symphony. I liked the jingling and jangling of the assembly lines, stainless steel's crisp pitch, titanium's dull thump, magnesium's cheerful chirping, aluminum's sullen echo, chromium's hushed drone, and cadmium's low murmur. The music of modern industry was beautiful to me and rekindled pleasures and interests that I had had since I test-fired my first bamboo rocket in the fourth grade. The technology nerd in me had found a perfect playground.

I was grateful that fate had provided me with the opportunity to follow in my father's footsteps, something my mother would be proud of. After the war, my father, whose formal education ended at the sixth grade, studied on his own and became an outstanding mechanical engineer and inspector in the army. And now I had the chance to become an engineer like him.

Like all the Beijing Kids, I would start at the bottom and serve as an apprentice for three years, at a monthly stipend of eighteen yuan (nine dollars at the time). The amount was just enough to cover my meals (if I did not eat meat dishes too often) and dormitory fees. In my fourth year, I would become a probationary worker, with a monthly wage of thirty-six yuan. In my fifth year, I would become a regular worker, earning forty-two yuan and fifty-two cents a month. That would be my permanent wage, but it might be raised slightly every five or six years. The low wage, however, did not concern me at all, for I was confident that I would make something out of myself before long and would rise far above the ordinary rank of assembly worker.

I had set my eyes on a higher goal even before I arrived at the factory in 1972. While I was in Yan'an waiting for my physical examination, I scoured the secondhand bookstores there and bought two books that I thought would get me started on my way to becoming an engineer. One of them was *The Biography of Yakovlev*, a well-known Soviet aircraft designer during World War II. I was very excited to read the story of how he labored in a factory and eventually taught himself college courses to become an engineer. After reading the book in one night, I told myself that I would become a Chinese Yakovlev through self-education. I knew that since I had only a fifth-grade education, my desire was very ambitious—one could say that it was like a mouse wanting to soar to the sky like an eagle, but I never doubted that I would succeed.

The other book I bought in Yan'an was *An Introduction to Relativity*, which showed how ignorant I was at that time. Not even knowing that a mechanical engineer had no use for theoretical physics, I thought becoming an engineer meant that I must begin my studies with the theory of relativity. And that was what I did. I began studying the book on the train to the East Wind Aircraft Factory and found that I could not understand a single mathematical equation in the book.

I was undaunted by the setback, though, but only because I had a great deal of youthful confidence and even more youthful ignorance. All I needed to do, I figured, was understand the details. The fact that I never had the chance to go to high school to study mathematics did not deter me, nor did I bother to feel sorry for myself for having been denied the opportunity because of the revolution. As soon as I settled down in the factory, I began looking for high school math books. It wasn't easy in those days, but I was lucky to find an ancient high school math textbook, whose pages were made of rough straw paper, in a co-worker's room, under his bed. The co-worker graciously gave the book to me. Following

Yakovlev's example, I drew up a detailed study plan with the book, which I posted on the wall by my bunk bed.

With the plan in place, I officially launched my ambitious study on the day I started working as an apprentice in the No. 8 Workshop. For the next few years, I adhered to my plan, down to the minute and virtually without interruption. But managing time was the easiest part of my self-improvement, and I soon ran into many other impediments. On the second day of my studies, for instance, the lights in the whole building went out. The power outage, I discovered, was almost a daily occurrence, which was mostly due to a blown fuse in the old building. But this did not deter me from studying. When the power was out, I resorted to candles, keeping a large supply by my bed. Having acclimated myself to candlelight in the cave-house in Shaanbei, I was not too distressed by its dim, unsteady light. In fact, sitting in the dim candlelight, I sometimes even felt fortunate, and was reminded of the story of an ancient scholar I read in the second grade. The legendary scholar was so poor that he could not afford even candles, and so to read at night, he would go to the fields to catch fireflies in the summer and bring them home in a bag, so that he could read by the light from the bugs' tails. And in the winter, he would drill a tiny hole in the wall which his house shared with his neighbor's, and read by the light of the neighbor's candle. That was the spirit of the Chinese scholar that I admired.

Another problem I faced was fatigue. Only a few weeks into my studies, I often found myself too tired to concentrate after eight hours of work and the hour of political study that all workers had to attend. Sometimes I simply fell asleep on my books. My fatigue was exacerbated by the fact there was no table in the dormitory room and I had to use one of the stools for my desk. Curling up like a prawn on it every night, I started to have back pain after a week. To combat fatigue and back pain, I tried to emulate another legendary Chinese scholar. To prevent himself from falling asleep during his studies, the ancient scholar tied his long hair to the beam of the house, thus when his head slumped forward, his hair would be pulled and he would wake up. Besides that, he put an awl by his stool, and, whenever he was drowsy, would stick the awl in his thigh, so that the sharp pain would keep him awake for a while. I did not have a beam to tie my short hair, but I tried the awl method for stimulation, which I found quite effective. To this day, I still have a few scars on my thighs.

Aside from power outages and fatigue, I also ran into a problem far more distracting, one that few ancient scholars had to contend with: the noisy, lusty stories that my roommates told while they were playing cards at the other end of the small room. They were led by Bean Sprout, and joined by other fellow workers such as Master Pan and Little Lenin. They played their favorite game, "driving the pig," every night and the loser had to crawl under a makeshift table and endure loud jeering and prodding from the spectators. But it was the lascivious stories that Bean Sprout told the rowdy crowd—stories that stirred up hormones—that I found most distracting. One night shortly after I began my studies, for example, Bean Sprout told a long and lusty story about Old Revolutionary, which completely ruined my whole evening.

To his credit, Bean Sprout was a sensational storyteller like Smoking Devil. His real name was Nan Boqin, but because of his long fragile neck, people called him Bean Sprout. Outside of the dormitory he was quiet and retiring, almost timid, reminding me of a skittish shrimp. But with cards before him, after the first pot of tea, he became a different person, excited, melodramatic, and eager to relate the most salacious stories about flesh in the factory.

"Have you heard the latest news about Old Revolutionary?" Bean Sprout began that night in his scratchy voice.

"What happened to our most senior Party member?" Master Pan asked, drawing a card. "I saw him only three days ago at lunch, and he was bad-mouthing Red Calf again, as usual." Red Calf was the Party secretary of the workshop. " 'Red Calf, that young fart!' " Master Pan imitated Old Revolutionary's contemptuous tone, " 'All he does each day is smoke two packs of cigarettes, drink half a dozen pots of tea, and flood the bathroom. That's what he does.' "

"Well, he'd be licking Red Calf's hooves now, if he could," Bean Sprout said. "Because he was arrested yesterday. They are still trying to keep it a secret."

Everybody's eyes shot up from the cards, astonished to hear the news. I too was surprised, because I was quite fond of the old man who guided our tour of the workshop on our first day.

"Red Calf arrested Old Revolutionary?" asked Master Pan, "How dare he? He was still in diapers when Old Revolutionary was throwing grenades at the Japanese. What's the charge?"

"Well, it's a long story," said Bean Sprout. "Serve a new pot of tea first, will you?" That night, Bean Sprout was at his best as he wove all the available facts and fantasy into a juicy, colorful story about Old Revolutionary's tragicomic love affair.

"You have all seen Old Revolutionary's aunt, right? But did any of you know that Old Revolutionary has been sleeping with his aunt?" began Bean Sprout. "That's the story. She was not his aunt at all, but a former lover whom he brought back from his native village two years ago when he went back to attend his mother's funeral. After he brought her back, he ordered his wife to sleep in their daughter's room, because the aunt was ill and needed special care from him at night. I don't know how his wife swallowed the lie and let them sleep together for two years! Since she said nothing, his neighbors never suspected a thing. But finally, last week, his wife could not bear the shame any more and told the factory authorities about it. Red Calf immediately called a secret emergency meeting of Party officials, and they decided to catch Old Revolutionary red-handed the next night. They mobilized a dozen militiamen and issued them rifles. The militiamen waited in the nearby apartment for the signal from Old Revolutionary's wife.

"When the signal, a red flashlight blinking on and off three times— Red Calf must have seen a lot of spy movies—appeared in the window at two o'clock in the morning, Red Calf and the militia quietly entered the apartment, using a key supplied by the wife. The attack was so swift, so silent, so unexpected that they caught the two naked bodies literally in the act. They did not have time to even unlock themselves from each other before they knew what had happened. What a sight! There were viscous fluids all over the bed and their bodies, according to someone I knew who was present.

"Old Revolutionary tried to protest: 'What are you doing breaking into a civilian's house? This is illegal! I will tell the Party secretary to-morrow!'

"And Red Calf emerged from the shadows and answered: 'The Party secretary is here. You will have a lot of questions to answer at Party headquarters.'

"The lovebirds were brought to the detention center and interrogated separately. Both confessed their 'crimes' right away. The lovers were made to describe in detail what they did and how they did it. According to someone who was at the interrogation, Old Revolutionary's confession reads like a book of pornography."

Those were the kinds of stories that I had to listen to. Needless to say, I solved not a single trigonometry problem that night.

The first summer presented me with yet another irksome distraction: bedbugs, which we called "smelly bugs." They look like white, flattened sesame seeds when empty and miniature footballs when full of blood, and they were the most aggressive and tenacious bloodsuckers that I have ever encountered. Although the factory had regularly scheduled "bed-bug days," when entire dormitories were sealed and fumigated with in-secticides, the bedbugs always returned with a vengeance the next day to make up for the previous day's inconvenience. For the entire sum-mer, my study sessions were punctuated with incessant slapping and scratching. One night, however, I discovered a whole colony of well-fed bugs behind my study plan hanging on the wall. With a force as decisive as Eisenhower's "Operation Overlord," I struck the enemy and annihi-lated the entire army with my bare hands. My heroic study plan was red with the blood of tiny anti-revolutionaries.

Despite all the distractions, I pressed on with my books and made slow but steady progress. By the end of the first year, I was ahead of schedule, having worked my way through high-school mathematics. I then plunged into the books on physics and aviation mechanics. The more I studied, however, the more I realized how little I knew. I had long abandoned the hope of studying relativity and I knew I had to go college someday if I wanted to be a real engineer. But going to college was out of the question then, because all colleges had been closed since the begin-ning of the Cultural Revolution.

While I studied my books, I had also diligently learned the skills of the trade and had quickly become an efficient assembly worker. Before six months had passed, I was able to assemble two complete gearboxes a day, the same amount of work a veteran regularly did. But I knew this was only the beginning of what I wanted to accomplish.

## Li Ling

The Chinese have a saying: *There would be no books if there were no coincidences*. And that was what flashed through my mind one Saturday afternoon in the factory's puny library, a single room that contained little more than a few technical magazines. It was my habit to come here after a week's work to browse through the magazines. The room was always quiet, always empty, and it had become my "Lotus Bower," where I could enjoy the luxury of quiet for a few hours each week. Only occasionally would an engineer or technician come in to check something. Most of the time, I was the only one in the room.

About six months after I came to the factory, I was flipping through an issue of *Modern Aviation* when the door opened and a girl quietly slipped into the room. She took a magazine and sat down opposite me at the big oval table, the only table in the room. Over my magazine, I stole a glance at the unusual visitor and was startled to notice a pair of eyebrows that arched upward like Turkish swords.

Instead of the "combat style" short hair of the Cultural Revolution, however, her hair was now long, and tied up with a black silk band. Her face was tranquil and smooth, with a touch of healthy pink in the cheeks, and her large eyes, fixed on the page in front of her, looked thoughtful. She was wearing a dark-green plaid jacket, which might have been a man's jacket.

For ten minutes, I observed my new companion over the magazine. Finally, I got up my nerve and put down *Modern Aviation*.

"Aren't you Li Ling?" I asked. "I used to be a barefoot doctor, and I treated your back at the reservoir construction site last year."

For an instant, she seemed surprised, but her large and shining eyes quickly resumed their tranquility. "I thought you looked a little familiar. So you are the barefoot doctor who saved my life," she said, her words flowing like a leisurely mountain stream, cool and pleasing. "I never had a chance to thank you. What's your name?"

"Fan Shen," I said.

"Ha, one of the masses. Your parents must have wanted you to be a revolutionary," she said, smiling. I blushed a little. I felt uncomfortable when she caught the meaning of my revolutionary name but I did not tell her how I felt about revolution now.

"How is your back now?" I asked, trying to change the subject.

"It still bothers me from time to time, and sometimes it is quite bad. I have been to several hospitals in Beijing, and have had countless acupuncture treatments, but nothing can completely cure it. I had a fracture in one vertebra, and it did not heal properly."

"Sorry to hear that. Do you read technical magazines too?" I said, knowing I was asking the obvious.

She smiled mysteriously. "Do I look like someone who cares about MiG-19 and F-4 Phantom Fighters?"

"But aren't you reading *International Aviation Today*?" I nodded at the magazine in her hands.

"That's the cover. You can never judge a book by its cover. Don't you know the saying?" She laughed. "I sense that I can trust you. You seem to be a bookworm, too. I have seen you coming here before. All right, I'll let you know my little secret, but keep your mouth shut." Slowly she lifted the technical magazine and revealed a small book behind it. It had a crude brown paper cover. In large block characters, neatly written by hand in black ink on the cover, was its title: *The Biography of Karl Marx*.

I was more confused than ever. There was no need to be so secretive and sly when you were reading a book about the founding father of communism. "Oh, Karl Marx," I said. But why in the world she would be interested in the man who wanted to eliminate bourgeois families like hers?

"Didn't I say 'don't judge a book by its cover'?" She giggled, obviously enjoying her second triumph. Closing the book, she slid it across the table.

I took it and turned the cover page. On the inside was a very different title: *The Prince*, by Niccolò Machiavelli. I had never heard of the book. The pages were old and yellow, and the text was in old Chinese characters. It must have been translated and printed before the language reforms of the late 1950s.

"This is my favorite book, together with Friedrich Nietzsche's *Thus Spake Zarathustra*," she said, smoothly pronouncing the long foreign names without a hitch. I was amazed. "These books teach you not to trust anyone," she smiled. "That's why I like them."

But this was wholly at odds with her behavior toward me and I did not detect any distrust in her smile. "What kind of books are these?" I asked timidly, embarrassed for my ignorance.

"I call them miscellaneous books. About everything, or about nothing, or about nothing useful, I should say. That's the kind of book I like to read," she said. "Real philosophy, political science, history, economics, and all kinds of miscellaneous, good-for-nothing, get-you-into-trouble books. Do you read other things—I mean, idle stuff, besides magazines on MiGs and Phantoms?"

I nodded eagerly, and I told her about the stolen books that I had read in Beijing. Although we had officially met only a few minutes ago, I felt a strange bond between us.

"If you would like to read some of these books, I can lend you a few. But," she added, her face drawn and her voice sober, "you must remember the Austrian philosopher Ludwig Wittgenstein's famous words: *Whereof one cannot speak, thereon one must remain silent.* You must never talk to people about these books."

"Of course," I said. I was awed by her knowledge. She seemed to remember everything she had read. How did she do it? Just as I was once keenly aware of my sweat-stained rubber shoes at her house, so was I keenly aware of my shabby hoard of knowledge. My ignorance created a deep chasm between us, a chasm so deep that I doubted that I would ever be able to cross it.

It turned out that Li Ling worked as an archive clerk at the testing bay, which was part of my workshop but in a separate building. In the months that followed, I borrowed a book or two from her every week. I did not know how she preserved those forbidden books through the Cultural Revolution, perhaps by wrapping all of them in cheap brown paper and giving each a different title on the outside cover. After reading the books, I would talk to her during the breaks outside her office when no one was around. The haphazard reading often did nothing but reinforce my awareness of how deeply ignorant I was. Some of the books were so difficult that I could hardly finish them. I did not understand, for example, much of Machiavelli, and even less of Nietzsche, and I felt palpable relief and satisfaction—unjustifiable, but palpable nonetheless—when Li Ling told me that Nietzsche went crazy later in life. Maybe that's why I could not understand him. The books that offered practical advice on life were my favorites, books like Robert Schumann's *On Music and Musicians* and Benjamin Franklin's *Autobiography*. Franklin's model of self-improvement was most inspiring to me. His thirteen "commandments" that he offered to his son became my guide for many years to come. From him I learned to set practical goals, plan my course of action, and work tenaciously to achieve those goals, even in the face of seemingly insurmountable obstacles.

I often feel very fortunate, even today, that I had met Li Ling in the factory and had read those forbidden books from her. If Smoking Devil was my practical teacher who taught me techniques of survival in life, then Li Ling was my spiritual teacher who stretched my imagination and stoked the fire of my ambition.

There was a consensus at the East Wind Aircraft Factory that Li Ling was the prettiest girl at the plant. Men always ogled her—lusty toads gaping at a white swan—whenever her slender body and long legs whisked by. She walked fast, with her eyes fixed on the ground, her arms swinging straight back and forth. But for some reason, I did not think of her sexually. She was far too superior to me, both in knowledge and in looks. It was true that in the last few years I had grown taller, but I was still thin, and when I looked at my naked body in the mirror in the public bathhouse, I saw nothing I could be proud of. I felt certain that Li Ling would never be interested in me, with my small eyes, dark skin, and awkward and shy manner. Besides, she was seven years older than I was, and was rumored to have a boyfriend who worked in a factory in another city. I often wondered who the lucky guy was. To me, she was my teacher and mentor, and it would have been sacrilegious to think of her any other way.

Only once did our platonic relationship appear to move in a different direction. That was when Li Ling invited me to her dormitory room to look at her stamp collection. The room, more a cubicle than anything else, was on the third floor of a drab brick building. It was barely bigger than a king-size bed. There was no desk, chair, or dresser. Against the window was a narrow cot, whose clean, white sheets did not even attempt to hide the rickety wooden legs. A cement sink stood opposite the cot, by the door. There was a three-level makeshift bookshelf of thin pine boards against the wall between the sink and the cot. Six or seven rusty pipes, like a family of copperheads, crawled over the walls and the ceiling. I realized that the room was once a kitchen.

"I was assigned to the dormitory room next door with three other girls," Li Ling said, pouring hot water into a teacup for me. "But there was no privacy there and I could not read late at night when they wanted to turn off the light to sleep. So I hijacked the kitchen. Now they have to go down the hall to the toilet to wash their faces. Sit down, here is your tea."

I sat down on her narrow bed, and she handed me the first album that she took out from a trunk under the bed. She had a very large collection, the best that I had ever seen, with many beautiful stamps from Poland, Czechoslovakia, the Soviet Union, Romania, and other European countries. As she was handing me the second album, she sat down very close to me, so close that I could feel her leg lightly touching mine and sense the heat from her body. My heart skipped a beat or two, and then I lapsed into total confusion, almost a state of shock. For the next few minutes, I hardly heard anything she said, and fought very hard against the urge to touch her hand. She looked so delicate, so inviting, so pretty. My heart throbbed and pounded as I discreetly smelled the faint scent of the soap she used to wash her hair. She was talking about how she used to go alone to stamp shops in Beijing when she was only seven, and was always very happy to travel around the city to buy or trade stamps. So freely and calmly did she talk that I decided that her sitting so close by was accidental. It would be very embarrassing if I touched her and she turned out to have no romantic intentions at all.

Despite the urges that young men have when sitting alone with a pretty woman, I felt that I could not get any closer to Li Ling. What prevented me, more than anything else, was her superior attitude. How I longed to be treated as her equal, but I felt that she talked to me as if I were her ten-year-old brother and she were my seventeen-year-old sister. There were also occasional sarcastic remarks and taunts that wounded my pride. Once, for example, after a volleyball match between the No. 8 Workshop and No. 14 Workshop in which my cunning spike saved the game, I proudly turned to Li Ling. She and a girlfriend had been watching it from the sidelines. My face was flushed, still half intoxicated by the loud cheers of the spectators.

"Did you notice," she said to her friend, as I wiped the sweat off my face with a towel, "that he has bowed legs?"

The smile froze on my face. What had I done to deserve such gratuitous cruelty?

In March, a year after my arrival at the factory, Red Calf, the Party Secretary of the workshop, called me into his office. This was the first time that I had been officially invited there and I was quite apprehensive. Still a young man of about forty-five, Red Calf was quite friendly and did not have the typical drawl of a Party secretary when he spoke.

"Want a cigarette?" Red Calf pulled out a pack of Front Gates and waved it at me. I declined. I did not smoke. The Party secretary lit one for himself.

"I have been watching you since you arrived here," said the secretary. "You have been doing a good job, and everybody praises you, especially for your studies. We have all seen you study night after night on your stool, and you were the first apprentice in the workshop to work independently. That is the kind of spirit the Party needs. We wish we had more hardworking young people like you. The Party Committee has decided to give you a new challenge. We have decided to transfer you to the testing bay, to be a special circuit electrician apprentice. You know in the last few months we have lost a number of workers at the testing bay because of illnesses, and we need urgently someone to learn the job quickly. It's the most important job in the testing bay. Whenever there is a problem, the circuit electrician has to diagnose it fast, or all work at the testing bay comes to a stop. This is a tremendous honor for the Party to trust such a young person as you, and we are confident that you will not disappoint us. I have designated Master Deng as your mentor. He is the ranking Party member at the testing bay and will be a good guide for your political growth."

I eagerly accepted the appointment, but for my own reasons. I thrilled at the prospect of working in the same building as Li Ling and seeing her every day.

The next day, I reported to Master Deng at the electrician's office on the second floor. Master Deng had a white puffy face and heavy eyelids (from kidney problems, as I later learned), and was half dozing over a cup of tea when I entered.

After briefly greeting one another, I anxiously asked Master Deng: "Where should I begin? What books should I read?" Master Deng was obviously annoyed by my eagerness. He slowly ran his sleepy eyes over me, and then reluctantly straightened his back and reached into the desk drawer, from which he withdrew a thick book and pushed it across the desk.

"Read it," he tersely said, and returned to his teacup.

The greasy book, *Basic Electrical Principles*, was an outdated vocational school textbook. It was printed on dark straw paper, the pages so fragile that many had fallen out and had to be glued back in. I plunged into it nonetheless. I studied ten hours a day and took extensive notes. In less than a week, I finished the book. But, as before, I was more dissatisfied than ever. I knew that theory alone was not enough to make me a good troubleshooter and I also needed practical knowledge, knowledge of how things actually worked. By the second month, I had begun studying blueprints of the wiring and circuitry of the entire building. Armed with a flashlight and a roll of wiring maps, I set out to explore every nook and cranny of the vast building. On some days, I spent hours crawling under each of the testing platforms. Like Michelangelo patiently lying on a scaffold under the ceiling of the Sistine Chapel, I would lie on the greasy floor under each switch box and slowly sort out the confusing maze of colored wires. Whenever I found a discrepancy between the prints and the actual wiring, I would make a note in my notebook. Before six months were out, I had mastered the wiring of the testing bay and the special circuits of the jet engine. Not only did I learn to analyze the problems, but also where the problems were like to occur. Sometimes, I discovered, the best way to get the antiquated Soviet circuit boards to work properly was to give them a swift kick. In that respect, I later discovered, they were like a lot of people.

Within ten months, I was a de facto circuit master, without the title. Technically, I was still an apprentice. But whenever there was a major problem, the testing technicians often called on me instead of Master Deng. I could have studied further and worked toward a career in electrical engineering in the factory as I had originally planned, but I did not. By this time, I had learned something else about the factory that made me realize that this was not a place I could stay for long. The factory that I had so enjoyed because it marked my escape from the dreadful mountain village turned out to have some very dark and terrible secrets, and I found that by escaping from the village, I had fallen into another dreadful trap from which I had to struggle to escape.

# 18  "Another Jumped Last Night"

After I began working in the same building as Li Ling, we spoke almost every day, and our conversations gave me great pleasure. Sometimes we saw each other twice a day, in the morning and during the afternoon break. I lived for these conversations. When I came back from a talk with Li Ling, I frequently found myself with a burning desire to study philosophy and history, subjects that she knew so much about. I wanted to know as much as she, in order to say something worthwhile to her, to attract her attention, to win her praise.

But wanting to be Li Ling's equal was not the only thing that pushed me to study hard. Another, equally strong, motivation to study was the desire to go to college someday so that I could flee the factory that I now came to dread. In fact, by this time, I had learned that there was something mysterious and terrible in the factory that made everyone want to escape. The factory was not at all what it appeared—a cheerful place full of happy, dedicated workers and their families.

To a newcomer, the campus of the factory looked clean and orderly, so much so that it did not look like a factory engaged in heavy industry, but a resort hospital. The roads were paved and lined with shady maple and birch trees. Encircled by evergreen bushes, the white buildings glittered in the bright spring sun.

But only after a few months, I began to feel a vague oppressiveness about the white buildings and walls. A short distance from the factory entrance was the gate for the residential area, also closed in by a high white wall. At any given moment, I was in one or the other of the white enclosures. The only difference between the facilities was that in the residential compound the buildings were smaller and crammed in tight rows like military barracks.

The oppressiveness came first of all from the fact that the factory was a completely isolated community. The nearest town, Yanglin, was twelve miles away. The people who lived there were not allowed near the factory.

Life here was highly regulated, like my boarding school in the Big Courtyard. Every daily activity—getting up, breakfast, lunch, afternoon political study, dinner—was announced by a military bugle blaring over the loudspeakers at precisely the same times. At six-thirty every morning, I shuddered when the first blast of the bugle broke through the window and rudely awakened me, reminding me of the dreaded rapping of Uncle Cricket. As in the countryside, I dared not be tardy. Throwing on my jacket, I would hurry out of the room to one of the three identical gigantic white public dining halls at the center of the residential compound. Like a Roman pantheon, each dining hall had a row of tall doors on three sides. The rush was necessary: not only were the queues to the food windows long, but it was necessary to go through three lines for a typical meal, steamed bread being bought at one window, the vegetable dish at another, and the porridge or soup at still another. On a good day it took about twenty minutes to buy anything remotely like a decent meal.

The dining halls also served as auditoriums for political rallies and funeral services. That was one of the reasons that I hated eating meals in the halls. Amid the aroma of boiled vegetables and corn bread, there was always an alien smell in the air, the smell of death. By the third year of my apprenticeship, I had attended six funeral services in the dining hall where I ate, services for people who had eaten meals with me and died prematurely. There was something cryptic, almost sinister, about this place that seemed to drive people out of their minds and to their graves.

The first mysterious death that I witnessed occurred during an afternoon nap, just a few months after I began my apprenticeship.

When I came back from a late lunch that afternoon, the dormitory was very quiet and everybody was asleep. Cha Nong, a young man of twenty-six who occupied the lower bunk bed opposite mine, was lying on his side, already asleep. A slender and good-looking young man with large slanting eyes and a quiet voice, he was the center of many young female workers' attention. A few weeks earlier, he had become engaged to the best-looking girl in the workshop. He was a skilled worker, a graduate from a school of aviation mechanics. Everybody, especially young men like me, admired and envied him for his skills and his success with women.

I climbed onto my bed quietly and closed my eyes. Scarcely ten minutes later, however, I was started from my sleep by the sound of loud and very hurried steps in the hall and a voice yelling out: "Someone jumped off the roof!"

Together with many people in their shorts, I rushed down to the ground behind the building to see what was the matter. And I will never forget what I saw: my roommate, Cha Nong, was lying on his back, his face liverish-purple, his eyes wide open, staring at the bright sun without care. Even though there was little blood on his face, his body looked just as grotesque and frightening as that of General Hei in the Big Courtyard. One of his legs was twisted under his body, while the other twitched in irregular spasms. There was a faint, low gurgling sound bubbling away in his throat. Three or four other people were standing over him; they were debating whether to lift him up or call an ambulance. Time seemed suspended there and each minute stretched on and on and on. Finally, we lifted him up and carried him to the hospital, which was just three or four blocks away.

The official cause of death was insanity. His fiancée wept for weeks. But the question has puzzled me ever since: Why did he jump off the roof on such a beautiful afternoon, when such a beautiful girl was waiting to marry him?

Cha Nong's death was the first of many enigmatic deaths that had occurred in the factory. Three weeks after his death, a security guard blew his brains out with a service revolver. A month and a half later, on a Sunday afternoon, a twenty-seven-year-old woman from the No. 11 Workshop lay down on the tracks in front of an oncoming train just outside of the factory wall. In September, just before the National Day, a man in his forties, a Party member in the No. 3 Workshop, jumped off the crane he operated right after his shift was over, leaving behind a wife and two infants. There seemed no pattern to the deaths. The suicides seemed unrelated, but their rate was so alarming that the Central Committee of the Communist Party in Beijing ordered an investigation. The three-member team, headed by none other than the Great Leader's nephew, spent six months at the factory, but left quietly without issuing a public report. During those six months, they themselves witnessed two more suicides. After they left, the suicide rate picked up again, as if to make up for lost time. Within two weeks, a young apprentice from the No. 17 Workshop slashed her wrists in a restroom but was rescued by her co-workers. A little more than a week later a veteran cook of twenty years hung himself in the kitchen of the No. 2 dining hall while alone on the night shift.

To ward off the new wave of mysterious deaths, the Party Committee launched a massive political campaign, which required an additional hour of political study after work. As a result, after eight hours of work, we had to spend one more hour studying the Great Leader's words on selflessly serving the cause of communism. But despite the educational programs and precautions taken by the authorities, workers still found reasons for killing themselves and the means to do so. The suicides continued at the rate of one or two a month. Once, when a month and a half went by without a death, the factory Party secretary, Comrade Thus— he had a penchant for sprinkling the word *thus* in original and unexpected places throughout his sentences—jubilantly declared at the next mass rally: "*Thus*, our new educational program has heightened the revolutionary consciousness of the factory and *thus* has achieved significant results. We have *thus* beaten the bourgeois ghost of escaping to another world." But in the week following his speech, two people killed themselves. A thirty-four-year-old welder from the No. 14 Workshop, where jet engine parts were electroplated, filled a ladle with the cyanide solution used in electroplating, walked to the gate of the workshop, smiled to a horrified crowd of workers who were leaving for lunch, and drank the fluid. He staggered a few steps and, like an electroplated sheet of metal, stiffly fell to the ground. Three days later, a thirty-nine-year-old electrician from the No. 1 Workshop walked into a restricted area containing 6000-volt transformers and threw himself on the naked wires before his fellow workers could cut the current. He was incinerated instantly.

My fear of the white factory had increased steadily with each new death. By the end of my third year, when I finished my apprenticeship, the number of deaths stood at thirty-seven.

But apart from Cha Nong's death, all the other suicides were somewhat remote. They were not people I knew personally. The scenes of death were always cleaned up quietly, quickly, and thoroughly, so that no traces remained. Comrade Thus had made it very clear that people who spread "rumors" about suicides would be severely punished. Deaths resulting from suicide were never publicly announced; word was spread sotto voce, and quickly and secretly: "Another one, from the No. 6 Workshop, cut his wrists in the toilet room last night." That would be the extent of the information anyone dared communicate. No one said anything but we knew that few of the sudden deaths were from heart attacks, which was often the official cause of death.

Besides the suicides, there were also odd illnesses in the factory that further increased my fear of the place. There was, for example, the racing heart syndrome. Within a period of three months, a large number of healthy young men suddenly developed the illness. With a resting heart rate of one hundred or more beats per minute, many had to be hospitalized. At one point, the heart problem was so bad that nearly half of the workers at the testing bay were afflicted. In the winter of 1975, when thirty-three of the sixty-four workers at the testing bay were sick, Comrade Thus announced that he was launching a factory-wide emergency campaign to recruit new workers for the testing bay. Because workers at the testing bay had shorter working hours—six hours a day, with three shifts doing duty each day—and also were allotted extra cooking oil and larger rations of grain, there was no shortage of volunteers.

Then, just when the heart problem seemed to have subsided and new recruits had breathed fresh life into the place, there came another strange epidemic: facial paralysis. Like a contagious disease, within a week, as many as a dozen young workers woke up to find half of their faces "gone," without sensation and no longer capable of moving. Giant Wu, a hulky basketball player on the factory team, appeared one morning at the door of my room. The left side of his face was covered with a dark purplish jam-like stuff.

"Don't laugh at me," he said, trying to smile. The corner of the right side of his mouth lifted up and his right eye narrowed as his facial muscles tried to present the smile. But the left side of the face did not move. His left eye was still wide open, staring at me. The left side of his mouth was drooped, half open. I could hardly suppress a smile, although I tried to pretend that I did not notice anything unusual.

"That's eel's blood," he explained, pointing to the purple jelly on the left-hand side of his face. "I was told it's the best remedy for facial stroke. I woke up with half of my face frozen two days ago. Just like that. It must have been the cold draft in my room during the night that caused it. I have tried everything since then—dung beetle jam with honey, electrical acupuncture, dog blood, you name it. If you know any folk remedies, be sure to let me know. I'll try anything. I am only twenty-four, and if I don't cure this I won't be able to find a wife, and my mother will go crazy."

Fortunately, most of the cases of facial paralysis were temporary and disappeared within a few months. Since no one was dying, there was no official investigation to determine the cause of either epidemic.

In fact, no one talked about them openly. But in private, there was plenty of talk about these uncanny phenomena. In groups of three or four, over lunch breaks, people speculated in hushed tones that there must be some bad feng shui, or evil spirits, at the factory. Some people even took surreptitious action to protect themselves. For example, after the outbreak of the heart problems Master Pan, who was a secret believer in feng shui, burned a tiny evil man made of wheat flour along with a bundle of incense in the office in order to drive away the evil spirit. When facial paralysis hit, he killed a frog and splashed its blood on the beam above the door of his office. The next day, he and Bean Sprout and Little Lenin and I all walked through the beam solemnly, to receive the protection of the blood. Of course we did not talk about such things publicly, even though everybody, including Party members like Master Deng, knew his purpose and was even eager to stand under the blood-stained beam, hoping the protection would rub off on him, too.

By the end of the first year, I had realized that by escaping the village of Big Porcupine I had stepped into an even more sinister and dangerous trap. I never found out what caused the suicides and strange illnesses at the factory. Were they caused by the heavy metals used in the factory, or by the polluted groundwater, or by the tension of an isolated military life? I never knew, but I did know that I had to get out of there as soon as I could.

## *19*  The Year with Two Augusts

New Year's Day 1976 was bitterly cold. The sky was gray and a strong northeast wind howled all day. A mighty Siberian storm had crossed the border and swept southward, freezing and paralyzing much of China, marking the beginning of a year that would bring the country unprecedented natural and political disasters and bring me the most terrible grief of my life.

Long before New Year's Day, Master Pan had informed us that 1976 would be a year of trouble, for it was a leap year with thirteen months on the Chinese lunar calendar. Worse still, the intercalary month fell to August, so there were two Augusts. For the superstitious Chinese, two Augusts is the most ominous celestial combination and will always bring misery to mankind. Master Pan, who had an extensive knowledge of the folk "yellow calendar," had told us to lay low in the coming year. "Stay away from this place if you can," he said. "Look out for trouble and take cover next year. It's going to be a bad year." I did not pay much attention to him. I was brought up by Marxist atheists and was taught not to believe any superstitions. Li Ling, however, heeded Master Pan's warning and took a leave of absence; she stayed in Beijing for nearly six months. She used the pretense that her back injuries had flared up again and she needed to go home to have them treated.

But true to Master Pan's prediction, three major natural disasters—all of epic proportions—hit China that year. All three occurred during the two Augusts. On the first August 9 (of the Yellow Calendar)—July 28 on the Gregorian calendar—the worst earthquake in two centuries hit Tangshan, a coastal city one hundred miles north of Beijing, killing 225 thousand and wounding 500 thousand. Eleven days after the Great Tangshan Earthquake, on August 20, the main dam at the Madian Reservoir—the largest reservoir on the Yellow River—collapsed during a torrential rain, and in less than three hours the deluge swallowed Madian and its surrounding villages, drowning thousands of people.

"Well, this is not over yet," Master Pan said gravely during a lunch break. "When there is a flood in the North, there will be a drought in the South." And he was right. That summer, the worst drought in a century hit most of southeastern provinces in China. Hundreds of thousands of people starved to death.

But the horrid natural disasters were only half of what would befall the nation. The political disasters of that year shook China even more. The country had just emerged from the political turmoil of the Cultural Revolution, and we had finally started to feel a sense of normalcy returning. But then came the political earthquakes: the deaths of the Big Three. On January 8 Premier Zhou Enlai died of bladder cancer. His death shocked the nation, for he was considered a political moderate, an essential mediator between different political factions. His death brought fears of a return to massive political unrest. In July our fears were deepened by the death of another political moderate, Marshal Zhu De, vice chairman of the Communist Party.

The final political earthquake that overshadowed all the disasters of that year occurred on September 9. Chairman Mao, the Great Leader himself, died. We at the East Wind Aircraft Factory were shocked and dazed when we heard the special news bulletin on the loudspeakers at 4 P M. After so many years of shouting "Long Live Chairman Mao," I thought the saint would live forever. Like a colony of ants that had suddenly lost its queen, people scurried in all directions, as if their lives had lost all meaning.

For me, the national disasters were not the end of the troubles brought by the double Augusts. There was still one more horror to test my already wrecked nerves. In the week following the Great Leader's death, the East Wind Aircraft Factory was a terribly gloomy place. There was no popular music, no entertainment of any kind, no laughs. The loudspeakers incessantly blasted the music played at the Great Leader's funeral. We spoke to each other in low, hushed tones, as if we were afraid of being accused of irreverence. The whole factory campus was like a ghost town. After Friday evening's political seminar (the day was marked "DO NOT GO OUTDOORS" on Master Pan's Yellow Calendar), I walked through the quiet streets back to my dorm. The sky was dark, and it was about to rain. Except for the occasional slight tremors caused by the roar of the jet engines at the testing bay, the air was stagnant and dead. I slowly dragged my tired legs up the stairs to the third floor as several people wandered down to the dining hall. They all looked at the ground as they passed, trying to avoid eye contact and conversation. There was a bleak chilliness in the hall on the third floor, and in the darkness my steps sounded hollow on the thin concrete-slab floor. I stepped to the door and fumbled for the key in my pants pocket, and I discovered that the door was unlocked. I nudged it slightly and a shaft of faint bluish-gray light slid out of the opening and then shot to the opposite wall of the corridor.

For a moment, standing in the doorway and pocketing my keys, I was not sure what I was seeing on the window. It looked like the blurred silhouette of a gigantic bat. I took two steps into the room, and then dropped my bag and froze. A man was hanging from the window frame! It was Bean Sprout! A thin electrical wire, almost invisible at first, cut deeply into his neck. It was tied to a nail on top of the wooden window frame. On the floor, there was an overturned stool and, scattered around it, dozens of playing cards. Bean Sprout's eyes squinted, almost smiled at me, as if he were about to tell me one of his dirty jokes. I was too shocked to scream or cry the way people often do in such situations. My emotions couldn't change gears that quickly. Instead, I rushed forward and wrapped my arms around Bean Sprout's legs, trying to raise him up to relieve the pressure on his neck. His body was heavy and rigid, and his pants were cold and wet. Realizing that I could not get the electrical cord off the hook, I tried to catch the overturned stool with the top of my right foot so that I could stand on it and untie the wire. But the stool was out of reach. Holding the stiff legs of Bean Sprout, afraid that I might do more damage if I let go, I finally found my voice when I heard some people passing by in the corridor.

"HELP! SOMEBODY HELP ME! BEAN SPROUT HUNG . . ." My voice cracked as I choked back tears. In the blurred darkness, several shadowy figures rushed in and grabbed his legs and raised them up; another climbed up the windowsill.

"What the hell is going on? I just saw him ten minutes ago in the dining hall!" A man said, panting heavily.

"He can't have been up there very long. Did he urinate?" another asked.

"I don't see any on the ground. There's still hope." The body was cut down and laid on the floor. A person straddled Bean Sprout, sitting on his stomach, and started pounding on his chest.

"Did anyone run to the hospital for an ambulance yet?" asked a voice, which I recognized as Giant Wu's. The factory hospital was four blocks away, and we had no telephone in the dorm building. "I'll go," I said and ran as fast as I could to the hospital.

I do not remember much of what happened after that. The ambulance took Bean Sprout to the emergency room and we learned that he was still alive.

I visited Bean Sprout the next day with Master Pan in the emergency room. Bean Sprout was breathing heavily with the aid of a respirator, and his face and naked body were covered with white and brown plastic tubes connected to various machines by his bed. We quietly stood at the door, looking at the two large, almost black, bony feet stretched out toward us. That was the last I ever saw of Bean Sprout. Later that day, Master Pan, Little Lenin, and I caught a ride on an army truck to another hospital forty miles away to bring back five tanks of oxygen for Bean Sprout. The fresh oxygen kept him breathing for another day, but he died on the third day.

I never found out why Bean Sprout killed himself. He had been plagued by chronic liver disease and a strained family life—his wife and children lived in his native village forty miles away, and he could see them only on weekends. But somehow I don't believe these are the reasons that drove him to his death.

The funeral was held two days later in the dining hall where Bean Sprout and I used to eat our meals together. It was the saddest of all the funerals that I had attended in that dining hall. All three hundred workers from the No. 8 Workshop attended. "The Painter," the factory's self-taught unofficial artist, drew a large portrait of Bean Sprout from a one-inch black-and-white photo, and it was hung on one of the dining hall windows. Several wreaths were placed on either side of the picture. In the front row, facing the picture, stood Bean Sprout's four children and his wife. They had been transported to the factory by military truck. On their arms they wore a black silk band bearing the large white character *Xiao*, or "Mourning." Behind them we stood in neat columns, dressed in our white work uniforms. On each person's breast was a single white paper flower.

The funeral was brief. Following a short moment of silence and funeral music played on an old gramophone, Red Calf, the Party secretary, delivered a standard revolutionary eulogy, as was required at revolutionary funerals. On this occasion, however, the Party secretary struggled to find the right words to praise Bean Sprout for serving the Party well even though he committed suicide, which was considered a treacherous act by the Party. Following the short eulogy was the final item: everybody walking past and bowing to the picture of the deceased. The funeral would have concluded here in the unemotional and matter-of-fact way that so many Chinese funerals do, but for a sudden, bestial howl from the dark-faced woman in the front row. The woman had not cried or made a sound throughout the ceremony. The shriek that startled everyone was not a tearful paroxysm of grief from a mourning wife, but a sharp menacing wail from a wounded she-wolf preparing to launch a final desperate attack. The violent, wild ululation seemed to hiss through the air like a serpent looking for an adversary to strike. The single-file procession that was just beginning to pass Bean Sprout's portrait stopped in its tracks, and before anyone of us fully realized the source of the chilling howl, the small figure in the front row shot forward and clamped a pair of powerful peasant hands around Red Calf's throat. The Party secretary fell backward to the ground, knocking over the small table with the gramophone. A second later, the orderly funeral was in total chaos. We rushed forward from several directions to save the secretary. Someone fell and was trampled, but his anguished cry only seemed a sad, weak commentary on the woman's wail and animal vitality. A few others grunted in anger. Like the jaws of a ravenous snapping turtle, the pair of black hands that held the secretary's throat refused to open. For what seemed like minutes, no one could dislodge her. Finally, Giant Wu hit the woman on the head with a wooden board, and her face dimmed and then blacked out altogether as she slumped to the ground. The funeral thus ended abruptly. Several of us dragged the powerful peasant woman out of the room, and others carried away the broken gramophone and the half-strangled secretary.

In the next few days, from early morning till dusk, the little dark woman planted herself in front of our dormitory where her husband used to live. Pacing back and forth, pointing a dark finger at the window from which Bean Sprout hung himself, she cursed, croaked, and bellowed. No one could understand what she was saying, in part because she was cursing in her peasant dialect. At first, she seemed to be cursing Red Calf, but then she started to curse the building, the window, the sidewalk, and eventually everyone who passed by. Master Pan, Little Lenin, and I tried to persuade her to go home, but we soon retreated when we found ourselves the target of her venom. After three days, few people paid much attention when they passed her on the way to work. The woman continued to sit below Bean Sprout's window and erupt into angry outbursts every once in a while. Some children then noticed her and began to taunt her, as if provoking a chained dog. When the woman sat down, taking a break from cursing the third-floor window, the children would inch forward to imitate her, pointing a finger at the window and skittering back and forth, chanting: "Shoe Awl, Shoe Awl, Howl like a Barn Owl!" Like a tired but defiant old dog, the angular little woman would be energized by their taunts and would jump up, point her crooked finger at the children and curse them. They would then disperse with laughter, ready to start the game all over again in a few minutes.

I felt sorry for the woman but could do nothing to help her. I do not know where the woman stayed at night, where her children went, or if she ate anything during those days. I lost count of how many days she battled the factory children and cursed the window. But one morning when I went out of the dorm, she was no longer by the curb. Bean Sprout had no life insurance or pension, despite the fact that he had worked for the state for twenty-six years. It was rumored that the factory paid her 250 yuan to go home.

After listening to Bean Sprout laugh, tell dirty jokes, crawl under the card table, and argue with everyone for three years, I was hit especially hard by his sudden death. The winter that followed Bean Sprout's death came early and seemed particularly harsh. In mid-December 1976 the temperature plummeted to fifteen degrees below zero. So cold was our unheated dormitory room that in the mornings my wet towels were frozen into solid sheets, strong and stiff.

For months following Bean Sprout's death, I was anxious and restless. The anxiety was indescribable, vague but lodged deep in my heart. It was not a fear of Bean Sprout's ghost; I was an atheist and did not believe in ghosts. It came only at night, like the misty, cold draft that forced its way through the cracks of the window and wrapped itself slowly around my body, seeping into my pores and numbing my limbs.

It was in those nights that I started to have dreams of flying away, of silently propelling myself through the air, swimming like a frog. After I had had several of these dreams, my breaststroke seemed to improve steadily and I flew father and faster in each successive dream. Several times, I flew so high and so far that I felt certain that I had finally escaped my dark fear and it would never touch me again. But at the end of each dream, I would find that I had gone nowhere—just like the monkey who could travel ten thousand miles in a single somersault, but always found himself merely bouncing stupidly and comically in the infinite hand of the Buddha.

**"The Goal: Join the Party"**

To keep my mind from thoughts of Bean Sprout and the terrible dreams, I studied even harder, spending all my spare time on books. I made good progress when I completed my apprenticeship at the end of the third year: I had mastered high school mathematics and physics and had even gone on to study calculus and differential equations. But still I did not know how I would ever use the theoretical knowledge I acquired. Nor did I have any idea how Newton's laws and differential equations would help me escape the dreaded factory and get me into college. As far as I could see, thirty years from now I would still be working at the testing bay and hearing the roaring engines if I did not find another way out.

A few weeks after Bean Sprout's funeral, I received two letters that suddenly pointed a way out for me. The first letter was from Smoking Devil, from whom I had not heard for more than a year. After talking happily about his two girls and his wife, he revealed his strategy to better himself in the communist society. "You will be surprised to hear this," he wrote. "I have just joined the Communist Party! I have figured out that joining the Party is the best way to advance in one's career in China. . . . Have you thought of joining the Party? You should."

The second letter was from Baby Dragon, my fellow Red Guard of the Great Wall Fighting Team, who had joined the army. Strangely, in his letter he took the same attitude as Smoking Devil toward joining the Party. After four years in the service, Baby Dragon had advanced significantly in his career. He, too, had joined the Communist Party and had risen to the rank of an officer. Because of his Party membership, he had been chosen to be among the first "new students" to enroll in the army's Infantry College, which had just been reopened together with many civilian colleges as part of the Communist Party's new educational reform. The "new reform" mandated that all colleges must recruit students based on their political loyalty to the Party.

Both Smoking Devil and Baby Dragon were right, I thought. Party membership was a way for me to fulfill my dreams of going to college and escaping the factory. Not long after I received these letters, the East Wind Aircraft Factory announced that it too would soon select a few Party members to study at Nanjing College of Aeronautics. It was a chance I could not afford to miss.

"A sacrifice I must make—THE GOAL: JOIN THE PARTY"—I entered the elliptic command in my secret diary, which I had been keeping for some time. I used only elliptical phrases and cryptic symbols to remind myself of my decisions. The decision meant that I would have to sacrifice my academic studies and to devote my time to political activities, activities that I had always loathed. I hated those vulgar and hypocritical Communist Party officials, but I now must work to win their favor, just as I had with Uncle Cricket. As with my studies, I devised a plan and immediately began to execute the plan.

As a first step in my campaign to join the Party, I started a second diary, an "open" diary that I would deliberately leave in places where it would be easily discovered. It was full of revolutionary thoughts and praise for the Party. Years of exposure to communist propaganda made writing such a diary much easier than working out calculus problems. Before long, I filled three volumes, which I was careful to wrap with bright red plastic covers. I was also careful to leave my bright Red diaries carelessly—but not too carelessly—on my office desk and on my bed, and I noticed that Master Deng occasionally glanced at them. Not long after I planted my diaries in strategic places, Master Deng took me aside during a lunch break.

"We are impressed by the thoughts expressed in your diaries," he said, unabashedly admitting that he had read them. "The Party needs young people like you, people who have both technical skills and a Red heart."

He took a long sip from his large teacup, letting the water roll around in his mouth noisily from side to side, and sighed with happiness as the aroma soothed his body. For Master Deng, the monstrous teacup was as good as an opium pipe. Turning to me again, he confirmed as much: "Having a pot of tea after a meal makes one happier than a little Buddha. Either Confucius or Mencius said that. Anyway, to get back to your diary, you should get closer to the Party, talk more with Party members, do more volunteer work for the Party. I have reported your political progress to the Party secretary and he will speak to you soon."

The meeting with Red Calf, the Party secretary, took place two days later and gave me much hope. "We are pleased with your desire to join the Communist Party," said Red Calf, "and I want to personally invite you to join the Communist Youth League, which is the first step toward Party membership. There you will have a chance to demonstrate your determination to serve the cause of communism. These days, young people's enthusiasm for communism has been declining and we need people like you to re-energize them. We are glad that you are following in the footsteps of your parents." Of course, the secretary knew from my personal file that both my parents were longtime Party members.

I nodded eagerly and piously, like a little monk listening to a lecture by Buddha himself. I took note of everything that Red Calf said. "I will do the best I can to serve the Party," I said.

A month after my talk with Red Calf, I was admitted to the Communist Youth League, and I devoted even more time and energy to making a good impression on the Party secretary. On my office desk, I kept an impressive pile of books by Marx, Engels, Lenin, and Chairman Mao, and I studied them during breaks for the show. Every Tuesday night, I led a study group that discussed dialectical materialism, historical materialism, and the theory of class struggle. At the daily political seminars, I aided Master Deng by reading the editorials in the *People's Daily* and quotations from the Great Leader's Little Red Book. On the bulletin board at the entrance of the testing bay, I wrote a weekly column about good deeds performed by Communist youths the previous week. And at the workshop's political rallies, I sat conspicuously in the front row and enthusiastically shouted slogans.

Once again, my efforts soon paid off. I was appointed Deputy Secretary of the Youth League in February; not long after that, I was made commander of the Young Militia of the workshop. Besides the lectures and study groups, I also organized "extra contribution days," when we Communist Youths volunteered to put in a day's work without pay. Finally, with the help and encouragement of Master Deng and Red Calf, I submitted a lengthy application to the Communist Party. Everything seemed to be on track. Upon receiving the application, Master Deng smiled broadly and promised that he would personally sponsor my membership at the next Party meeting. During a weekly political rally, Red Calf praised me and my work in the Communist Youth League, and my heart leapt with joy when the Party secretary added, "The next time we choose someone to go to college, we will first consider revolutionary youths like Fan Shen."

Becoming a Party member, however, was a slow process. A person had to pass many tests to prove his loyalty to the Party. One of the last tests was regular confessional meetings with an appointed Party mentor. The applicant must confess all his past sins and un-revolutionary thoughts and seek guidance from the mentor. When the mentor felt that the applicant was ready, he would make a formal recommendation to the general assembly of the Party and a vote would be taken. It was here that I unexpectedly stumbled and ruined my chance to join the Party and go to college.

The Party mentor that Red Calf appointed for me was Master Zhu, whom the young people in the workshop called "Combat Zhu," both for his long service in the army and for the cigarettes he smoked—Combats, the cheapest brand on the market, priced at just nine cents a pack. He was the only one I knew who smoked the brand. An old bachelor, about fifty, bald and barely literate, he slurred his words and was sometimes hard to understand. Listening to his gibberish was pure torture for me. But Combat Zhu took his job seriously and insisted on meeting me twice a week to hear my confessions and to discuss my political progress. During those tedious counseling sessions—called "heart-to-heart" conversations—I would nod from time to time, staring fixedly at old Combat Zhu puffing away on his cheap cigarettes. Combat Zhu did not speak much because he obviously disliked doing so, but there was no doubt that he enjoyed lighting up cigarette after cigarette as I sat by his side.

One day after work, we sat down on one of the benches arranged in a circle in the bushes outside the workshop, and Combat Zhu offered me a cigarette, which I politely declined. After finishing a second cigarette, he started to grind out—slowly—the story of his life. He told me how hard life was in his native village, how he left the child bride whom his parents had chosen for him when he was eleven and she was thirteen, and how he still supported her financially, for he did not want to disappoint his parents by divorcing her. That was why he was so poor and had to smoke the cheapest cigarettes. He asked me whether I had a girlfriend. I shook my head.

"Good. Don't have a girlfriend at your age," he said. His eyes had a peculiar look to them as he glanced at me and said this. Then he drew a fresh cigarette from the pack and tossed the pack on the bench. "The Party has taught us that young people at your age are like the sun at 8 A.M. You have the whole future in front of you and you should concentrate on improving yourself and on serving the Party's causes. Girlfriends are too distracting. You are only twenty-three. It's a bourgeois thing to think of women at your age."

I smiled and nodded innocuously.

"It is good that a young man like you is concentrating on joining the

Party," he continued. Out came the words one by one, as if he were pain-stakingly picking them out from between his yellow teeth with a tooth-pick. "Women are not good for a career. If you want to succeed, you must avoid women and get closer to the Party members."

While emphatically and respectfully nodding at the old bachelor, I thought to myself that if I could, I would rather give up my career and have a lovely girl. I remembered how during those long nights of solitary study I fantasized about touching the pretty hand of the new secretary at the workshop and telling her my grand ambitions, and then sweetly, my mind drifted off to Li Ling and the time when we sat—so close that our thighs touched—in her secluded alcove looking at her stamps. I could still feel that gentle touch.

"When it comes down to it, you can only trust men," Combat Zhu said, smiling but very serious. He stared at his greasy homemade shoes as he drawled, "When I was young, my cousin and I used to play this game of pulling carrots." An odd grin appeared on his face.

"Pull . . . Pulling carrots? What's that?" I asked absentmindedly, still thinking of Li Ling.

"This," Combat Zhu said, laying his hand suddenly on my crotch and pulling at it.

As Combat Zhu leaned sideways toward me, the strong smell of cheap tobacco hit my nostrils and then slunk down my body like a slippery yel-lowish eel. I jerked backward convulsively, not so much because of the groping hand as because of the smothering stench. Combat Zhu imme-diately withdrew his hand. I was confused, but it was not my nature to have an outburst of anger. Not wanting to offend him, I smiled awk-wardly and mumbled, "That . . . That's a funny game."

"The game is to pull each other there," he said, pointing to my groin, "and to see who can get the white juice out first. Do you want to try it?" Combat Zhu sidled over toward me, as if he were about to grab my groin again.

"No, no, no, Master Zhu." I abruptly stood up and backed toward the gap between the benches. "I, I need to go the restroom now." I was afraid and repelled. The nearness of Combat Zhu's heinous face and disgusting tobacco stench threw me into a panic. I stumbled backward and fled, and I did not come back to the session.

Although I did not report the incident to anyone, I refused to have any more "heart-to-heart" confessionals with Combat Zhu. What kind of reports he sent to the Party's general assembly I do not know, but my ap-plication was rejected at the next Party meeting and Red Calf told me politely that I needed more time to develop my loyalty to the Party. "But don't be discouraged. The door of the Party is always open. Do keep trying," he encouraged me.

I was desperate enough to believe him. I sent in application after application, one every two weeks, to show my enthusiasm for the Party and determination to join it. But the Party's door was still closed to me.

That summer, the Party committee chose a young Party member from my workshop who had never finished eighth grade to attend Nanjing College of Aeronautics, the college I had dreamed of attending. My hopes were crushed. Although I dared not show it, I hated this system of selecting college students, and hated myself for wasting so much time writing stupid applications to join the Party.

While I was busy composing increasingly elaborate and glowing applications to the Party, a group of college students from Nanjing College of Aeronautics came to the East Wind Aircraft Factory for their internship training. They were the first group of college students selected by the Party from workers, peasants, and soldiers. Every evening when I left the workshop, I would watch them with envy as they played volleyball or sat in small groups studying. Young men and young women my own age who sang and played and laughed! And they laughed so differently from the workers in the factory! They did not know about the suicides and the strange illnesses. The aircraft factory was a fun place for them, a kind of interesting vacation. When they finished their two-month internships, they would leave the factory and go back to college, back to their studies. When they walked into the workshop, everyone's eyes followed them. They were the chosen ones, the ones the Party trusted.

What could I do to gain the Party's trust? How did they gain the confidence of the Party? How did they please people like Master Deng, Red Calf, and Combat Zhu? I thought often these questions and sometimes even seriously contemplated going back to Combat Zhu and playing "pulling carrots." Those were the most desperate moments of my life. A few months later, I was relieved when the odious option was taken away from me.

One day, the whole factory was shocked by the news that Combat Zhu had been secretly arrested. Red Calf announced to the assembly of the workshop that Combat Zhu, a corrupt enemy hidden in our factory for many years, had been expelled from the Party and fired from the factory. The exact nature of his crime was not stated, or even hinted at. Rumor had it that he was charged with the strange crime of "sperm robbery," a crime no one had heard of before. Later we learned that two thirteen-year-old boys had told the authorities that he had "robbed" them, promising them candy in exchange for their sperm, which he said was used for curing an illness he had. But he was late in his candy payment and the boys told their mothers. He was sentenced to five years of hard labor.

The arrest of Combat Zhu marked the end of my efforts to join the Party and I was left where I began: searching for a way to go to college and to escape the dreaded factory.

My failure to join the Party threw me into a depression that lasted several weeks. All those months of political activism, all those revolutionary diaries, the hundreds of pages of applications, the countless hours of torture at confessional meetings—all of it wasted. In those depressed weeks, the only book I could read was Stendhal's *The Red and the Black*, and I read it over and over again. Each time I drew a few drops of strength from the story of Julien Sorel, the son of poor peasants, whose unwavering drive for success, determined pursuit of knowledge, and passionate audacity in love struck a chord in my heart. With the help of the book and the passage of time, I slowly regained my hope and resolve.

I abandoned writing silly applications to join the Party and went back to my serious studies. Besides reading the philosophical books that I borrowed from Li Ling, I decided to begin studying English. I had a vague hope that the language might help me get into college someday. But just as I had when studying other subjects, I had trouble finding textbooks. Most of the English books had been labeled imperialist books and burned by the Red Guards. I searched the factory bookstore and library and all I could find was a thin pamphlet that accompanied a new radio program called "English by Radio," which was meant more for political indoctrination than for teaching English. It contained next to nothing except for some political slogans, such as "Long Live Chairman Mao!" and "Long Live the Great Proletarian Cultural Revolution!" But I was not one to give up easily and on Sundays, I borrowed Master Pan's bicycle and rode to the high schools in the surrounding area to search their libraries.

In my visit to a country high school one Sunday, I was very lucky to meet an English teacher who became my friend instantly and who lent me several precious English textbooks that he had kept hidden from the Red Guards. His name was Liu Gong, but I later jokingly referred to him as "Fountain Pen," for he was so fond of fountain pens that he always had four or five in his breast pocket, glittering from his chest like a row of medals. A college graduate and a real scholar, he was well versed not only in English but also in history, politics, and literature. In the course of a year, I went to Fountain Pen's school nearly every Sunday to borrow books and to study English with him. But the real pleasure of seeing him was the talks we had after our lessons, during which we passionately debated about the future of China.

From the very beginning, I loved the English language and I studied hard. In fact, I was so enthralled with memorizing English words in those days that I got myself into several accidents. One day, when I was reading flash cards while walking to the dining hall, I walked right into a large poplar tree and got myself a bump the size of a walnut on my forehead—a badge of a budding scholar. Another time, I was riding a bike to see Fountain Pen and started thinking of the words I studied that day. All of a sudden my bike careened, seemingly of its own will, and shot into an irrigation ditch filled with manure. My only Sunday jacket was ruined. Fountain Pen jokingly said that this was God's punishment for studying a forbidden language. Obviously the Party did not want me to study English, the language of evil capitalist countries. And in China, the Party was God.

Even though he said it in jest, we both knew that there was some truth to it. More than once I had grave doubts about what I was doing. Sometimes books and learning seemed to me merely a grand mirage, a siren's song. What was the use of studying English? What was the use of reading philosophy and novels? Could they ever change my fate without the blessing of the Party? Such moments of doubt, however, faded like the tails of fireflies the moment I walked out of the dormitory. Seeing the familiar white dining halls where all the funerals were held, I would remember Bean Sprout and all the other deaths, and I knew that I could not give up books: they were my only hope; perhaps they would someday help carry me away from the place.

Little did I know that the first place where I would use "the idle books" was not college as I had imagined, but an even more dreadful place than the factory. There, the books, whose usefulness I once doubted, proved to be a lifesaver.

I was arrested on the evening of August 15, 1977—the day of the Moon Festival. When I was led away by three plainclothes policemen in a dark green police jeep, I felt like I was in one of my dreams again, and half hoped that I would wake up to find it was just another nightmare. Even the pain in my arms and wrists felt unreal, since I had never been bound before. An hour later we arrived at a dark building and a guard led me to the basement, where we walked through a long corridor of prison cells. Before he shoved me through a black iron door toward the end of the line, I looked up and was alarmed to notice the big white "No. 4" painted on the doorframe. It was a bad omen. Four is the most ominous number in Chinese: it has the same pronunciation as death.

The heavy, rusty metal door clanged shut behind me and I realized this was not a dream. The air became immediately thicker, almost tangible, with a sour decaying smell like that of spoiled food scraps. After my eyes grew more accustomed to the dim light, I stepped forward and looked around. The cell was a narrow single-person unit. On the floor, at the left end of the wall, was a bare wooden board serving as a bed. Barely two steps from the bed, in the right corner, was a wooden barrel with a hole in the cover, a toilet barrel like the ones I had seen in peasant homes. A nauseating stench surrounded the barrel, and a small army of large green-headed flies rested comfortably on the cover.

Confused and tired, I collapsed on the hard board, but I could hardly sleep. My arms and wrists stabbed me with a numbing pain whenever I moved and I tried to shelter my face from the stench of the toilet barrel, but the almighty stink always found me within seconds of taking a new position.

But I knew this was no time to dwell on such petty things as the terrible odor. I had to concentrate on more urgent problems. I did not know why I was arrested, but I knew I was in grave danger. Few people ever get out of a Chinese prison without losing at least a layer of skin. I tried to think of what I had done that prompted my arrest. Since the death of the Great Leader the previous year, police had been rounding up "criminals," from petty thieves to political dissidents, and punishment had been swift and severe, "to ensure the political stability of the country." In the last two months at the East Wind Aircraft Factory, there had been two "public arrest rallies" whose sole purpose was arresting and condemning "criminals," but I could hardly see any similarity between me and the people arrested at the rallies. The first rally was to arrest "The Painter," the man who had painted Bean Sprout's funeral portrait. He was a technician and an amateur artist who painted funeral portraits and taught a few private students in his spare time. His crime: "bourgeois corruption"—showing nude paintings to female students.

A few weeks later came a second mass rally to arrest "Singer," a worker in my workshop. Singer was a dark faced young man who always hummed while he worked. I considered him a friend. His arrest was a shock to the whole factory. And the way he was arrested struck a deep fear in me.

It was a rally designed to create fear. All the workers, more than five thousand, were assembled one afternoon in front of an open-air stage surrounded by the factory militia armed with semi-automatic rifles with shining bayonets. Hanging on two tall poles and spanning the entire stage was a long banner: "MASS MEETING TO ARREST AND CONDEMN CHILD CORRUPTOR JIN LI." Jin Li was Singer's real name.

As with many political rallies of the Cultural Revolution, the rally began with the singing of the Great Leader's song "Harden Our Hearts." After the song, the head of security ordered to bring up the child corruptor Jin Li. Then the loudspeakers, turned all the way up, violently jolted everyone with slogans. "DOWN WITH THE CHILD COR-RUPTOR JIN LI!" shouted a male announcer. "LENIENCY WITH CONFESSION! PUNISHMENT WITH RESISTANCE!" shouted a female announcer. "LONG LIVE THE PROLETARIAN DICTA-TORSHIP!" both announcers bellowed through the microphone together. Singer was dragged onto the stage by two large policemen in green uniforms. The shouting of the slogans continued for another ten minutes.

The booming slogans always had their intended effect. The voice sheared over our heads, making every one of us shrink a little, afraid to be taller than the rest. We were cowed into submission, if only by noise.

My eyes were fixed on Singer's face; I feared for my friend. This was not just a routine "struggle meeting." The guns and bayonets foretold his fate.

Looking at my friend's face, I could see the fear he must be experiencing: the fear of total loneliness, of being completely forsaken, of being condemned by everyone he knew, spit upon and shunned by the entire society. Some of the militiamen holding shining new AK-47s were Singer's co-workers, and had played volleyball with him just two days before.

The head of the Civil Militia announced Singer's crime. The charges were two counts of child corruption: on two occasions he had taught several teenagers two songs that were "bourgeois," one a love song from the pre-revolutionary era, and one a supposedly pornographic ballad. The charges were ridiculous, but they were high crimes at the moment.

Next came the most dramatic part of the public arrests, a part that everybody was expecting: the ritualistic tying of the prisoner. A burly policeman came onstage with a thin, white nylon rope. While his two colleagues stretched out Singer's arms, he skillfully encircled the rope several times around each arm and pulled both arms tightly together behind the prisoner's back. Then, with a sudden jerk, he lifted the prisoner by the rope, leaving his feet high above the ground, dangling in the air for a good ten seconds, and then dropped him. An agonized cry came from Singer. This was the modern Chinese art of tying a prisoner that everybody had whispered about. A public tying performance was just not good enough if the prisoner was not lifted and dumped. Hanging in the air, the weight of the prisoner helped tighten the rope, and forced it to cut deeply into the flesh. From Singer's distorted face, no one could doubt that the pain was excruciating. And the message was communicated: everybody had been warned.

I never saw Singer again. It was said that he was sentenced to six years of hard labor but died of acute hepatitis at a labor camp in the second year.

Throughout the night, I contemplated my fate. Would I be arrested publicly like Singer? What was my crime? I'd never taught young people "anti-revolutionary songs" or showed people pictures of naked women. It was true that I still had the book with paintings of naked women, but it was securely wrapped and hidden in my bag and I had not touched it since I came to the factory. Did someone search my bag and find the book?

Toward the morning, a sharp metallic noise woke me. Raising my head, I saw a dirty enamel plate slid through the hole at the bottom of the door and come to a stop not far from my head. The plate was practically a sheet of black metal, the white enamel having largely flaked off. On it were a small wotou—cone-shaped corn bread—and two ugly pieces of salted turnip that looked like dried goose droppings. Jammed between them was a cracked enamel cup filled with water. The flies immediately took notice and started circling the plate.

Pushing myself up, I reached out for the food instinctively. I picked up the wotou, broke it into two, shoved half into my mouth, bit into it, and started chewing. The wotou was coarse and hard, and at least three days old, but it tasted good. I realized that I was very hungry because I did not have supper the night before.

The wotou was small, not more than three or four mouthfuls, and was gone in less than a minute. I put a piece of the goose droppings in my mouth. It tasted bitter and mushy, and I washed it down with a mouthful of water. The food whetted my appetite and left me hungrier. My mind turned to the dinner that Little Lenin's wife prepared the night before: stewed pork, stir-fried cabbage with bamboo shoots, and steamed white rice, all hot. It was a dinner to celebrate the August 15 Moon Festival, and I remembered how Master Pan and I, as guests of honor, were sitting down and Meatball was scooping rice into our bowls when the loud knock on the door came. I felt sorry for myself for missing the meal, and for Meatball, who had spent the whole day cooking.

After the meager breakfast, I returned to my thoughts. I knew I would be interrogated soon. I had to think about what to say. One word out of place, and I might be dead like Singer. Although I did not know the reason for my arrest, the charge had to be serious, for only prisoners charged with the most serious political crimes were confined to single cells. Common criminals were crammed into large, crowded cells. Over and over again I searched my memory for anything I had said in the past few years that might incriminate me. Was it a complaint about Red Calf, the incompetent Party secretary, that I made to two of my best friends at a dinner? Or did someone read my secret diary and decipher its encrypted meanings? Or was it for my secretly listening to the BBC and the Voice of America late at night?

There was one thing I was sure of: no matter what the charge, I should never admit it. Although the official policy was "confession earns leniency and resistance doubles punishment," it was simply not true. Convictions were often based solely on an inmate's confession. Smoking Devil had once told to me that I should never admit to anything if I was ever arrested. "Don't ever be fooled by the promised lenient treatment," he said. "I have seen too many people who, after confessing their crimes, were dragged out and shot. Confession is suicide." That, I reminded myself, I have to remember under any circumstances.

"I AM A TRUE REVOLUTIONARY! I AM NOT AFRAID OF DYING FOR TRUTH! I LOVE THE GREAT LEADER!" A loud voice suddenly broke the train of my gloomy thoughts. I recognized instantly the low raspy voice. The speaker could not have been anyone but Fountain Pen, my friend and English teacher. I jumped up and rushed to the door, just in time to see him pass my cell, escorted by two guards. Fountain Pen looked haggard. His sunken face was pale and long and his unkempt hair fell down over his face, covering one of his glasses. He still wore the faded blue Mao jacket that he had always worn, and four large fountain pens—the only luxuries he possessed—still protruded from his breast pocket. He was arguing excitedly with the guards and did not see me.

"I was not attacking Chairman Mao! My essay is about true Marxist democracy. I have nothing to hide." He kept repeating that as they walked toward the end of the hall.

"You'll have the chance to tell that to Marx himself pretty soon," a guard jeered at him.

Don't you know it is useless to argue with guards, Fountain Pen? I wanted to say to my friend, but bit my lips and did not utter a sound. What's the use of writing about true Marxist democracy? You are too idealistic and stupid. How could you write it down? I remembered cautioning him precisely against that a few months before.

They were out of sight soon. Only their voices could still be heard. "You are dead meat now, don't you know? Now get ready to see the Devil himself!" a guard chuckled with gleeful excitement.

"I am not an anti-revolutionary. I want to appeal . . ." Fountain Pen's words faded as the hall door closed behind them.

Recovering from the shock of seeing my friend, I began to understand why I was there. I was probably in prison because of him. From the prisoner next door, I learned that my friend had been charged with the most serious political crime.

During the month before the first anniversary of Chairman Mao's death, while everybody was supposed to study the Great Leader's works, Fountain Pen began writing a long treatise on Marxist democracy in an empty classroom. The principal, who saw part of the essay, tipped off the police. That evening while he was writing, the police rushed in. Fountain Pen panicked and tried to stuff the papers into his mouth, but the police officers choked him and pulled the pages out. It did not take them long to decide that the essay was a vicious attack on the Great Leader's socialist democracy. The head of the public security bureau personally reported the case to the Party's central committee, and he was ordered to arrest Fountain Pen immediately.

"This guy is as good as dead now, in my opinion," the inmate in the next cell said. "Doesn't have a clue about which way the political wind is blowing! Attacking Chairman Mao before the old man's body is cold— can you be more stupid than that? I think they are going to sentence him today. He's going to get the 'iron pill.'"

His words sent a shiver through my body. If my friend's crime was a capital crime, what kind was mine? Was I going to be charged as a co-conspirator? In that case, I could get the iron pill, too. What would the charge be?

I searched my brain to remember every meeting I had with Fountain Pen recently. I had had some dinners with him in the last year or so. People knew we were close friends. But the truth was I had always been leery of his political naïveté. He was too ready to talk to anyone about his lofty theories, and too careless in writing down his thoughts. I had told him never to write down his political thoughts.

What worried me was the two long letters that Fountain Pen had written me. In them, he expounded some of his ideas about democracy and Marxism. Fountain Pen was a very simple-minded thinker. He thought that the Party would be pleased with his efforts to explore the meaning of proletarian democratic dictatorship, an idea that Marx had written about. But I knew that that kind of original thinking was troublesome and had put his letters in an old shoe as a precaution. Did the police find the letters? How stupid of me not to have burned them!

Shortly after two o'clock in the afternoon, I was led into an interrogation room. Except for a wooden table and three wooden stools, the room was bare. A faded picture of Chairman Mao was draped on a green wall in the back of the room. Underneath it was the expected calligraphed slogan: CONFESSION EARNS LENIENCY; RESISTENCE DOUBLES PUNISHMENT! Behind the table sat two middle-aged men, both wearing the same white short-sleeved shirts and dark blue trousers. The vacant stool in front of the table was obviously intended for me. The man on the left had a square brown face and was reading a file. The younger man on the right had a fleshy, ruddy face. He smiled in a friendly way toward me and motioned to me to sit down. The older official looked up from his papers. He had a brown complexion, and his face had some large noticeable pockmarks.

"I think you know why you are here," Pockmark began. He spoke in a low nasal voice, and his eyes were transfixed on mine.

I instinctively raise my eyes and met his stare with an innocent look. Avoiding eye contact is a sure sign of guilt, I knew. "No, I have no idea at all," I answered without hesitation, and without any hint of anger or resentment. I was surprised by how easily the words came out. "I was about to eat dinner with Little Lenin and his wife when the officers came. Is this about my argument with Secretary Red Calf last week? It is not entirely my fault, you know. Yes, I admit I should not have called him Miser Calf—"

"Don't try to fool us!" Pockmark interrupted sternly. "You know what your friend Liu Gong did, don't you? He committed an anti-revolutionary act and he stubbornly refused to confess. He made up his mind to be the enemy of the people, so he got the most severe punishment. This morning he was executed. We must teach the people's enemies not to underestimate the strength of our proletarian dictatorship . . ."

I did not hear the rest of the sentence—my head whirled and burned with agony and fear. Fountain Pen dead! He got the iron pill! And I could easily get twenty years for being his friend.

The younger official's voice was a complete contrast to his colleague's. He smiled and tried to soothe my jangled nerves: "You know, our policy is 'confession earns leniency and resistance doubles punishment.' We know what you have done, but we want to give you a chance to confess first. The Communist Party wants to save people who make mistakes, not to punish them, unless they compound their mistakes by resisting confession. Now take a little time to think, and tell us about you and your friend."

He paused, his smiling face poised in the air. "You are a smart young man," he began again. "And you are from a good family. We have all your files here, from kindergarten onward," he said as he picked up the yellow manila folder on the table and waved it at me. "I am sure you understand the Party's policies. If you confess, I can guarantee you that you will receive special treatment, no matter how serious your problem is. You can leave here today. Your friend tried to resist, and see what he got? Do you understand?"

His voice sounded casual and pleasant, almost as if he were inviting me to a dinner at his home that night. But I knew better.

"Yes, I want to confess," I nodded eagerly and meekly. "I know the good policy of the Party. I will confess my mistakes and tell you everything . . ."

I smiled humbly and began elaborating on a long self-criticism. I was an expert at self-criticism; I had learned the trick when I was in the first grade. "I ask the forgiveness of the Party. I was too naïve. I was deceived by Fountain Pen. He asked me to dinner at his dorm and I went and he talked about Marx's *Capital*, which I did not understand. But I did not sense anything wrong. Enemies are sometimes well disguised, you know. Chairman Mao said so. I should have studied the Great Leader's works harder and should have discovered Fountain Pen's evil intentions earlier. It was my fault. I know I deserve severe punishment. If Fountain Pen dared to attack our great beloved leader Chairman Mao, then . . . then he deserves what he got. In fact, a bullet was too good for him. He should have been shot a thousand times. No, he should have been fried in a big pan of oil. No, no, that's not enough. He should have been crushed by a big stone and fed to vultures. He—" My voice became excited. The exaggerated rhetoric of the Cultural Revolution flowed from me like a flash flood.

"That's good, that's a good start," Pockmark interrupted. "Did he show you any of his writings? Did he ever write you a letter?"

I remembered well Fountain Pen's essay "What Is True Democracy?" and the two letters he sent me.

"No, he said he wrote something but I was not interested. Oh, I was so blind that I never recognized what a vicious enemy he was, pretending to be my friend. I am very glad that the Party has saved me from him. I am so grateful to you, for exposing this dangerous enemy. I am so ashamed of myself . . ."

"Do you know any other people who were close to him?" The younger officer asked pleasantly.

"Yes, I think Principal Tu was pretty close to him. Fountain Pen told me that he had dinner with him twice. But Principal Tu is a good Party member. Could he be—"

"Good. You should not exclude anyone," Pockmark said. He jotted down something in his notebook. "Anyone else?"

"I don't know."

Pockmark's nasal voice turned cold again: "From our experience, anti-revolutionaries rarely act alone. They often work in cliques and they protect each other. We must get to the bottom of this case. Have you seen anyone suspicious contact your friend?"

"No, I have not seen anyone that was suspicious around him," I said, after apparently thinking long and hard.

But they would not take a "no" for an answer. For a long time, they explained the Party's policy again and again, and Pockmark, apparently growing impatient, made it clear that this was my last chance to confess as if my execution were scheduled for the next hour if I did not. I was getting edgy too. Hungry and tired, my vision blurred by dizziness, I felt like giving up. I could feel my cold wet shirt against my chest. The craters on Pockmark's face seemed to loom larger and larger as the minutes ticked by. I wanted to run into the fleshy warm arms of the younger official, and fall under his protection.

Then, looking up, I caught the slogan on the wall and was startled to read: "CONFESSION EARNS DEATH; RESISTANCE EARNS DEATH TOO!" And I remembered Smoking Devil's advice.

Finally, Pockmark closed the file folder. "We will stop here today," he said. "I am sure that there is still something that you have forgotten to tell us. Keep in mind that the Party's patience is limited. We will find out about everything anyway, whether you confess or not. Remember: tomorrow is your last chance."

The young official gave me a final leering smile. "Your friends at the factory and your parents in Beijing are worried about you. They want you to confess and go home. Confession is the only way out of here. We do not arrest people without a reason. No one gets out of here without a confession."

His voice was soft but it turned my stomach. My parents! They would no doubt blame me for bringing trouble to them again, and were probably thinking of disowning me at that very moment. Maybe I could never go home again. And the humiliation of all my relatives! And what were they saying about me in the factory? Was Red Calf jubilantly declaring that the Party had ferreted out another hidden enemy?

Standing up stiffly, I turned toward the door. In my heart, I felt murder. A thick and odious sludge of hatred slowly swelled to fill my entire body. I wanted to strangle the young official with my bare hands.

To my surprise, I was not returned to the single cell, but led to another wing of the prison and shoved into a crowded larger cell. This was a good sign, I thought. The police evidently still did not find any evidence to charge me.

In the first week, I was interrogated two more times, and I stuck to my story that I had nothing to do with my dead friend Fountain Pen and knew nothing about his anti-revolutionary activities. Pockmark lost patience with me after the third session.

"Since you don't want to confess voluntarily," he said, "you will have to sit here for a long time until you are ready to confess. You can't hide anything from us and we already know almost everything that you have done. An early confession will save you a lot of misery. But if you want to sit here and feed the fleas, that's your business. We have plenty of hungry fleas for you."

Five weeks went by. I was never charged with any crime, and there had never been a court hearing.

Then one morning in late September, right before breakfast, I was called out of the cell.

"We'll save the breakfast for you," said Old Brother, an inmate I had befriended, as I walked out of the cell.

But I was not taken to the interrogation room. Instead, I was taken to an outer office near the gate of the prison. There, to my surprise, I saw Little Lenin and his wife Meatball sitting on a long bench beneath a large portrait of the Great Leader. Meatball beamed at me as I entered the room.

The two officers who interrogated me, Pockmark and the ruddy-faced young officer, walked in and shook hands cordially with Meatball. Turning to me, Pockmark said with a dry smile: "We have completed our investigation and have decided to release you. You can go with your friends now. Remember, do not say anything about what happened here, or it will bring you a lot of trouble that you don't want. Just remember that."

I did not move when the young officer opened the door. "I can't go like this," I said quietly to the officer. A bolt of anger suddenly welled up in me. My face burned and a volcano seemed to have erupted. "I want an explanation. I want to get my name back. I *want* an apology. I cannot spend five weeks in jail and walk out as if nothing happened."

Pockmark jerked around. "APOLOGY? What apology? Do you mean to say that the Party was wrong? You'd better appreciate the fact that you are getting out. After all, you are a close friend of an executed anti-revolutionary! If it were not for your friends, you would have spent a lot more time here. You are lucky to have a friend whose father knows the deputy secretary of the Public Security Bureau!"

"Please go, please!" Meatball stood up and tugged firmly at my sleeve, and I let myself be dragged out the door. I knew she must be the one who had found a connection to the deputy secretary and saved my life, and I should not give her more trouble. What would be the use of an apology anyway?

The metal door closed behind us with the kind of loud clang that I thought occurred only in movies. I remembered that I had not had the chance to say goodbye to my fellow inmates. With my sudden disappearance, perhaps they would think that I had been executed. I felt sorry that I left in such a mysterious manner as if I had suddenly abandoned a bunch of comrades who had fought a tough battle with me in the same trench. It was ironic, I thought later, that I should feel such a bond to the common criminals and such a hatred for the Party officials who had just released me.

The interesting thing is that my relationship with my fellow prisoners did not end here. In Beijing a few years later, I ran into one of them—Big Brother, who had been released after serving his term and had settled in the city. He became my friend again and would play an important role in my struggle and triumph against the Communist Party bureaucracy. For this, I have to thank Pockmark and Ruddy Face for giving me a valuable friend.

"This dinner is to make up for the one you missed at the Moon Festival," Little Lenin said, standing up and holding a cup of liquor in front of him. "Let me be the first to toast Fan Shen's safe return. Everybody, bottoms up!"

"We were really worried when we heard about the execution of your friend Fountain Pen," said Meatball, her face shining from the liquor. "You must eat everything on your plate today. I spent the whole day preparing this meal and you'd better show me some gratitude. Now, here, give me your plate." Before I could move, she leaned across the table and snatched the plate in front of me. When it was returned, it was filled with pork ribs with red sauce, stir fried young hen with green peppers, and a large five-flavored duck egg. That was the night's second course!

"I checked the Yellow Calendar," Master Pan chimed in. "Today is a good day to receive a friend from far away. The quote for today is 'After a nightmare comes bliss.' Something good is going to happen to you now. Let me fill your cup again, to celebrate whatever is coming."

I was very grateful to have these friends. Even though my head was spinning from the liquor and my shrunken stomach refusing more food (this was the second day after I came back from prison), I felt that I could not turn down another cup of liquor from Master Pan, or another plate from Meatball.

"The Yellow Calendar is right," Little Lenin added excitedly. "There is indeed some good news waiting for you. They have just announced in the papers that the national university entrance examination will be restored. You came back just in time to prepare for it. I know how much you have wanted to go to college. Let me show you the paper."

I could feel the thumping of my heart as I read the great news. The front-page editorial in the *People's Daily* announced that the Party was starting yet a new reform in education. It had abolished the system of recruiting worker-peasant-soldier students for colleges and reinstated a national college entrance examination. From now on, students would be selected on the basis of academic merit. The first national examination was set in December and anybody could take the exam. This was the chance I had been waiting for.

The news set me on fire. I had less than three months to prepare for the examination, and I knew I had a lot to do. I had to start that very night. I could hardly wait for the dinner to end so that I could go back to my dorm to plan my course of study. I had to brush up on math, physics, and history, and I had to study chemistry and geography almost from scratch.

The next day, I found out that I was getting a late start. While I was in prison, millions of young people across the country had already started preparing for the exam. Many of them had formed study groups and studied with hand-copied and mimeographed textbooks and old college exams used before the Cultural Revolution, which were passed among friends like sacred religious texts.

I joined a study group that included Li Ling and Little Lenin. Every Sunday we got together and quizzed each other on what we had learned during the week. In those months, I slept little. The examination would determine my fate and I knew the odds were against me. Nationwide, 5.5 million people were taking the examination, and only 280 thousand would be admitted. The odds were one in nineteen. But like everyone else, I was hoping for a miracle.

On December 21, the first day of the national examination, I got up at 4:30 in the morning. The room was dark and cold. I did not turn on the light so as not to disturb my roommates. Groping in the darkness, I quickly put on my thick woolen sweater, woolen underwear, and old blue winter jacket. With my brown army-style satchel over my shoulder, I stepped out of the room and went downstairs. In my satchel were my books and two hard-boiled eggs and two round steamed buns for breakfast and lunch.

The dimly lit street was completely deserted. On the bike rack behind the building, I located the bicycle that I had borrowed from Master Pan the day before. There had been a light snowfall and the street was covered with a sheet of white dust. I shuddered a little as a gust of chilly morning wind found its way into my winter jacket, but I paid no attention to the cold. Ahead was a fifteen-mile bike ride on a rough country road to the high school where the examination was being held. I tied my satchel to the bicycle's rack, jumped on the bike, and rode to the factory gate.

Soon Li Ling and Little Lenin appeared on their bikes. The three of us headed out.

The narrow country road was unpaved, bumpy, and frozen. There were deep grooves and occasionally large clumps of dirt left by the hooves of horses during the rainy season in the summer. We cautiously maneuvered along the edge of the road, trying to avoid the ruts and lumps. The chilly winter breeze sharpened my senses and I felt alert and excited. For once, and despite the darkness, I felt I had a good sense of direction in life and was in control.

An hour and a half later, we arrived at the country school. The sky in the east was beginning to show a gray fish belly of light. We were not allowed to go into the building before the exam began, so we sat down against the dirt wall. I took out my notes and began reviewing the mathematical equations that I had copied for a quick last-minute review. When the first bell rang, I could hardly stand up; my limbs were numb and my shirt, wet from biking, clung to my back like a slab of ice.

Two men wearing red armbands examined the seal and picture on my examination pass very closely before letting me in the classroom. Inside, another official with a red armband escorted me to my assigned seat at the back of the classroom. A young girl in a padded blue cotton coat was sitting next to me. She smiled nervously as I sat down.

The country school's classroom was damp and chilly. A sealed white envelope containing the examination paper was on my desk. The large red number on the envelope stared up at me like a Cyclops.

It seemed a long time before the second bell rang, signaling that we were allowed to open our sealed envelopes. My heart suddenly quivered a little as I opened the envelopes and took out the examinations. I was aware that I was holding my own fate, the means to escape the factory, right in my hands. For six years I had been preparing for this moment and I could not afford to let the chance slip through my fingers. Excitedly, I quickly scanned the twelve regular problems and the three bonus problems and plunged into solving them.

The problems were not very difficult, but I soon found that I had trouble concentrating. Part of the problem was the old school desk, which was like the surface of the moon, full of large and small craters and canyons, the result of peeling paint. It was impossible to write a straight line. But I could not have done that anyway, even without the "lunar landscape." Having sat in the cold classroom for ten minutes, I found my hands almost numb and I could hardly hold the pen steadily. The irregular surface of the desk, fatigue, and the cold all bothered me throughout the exam, and by the end of the two-hour period, I had solved only seven problems and given partial answers to two more. It was a very disappointing start.

The chemistry exam was next, starting in two hours. Outside the sun was shining brightly. Its light and warmth was a sharp contrast to the dark and frigid classroom. Picking up my bag, I joined Li Ling and Little Lenin and went out of the school gate. We sat down on a large pile of corn stalks facing the sun and opened our lunches. Everybody was reluctant to talk; we were all too exhausted from the bike ride and the first exam. I studied the chemistry notes while I munched on a half-frozen bun.

I completed the second exam confidently and solved nearly all of the problems, including the bonus problems. When I came out of the chemistry exam in the afternoon, I wondered whether it was the warm midday sun that had energized me and had helped me complete the exam so easily. I prayed that the next two days would be sunny. And indeed, the next two days were sunny, and I did better and better in each subsequent exam.

Except for math, on which I scored 57 out of 100 points, I did well in the other five subjects, with a total score of 509—comfortably above the 425 minimum needed for admission. Out of 156 people from the aircraft factory who took the exam, there were 11 who scored above 425 points. Li Ling was also among the eleven, but Little Lenin failed by nine points.

For me, six years of intense nightly study had finally paid off. I sent a telegram to my parents in Beijing, "PASSED COLLEGE EXAM." Although I knew that that was vain, I felt obliged to bring a little joy to my parents, who would proudly announce the news to their colleagues in the Big Courtyard.

Two weeks after the examination, a large red poster appeared at the main gate of the Aircraft Factory. The names and examination scores of the "lucky eleven," as we were called, were written in large black letters, surrounded by red flowers. My total score was the highest. There was a strange scene when I walked into the testing bay that morning; everybody shook my hand with such warmth, as if I were an astronaut who had just returned from the moon. Master Pan brought in a bottle of red wine, bought with "donations" from everyone in the office   meaning that most people freely contributed but extortion had to be used on a reluctant few, such as Master Deng. Master Pan poured the wine into small glasses and, clicking his glass with everyone else's, stood in the middle of the room to give the toast:

"This is a great day for our small, humble office. We have a college student among us now. As the old Chinese proverb has it, *this is a golden phoenix flying out of a poor mountain village.* Fan Shen—we are honored to have worked with you. When you graduate from college and achieve great things, I hope you will not forget us. Everybody, bottoms up!"

Although I smiled with my fellow workers, I did not dare to smile too heartily with joy, or to laugh that most pleasant of laughs, the inner one of pure ecstasy. Life had taught me that I could never take anything for granted until it happened. And at the moment, I was still in the factory and whether I would be able to escape the factory was still unclear. A true smile in my heart, I felt, would lead to disaster, just as gloating over a victory in a chess game before it is over inevitably leads to an unforeseen loss.

The day after the red poster was hung on the factory gate and red wine was consumed in my office, Comrade Thus, the factory's Party secretary, sent word that he wanted to see the "lucky eleven" in his office. On hearing the summons, my heart sank. Any time a Party official took an interest in me, I know something sinister would happen.

Comrade Thus's office was furnished with a thick red carpet and leather couches, and looked like it had been modeled on an office we had all seen in a movie: the office Lenin had occupied in the Czar's Winter Palace. From one of its windows I could see the enormous head and waving hand of the giant statue of Chairman Mao that stood at the center of the courtyard. I sat down on a couch with Li Ling and two other friends who had studied with me.

Comrade Thus arrived twenty minutes late. Tall and plump, with a reddish face and well-groomed gray hair, the secretary looked radiant as he shook hands with us. Naturally, we all stood up to greet him.

"Sit down, make yourselves comfortable," he waved at us as he sank into the leather chair behind his desk. Flanking him were four other officials—the second deputy secretary, the third deputy secretary, the secretary of the Communist Youth League, and the director of the factory who was the first deputy secretary.

"*Thus*, as you can see," Comrade Thus said cheerfully in the peculiar Sichuan accent that we had all heard many times. "The entire Party leadership is here today to congratulate you for your outstanding achievement. *Thus* you have made us very proud. The Party is *thus* very proud of you." At this, all the Party officials nodded and smiled. "You all have *thus* a great future in front of you. As you know, the Party has *thus* a great need for people like you. And *thus* so does our factory for people like you. Which is *thus* the point of this meeting."

Comrade Thus paused and quickly scanned our apprehensive faces. "We know that you all *thus* have your own personal interests, *thus* things you would like to study in college. But as the Great Leader has taught us *thus*, individuals must obey the Party, and personal interests must *thus* submit to the country's interests. As you know, our factory is at a crossroads and we *thus* need a great many skilled people, bright young people like you, and *thus* we cannot afford to lose you. Therefore, the Party Committee has *thus* decided that you must all study the specialties that our factory is in dire need of, and you must come back here to work after your graduation."

My heart nearly stopped when I heard that I had to come back. But neither I nor anybody else dared to protest. We were so used to being ordered around by the Party that we were afraid that the Party might revoke our eligibility to go to college if we protested.

Comrade Thus told us that the Party had identified four specialties that were needed by the factory and therefore would be the only majors we were permitted to study: non-metal material science, aviation hydraulics, the science of metal surfaces, and aircraft mechanics. None of the subjects interested me. The three colleges Comrade Thus had chosen for us were all third-rate colleges in Xi'an, close enough to the factory that the Party secretary could visit and supervise our study.

We silently slinked out of the administrative building like a school of eels sneaking along the muddy banks of a rice paddy. I felt ashamed of myself for not daring to utter a single word of protest. Just as we were turning the corner and about to go our separate ways, a soft female voice called to us from behind: "Wait a minute, everyone!"

We all turned around. Li Ling was standing a few steps behind us and her face was flushed. "Are we all going to swallow this stupid decision without saying a word?" she asked. "This is a typical self-serving local policy that is against the Party's best interests."

*Absolutely right*, I thought. The image of the little girl who had once spoken up against the Red Guards flashed through my mind.

"We have to do something. But if we want to fight this, we have to band together," Li Ling said. She surveyed each of us with her large, fierce eyes.

"I am with you," I said firmly.

"So are we," two others said.

"We can protest," a girl with short pigtails said quietly. "But I don't think it will make any difference."

"But at least we can have the satisfaction that we have tried," I said. I was disappointed by her timidity.

"The policy is certainly not right," said a man with thick glasses and a black cotton overcoat. "But what's the use? A few of us overturning the Party Committee's decision? Impossible! You are wasting your time. Besides, no matter what you study, being a college student is already much better than being a worker at the bottom of society. I don't want to take a chance that may cost me my opportunity to go to college."

"He's right," echoed another man with a woolen scarf wrapped around his neck. "Don't forget, 'A person who knows what is enough will always be a happy person.' If you can't win, why fight? I don't want to risk what I have already won. We all studied very hard, didn't we? And we are already the lucky ones."

"That's the sort of typical Chinese philosophy that has held people back for centuries." I couldn't hold back my tongue anymore. Stupid courage often comes at unexpected moments. "We Chinese never ask the question this way, 'If we don't fight, how can we win?' Times have changed. The Party is changing too. Don't you see? It's *our* life. We are not just cogs in a machine. Can't you say, for once, 'This is what I want. I want to study what interests me'?" My own last sentence startled me, and my internal watchman struck a warning gong loudly. Talking about personal interest is blasphemy against Party doctrine. I sensed danger and quickly added, "Of course we want to serve the Party and the country, but if we fully develop our personal interests, we would do a much better job, and would serve the Party better. Don't you agree?"

"Fan Shen's right," Li Ling said. "Let's draft a letter politely asking the Party Committee to reconsider its decision. Will you all sign it?"

"I support your effort 100 percent, but I can't sign the letter," said the man with thick glasses.

"Neither can I," said the man with the woolen scarf.

The rest of us agreed to sign the letter. I drafted the letter that night, but I was apprehensive about delivering it to Comrade Thus, which Li Ling and I had agreed to do. I knew Li Ling had the same fear: if the letter failed, we would be branded troublemakers for life.

But this time, the looming battle turned out to be only a test from God, like the sacrifice of Isaac that Abraham was prepared to offer on the mountain.

In the dining hall the next day, Li Ling ran to me and shoved a copy of the latest *People's Daily* into my hand. "Look at this," she said, pointing to the headline of an editorial on the front page. Her face was glowing with excitement. "We have won!"

The title of the editorial was "Against Provincialism."

"This must be divine intervention. What happened to us must have happened all over the country, and so the central government has forbidden any local government from restricting the registration of college applicants. I have just heard that Comrade Thus has rescinded his decision." I felt relieved, but I still could not allow myself the joy that the promise of a college education should bring. Even if this were true, it was only a small victory.

But Li Ling was right. Comrade Thus did rescind his decision and we applied to the universities of our own choice. I was accepted by Lanzhou University as an English major and Li Ling was accepted by People's University in Beijing to study accounting. Just a few days later after we received our papers, we went our separate ways. It was very strange that after six years of intimate friendship we parted so quickly and so uneventfully. We did not even shake hands when we said a quick goodbye on the day she left the factory for Beijing.

The day before I boarded the train for Lanzhou University, I went to the testing bay for the last time. Since it was a Sunday, the building was empty, except for a janitor. I walked quickly upstairs to the control room of the No. 4 testing platform. With both hands, I pulled open the heavy steel door that separated the control room and the steel platform where jet engines were installed and tested. I then turned on the floodlights inside. There was no engine on the platform right then, so steel and rubber pipes dangled around the frame like disheveled stalks of corn after a harvest. I walked down to the steel platform, and I could hear the sound of my footsteps rumble and echo back and forth across the gigantic hollow concrete box. I walked to the back of the platform where there was a steel exhaust tunnel, round and about my height at the entrance, but growing steadily wider until it opened into a mammoth concrete tower. Carefully, I stepped into the exhaust tunnel and I could feel the cold, steady draft that ran through the tunnel. The tunnel was dark and I moved forward cautiously and slowly, careful not to touch the steel wall, which had a thick layer of soot on it, the residue from burnt jet fuel. When I reached the third section of the tunnel, I stopped. From the army satchel that I carried, I took out three hand-sized objects and placed them on the steel floor of the tunnel. Their bright red color pleased me, and I felt very happy as I walked out the testing bay.

The next morning, as my train was humming toward Lanzhou, I

knew exactly what was happening at the testing bay. At 8:05, Master Bu, the head of the testing group at the No. 4 platform, pushed the lever for engine thrust to the maximum level. The jet engine roared, soon reaching 11,500 revolutions per minute. He let the engine roar for two minutes, and then checked the thrust indicated on the scale on the left-hand panel. The dial pointed to ten thousand pounds. Everything was in order. The examiner, Master Jin, gave a thumbs-up and wrote the result in his ledger. There was one last test to be performed. Master Bu pushed the button for the afterburner boost. A long orange flame shot out of the end of the engine into the exhaust pipe. The entire steel and concrete platform shook as the thrust scale registered an additional 3,500 pounds of thrust. In less than ten seconds, two thousand degrees of heat incinerated the three red volumes that I had placed in the exhaust tunnel. They were my revolutionary diaries.

I make myself laugh at everything, for fear of having to weep.

*Pierre-Augustin Caron de Beaumarchais*

# *4* Wood

## 23 The Heavenly White Pagoda

I arrived at Lanzhou Station on a bright morning in February 1978 in an elated mood. I would be in a university, the place I had been dreaming of for so long. For six long and grueling years I had been struggling for this day, and I had won. On that day I felt that I was truly happy for the first time in many years. The dreaded white factory, the mysterious suicides and grotesque illnesses, Comrade Thus and Red Calf and Combat Zhu were all behind me now, and I would never have to go near that place again.

From the train station, a school van took me and a few other new students to the university. It was a pleasant ride through the downtown and we arrived in just a few minutes. Lanzhou University has an impressive front entrance, consisting of two long cast-iron sliding gates between two pillbox-like towers and a giant statue of the Great Leader facing the entrance. When I got off the van and walked into the gate, I smiled happily and waved to His Excellency.

The student dormitory was a large L-shaped brick building. The corridors inside the building were dark and the uneven concrete floor sounded hollow, spooky, and fragile when I walked through it with my luggage. My room was similar to the one I had at the aircraft factory, but a little smaller, with two bunk beds on each side and a narrow walkway barely a yard wide from the door to the only window. Four people shared the room, but I certainly did not mind the crowded living conditions. From the laughter and happy shouting in the hall, I sensed that everybody in the dormitory shared the same elation. I heard genuine laughter everywhere, a laughter free of worries, a laughter I had never heard before in my life. This was the class of 1982, the first crop of students who had been admitted to universities and colleges solely on the basis of academic merit since the Cultural Revolution. All of us knew our elite status in society. Fewer than one in nineteen people who took the national examination were admitted, and we were the ONES. Parents and friends were very proud of us. The whole society looked up to us—partly in envy.

The three roommates who came early helped me unpack and get settled on the last bunk bed and we introduced ourselves. The one sleeping above me was Zhao Congming—or "Clever" Zhao. As he told me his name, he added, with a funny country accent, "Don't laugh at my name. This is not a nickname; it is my real name." Wearing a faded blue Mao jacket, with a square, deeply tanned face, Clever Zhao looked much older than the average student. Judging from his worn out shoes—homemade and hand-stitched from rags—he had to be a peasant's son. I liked him immediately.

The lower bunk bed facing mine was occupied by Qian Le, a chubby, happy-go-lucky young man, whom we would soon call "Squirm" because of his slow speech and uncoordinated movements. He had been a crane-operator at a coalmine in Datong, the coal capital of China.

In the bunk above him was the youngest member of the class, barely sixteen, from Xi'an. His name was Huang Laishi, but his nickname from the previous school, "Six-Finger Huang," followed him here. Next to his right thumb he had an extra finger, which he regarded as a lucky charm.

Having settled in, we went down to lunch. The dining hall was just across the street from our dorm. It was about the size of two basketball courts, similar to, but larger than, the ones at the East Wind Aircraft Factory. When I entered it, it was like walking into a steam bath, but a steam bath with a dank sour odor instead of the clean smells of steam and soap. The hall was jammed with people in long lines. Each line was for a different item of food. At the door, Clever Zhao suggested that we form a partnership to get lunch. "If you'll get rice for me, I'll get a dish for you. We have to get that boiled pork rind before it's sold out."

I gave one of my enamel bowls to Clever Zhao, who handed me an extremely large wooden bowl in return. I was stunned by the size of the bowl. "What's this?!" I cried. "I could use it for my washbasin. How much rice do you want?"

"Get me just a pound," said Clever Zhao, a little embarrassed. "I can eat more, but I have to watch my ration, you know." Each student was allowed a ration of thirty-two pounds of grain each month.

There were no tables in the dining hall, so we all carried our meals back to the dorm to eat. Our first meal in the new dormitory was as pleasant as my train ride. I never thought that watching someone eat could be entertaining and appetizing until I saw Clever Zhao with a pair of chopsticks in his hands. He attacked the giant bowl of rice mixed with vegetables with complete abandon, like a wild pig, his mighty jaws chewing noisily. Although he had only an average build, he seemed to have a bottomless stomach. "I am a pig," he said jocularly when he saw us watching him with amusement. He ate everything, and he ate twice as much as I did. He told us that his favorite dish was boiled pork rind, cheap and fattening. "Whenever it's on sale," he said, "make sure you buy me at least a pound, and I'll pay you later." He ate the pork rind with such relish that I was constantly reminded of the story of Emperor Zhu Yuanzhang eating the "pearl, emerald, and jade soup." At the end of the meal, he went around the room and collected leftovers from every-body—fatty meat, pork rind, anything. And he did that after every meal from then on. He had such a big appetite that he always exhausted his food ration by the twentieth of the month, and if my roommates and I had not donated a portion of our food rations to him, he would have starved. The high point of Clever Zhao's dinners was the finale, when he would perform an elaborate ritual of savoring the last mouthful. He would always save one piece of meat, the largest and the best-looking one, until the end. After everything else was gone, he would suck the meat clean, set it at the center of the plate, rinse his mouth with water, and in all seriousness, start a sort of meditation, as though mentally pre-paring himself for the divine feast that was about to grace his palate. Fi-nally, picking up the meat with his chopsticks and carefully putting it in his mouth, he would let it roll around between his lips and in his mouth for some time before very deliberately biting in. Eyes closed, his head thrown back, his whole body slightly trembling, he would chew in a slow, majestic manner. The meat was the final fifty measures of Beethoven's *Ode to Joy*, and Clever Zhao was the enraptured conductor. At such mo-ments, my roommates and I would watch with envy and admiration, wishing we could attain such nirvana at least once in our lives.

For the first year, I was in heaven. I studied hard and my mind was hun-gry and restless. Fortunately, the library that had been sealed by the Red Guards during the Cultural Revolution had been reopened for us. Now that I had all the time and books at my disposal, I felt like a happy young salmon that had finally swum out of shallow mountain streams and into the ocean. I let my interests lead me through the intellectual labyrinth. The classes were easy for me, and I again found myself spending most of my time reading "idle" books. Most of my classmates stuck with text-books, in order to get good grades, but I was hungry for real knowledge. I still remembered those days at the aircraft factory when Li Ling's vast knowledge on many subjects made me ashamed of my ignorance and I vowed to study hard so that one day I could speak to her as an equal.

I did most of my reading on the White Pagoda Mountains. Located on the western bank of the Yellow River, and not far from the campus, the White Pagoda Mountains are a series of lush rolling hills. The White Pagoda, a Buddhist monument, is on top of the highest hill. It is an impressive building made of gleaming white marble and shaped like a bottle-guard. From it, most of the city of Lanzhou can be seen to the east, winding along the banks of the Yellow River. To the west there are hills which gradually, little by little, turn into mountains. Most of the hills near the city are barren, but for some reason—perhaps it was the divine energy of the Buddha—there are willow and poplar trees and thick undergrowth of vegetation on the White Pagoda Mountains. It is like an oasis in the Gobi desert.

Every weekend, early in the morning, I would pack a lunch of steamed bread and climb to the top of the mountain. Sitting under my favorite willow tree, listening to the faint murmur of the city below and absorbing the warm sunshine, I would read away the whole day under the spell of the White Pagoda. It was there that I completed my university education. Clever Zhao or Six-Finger Huang would occasionally join me, but most of the time I went alone.

Under the willow tree, I felt that I knew joy and peace for the first time since the beginning of the Cultural Revolution. The rallies and fighting of the Red Guards, the harsh winters and famines in the village of Big Porcupine, the macabre deaths and dark fears in the white factory all faded into the distant past. I started to feel that life had just begun for me. No longer did I have to toil nine hours during the day and study by candlelight at night, fighting fatigue and bedbugs; I could read twenty-four hours a day if I wanted. Nor did I have to "pat the horse's behind," that is, to kiss up to Party officials like Uncle Cricket, Combat Zhu, and Red Calf, and waste precious time on shameful fake revolutionary diaries. I felt like a puppy dropped into a pool of water for the first time, thrilled and bemused, not knowing how to handle the unexpected joy that freedom had brought me. During my first semester, I bought a new diary covered with beautiful blue silk. A new diary for a new chapter in my life, I thought.

The only sad news during my first year at the university was that Li Ling, who had been my idol and mentor for five years, got married. When we parted hastily when she left for Beijing, she did not mention anything about getting married. Nor did she mention it in the only postcard that she sent me from Beijing. I heard the surprising news from Little Lenin. She got married right after she arrived in Beijing. Why she got married so suddenly, and to a man who was reported to be quite vulgar and inferior to her, confused me. In fact, according to Little Lenin, the entire factory was shocked to hear that Li Ling had married such a man. Even stranger was that after a simple wedding ceremony, she and her husband were to live apart for the next four years. She would live in Beijing and study accounting, and he would live in Harbin and study computer science. Half a country separated them. Even though we did not write to each other during the college years, I still thought of her from time to time and used her as my inspiration to pursue real knowledge.

Thanks in part to Li Ling's books, I was used to studying independently and efficiently, and I found most of the college courses slow-moving and tedious. I attended some classes merely out of respect for the instructors. There was only one course, however, that I genuinely detested and actively avoided: the so-called political science course. To me, it was no different from the political propaganda that I had endured one hour a day for six years in the aircraft factory. At the university I had to put up with it one afternoon a week, but I still hated it with a burning passion. It reminded me of Uncle Cricket's and Combat Zhu's lectures. Most students went to the class dutifully and took notes diligently for the sake of the instructor, Comrade Pi, who was the Party secretary of the Foreign Language Department and who would decide our fate upon graduation. But I felt hypocritical pretending to study something I knew was worthless nonsense, and I tried to skip the class as often as I could. It was not long before I found myself engaged in guerrilla warfare with Comrade Pi. Feigning illness or oversleeping, I avoided Comrade Pi's classes and the weekly political study at least two or three times a month.

The only thing I liked about Comrade Pi was his name. It made me smile when I crowed it with deliberate mindlessness. In Chinese, the name Pi and the word for breaking wind are homophonous—differing only in tone—and my friends and I were always careless in pronouncing our instructor's name, making it sound like *Break Wind*. Before long he was known simply as "Mr. Breakwind."

Mr. Breakwind was a retired military man with a medium build, short legs, and flabby arms. He was probably in his late forties. Anyone who saw him would remember him for one thing: his thick round glasses. The glasses were often broken and stayed in one piece only because of small but strange-looking pieces of white tape affixed to the edges.

Like Uncle Cricket, Mr. Breakwind was a conscientious communist and he considered it his duty to deliver all young people, both body and mind, to the cause of the Party. Every Thursday afternoon, he would walk through the student dormitory to make sure that all the students attended the political study session. He banged on each door and looked at each bed to catch anyone who overslept. Like a shepherd driving a flock of sheep, he would round up all the strays and drive them to the four-hour class. He was so determined to catch anyone who had wandered from the flock that he sometimes went to great lengths to catch us. Knowing I was the ringleader of the stray sheep, he was especially vigilant about me. Even so, I had successfully evaded him on a number of occasions. On the Thursday just before May Day, however, Mr. Breakwind's determined efforts paid off. He caught me and my friends and made us pay such a heavy price for our truancy that we did not dare to skip his class for many months afterwards.

On that day, after lunch, I proposed to my roommates to play a game of "driving the pig" instead of going to the hated political meeting, and Squirm, Six-Finger Huang, and Clever Zhao all eagerly agreed. We closed the door and played away. At two o'clock, our play was interrupted by Mr. Breakwind's loud voice rumbling in the hall: "Political study time! Don't be late! Anybody still sleeping? Get up!" As soon as I heard him, I shot up, ran to the door, and quietly bolted it. I then tiptoed back to my seat. We resumed the game in silence, but were mindful of Mr. Breakwind's rushed, shuffling footsteps as they became closer and closer.

It did not take long before the knocking started. BANG! BANG! BANG! Mr. Breakwind's voice erupted outside the door: "Anybody in there? Don't try to fool me. Fan Shen! Clever Zhao! You in this room are the worst. Get out!"

No one made a move. We were in the middle of the best part of the game. Squirm had lost the last game and was the "pig." He was crawling under the narrow desk, the standard punishment for being the pig. We were having fun seeing the pudgy Squirm trying to wriggle his ample paunch between the legs of the desk. He squirmed like a fat silk larva, and it took him a good while to get halfway through. At that point he became stuck, and the small desk became a turtle shell on his back. We could hardly suppress our laughter as he moved his helpless limbs to try to rid himself of the turtle shell. Then suddenly, the corner of the desk bumped into a leg of the bunk bed and the rap from the collision ricocheted across the room and then through the empty hallway. At the sound, we all froze.

"Aha! I knew you were in there," Mr. Breakwind's voice suddenly boomed at the door. He had been listening outside for some time. "Open the door! I know who you are. Fan Shen, Clever Zhao, Qian Le, Huang Laishi! Open up! Don't try to fool me; I know all your tricks. I will catch you all and make you study for a week if you don't!"

BANG! BANG! BANG! The fragile door, made of thin alder boards, almost split from his pounding.

For several minutes, we did not move, not even a finger. Squirm froze on the floor with his carapace on his back, and the rest of us leaned against the wall. We shuddered at each loud knock, hoping the door would hold.

After five minutes of heavy bombardment, Mr. Breakwind's voice softened. "Okay, Okay, I will not punish you this time if you open the door now. You hear me? If you open the door and go to the political study now, I will forget everything and will not report you. Fan Shen, I know you want to join the Party. This is your chance to show your loyalty to the Party. Huang Laishi, you don't want to be mixed up with these bad elements. You are still young; you have a bright future in front of you. Clever Zhao, I know you are innocent. You are from a family of revolutionary peasants. Don't be corrupted by the bad influences around you . . ." He paused. A hopeful eerie silence blanketed the room. It seemed that Mr. Breakwind was getting tired and he was starting to wonder if he had actually heard anything. Was he preparing to go away?

Bang! BOOM! Bang! The door again shook horribly. "You think I am going away?" Mr. Breakwind's voice boomed again and echoed in the hall. All the other students were at political study by now, "Don't pretend you are sleeping! I know what you are doing. Come out!" My friends and I could hear Mr. Breakwind panting as he rested. "You are not going to get away with this," he muttered, but his footsteps indicated he was walking away. He must have finally got tired and decided to leave.

We heaved a sigh of relief and jumped up to help Squirm extricate himself from his wooden shell. I grabbed his arms, and Clever Zhao and Six-Finger Huang each gripped a leg of the desk, and we pulled in opposite directions. Squirm grimaced and moaned as the desk was forced across his belly and hip and he was finally dislodged. But before he could stand up, an ominous thud outside the door stopped us in our tracks. A chair had been planted against the door.

Above the door there was a small glass transom. Two hands soon appeared at the bottom of it. Mr. Breakwind was climbing up the back of the chair!

As if a starting pistol had been fired, all four of us dove into the nearest beds, pulled the covers, and pretended to be sleeping. Over the blanket,

I peeped helplessly as the top of a gray head, then thick round glasses, emerged at the transom. Unfortunately, in their desperate rush, Squirm and Six-Finger Huang had jumped into the same bed. Squirm, being heavier and slower, lay on top of Six-Finger Huang and the blanket that Squirm had grabbed barely covered him. I wanted to laugh but that would have been very imprudent. No sooner had Mr. Breakwind's glasses appeared than we immediately fell to sound sleep. Squirm even managed to let out a whistling snore.

"Don't you try to fool me!" sneered Mr. Breakwind. The mouth that spoke those words was barely visible, and there was a scratching shuffle as Mr. Breakwind tried to balance himself on the back of the chair. "I saw you move. You are not sleeping. You, Qian Le, what are you doing in Huang Laishi's bed? Are you sleeping together? This is getting more disgusting now. Clever Zhao, I see you moving. You can't fool me." Through an opening in my sheet, I could see Clever Zhao shaking slightly with suppressed laughter. Then I was startled to hear my own name: "Fan Shen, I know you are the ringleader. If you don't stop this foolishness this instant and open the door, I will write to your father. I know he's a revolutionary cadre in Beijing. I have all your records in my office. If you don't open the door now, I will send you to Tibet when you graduate, you mark my words!"

I was alarmed by his last threat. Mr. Breakwind indeed had the power to ruin my life by sending me to Tibet. The joke had gone too far. I jumped up, took two quick steps, threw back the bolt on the door, and abruptly pulled it open. The chair which had been leaning against the door was immediately deprived of support and fell into the room. And there, hanging on the windowsill, legs kicking frantically like a giant spider, was Mr. Breakwind, desperately trying to hold on to the beam above the door. A few seconds later, he fell—right over the chair. As he rolled into the room, his glasses flew like a missile across the room and shattered on the floor. I jumped over his body and dashed out into the hallway. As if on command, my friends jumped out of their beds and charged the door. Scrambling on all fours, the nearly blind Party secretary made a futile attempt to grab the legs dancing past him.

Mr. Breakwind was not seen for two weeks. He was reportedly nursing a back injury that dated back to his service in the army.

But when he came back, he made sure that I paid a dear price for my prank. I had to write a thirty-page self-criticism and two reports on the Great Leader's essays, "Serving the People" and "The Foolish Old Man Moving Mountains." In addition, my cohorts and I had to clean the bathrooms in the dorm for a whole year. At the end of the semester, I barely squeezed past his course. He gave me a "C" for the final examination, the only "C" I received in college. But I was just glad not to fail the course. Failing Political Science would be fatal for my future career, not to say the potential danger of being sent to Tibet. When the new semester started, I thought I'd better not play any more tricks on the Party secretary and so I dutifully went to his class every week like all the others. After a while, Mr. Breakwind no longer came pounding on our door on Thursday afternoons and it seemed that my political trouble was over. I did not see, however, that another dark cloud—bringing even bigger and more sinister political trouble—was about to drift over my head.

## 24  "Two Uncles Are Here to See You"

Wherever I went, I seemed to have a knack for befriending "dangerous" people and getting myself into serious trouble with the government. In the countryside, I befriended Moon Face, the landlord's son; in the aircraft factory, Fountain Pen, the anti-revolutionary who was executed; and now in the university, I did it again unwittingly, befriending another "dangerous" person and finding myself in grave danger before my first year at the university was over.

When Jacquelyn and her husband arrived at Lanzhou University, they caused quite a stir—not only on campus but in the entire city. They were the first Americans to be permitted to work in the city, which had been the center of China's nuclear program since the founding of the People's Republic.

Tall, slender, and graceful, Jacky was a talented teacher, and I became the best and most interested student in her poetry class. Our friendship developed rapidly because we shared many interests: art, education, music, philosophy, and creative writing. After class, we spent hours talking about a million and one interesting things. With her encouragement, I began writing short stories and publishing them in the local newspapers. Since she was studying Chinese, on weekends I went with her to Chinese movies and acted as an interpreter. After the movies, we would take walks around the town. I was vaguely aware that there was something between us that went beyond books, but at twenty-three, I was still shy around women and never thought of a relationship with a teacher, which to me was sacrilege. That's why I felt surprised one evening when Jacky kissed me quickly on the cheek as we said goodbye after working on a joint translation at her apartment. I was flattered that she took an interest in me, but I was also apprehensive about where it might lead us. An intimate relationship with an American would mean big political trouble for me. I knew that. Despite the Party's new Open Door Policy, most officials were still deeply suspicious of foreigners, especially Americans.

I was not the only one, however, who sensed the danger in my relationship with Jacky. Clever Zhao pulled me aside one day and warned me in grave terms: "I want to tell you this as a friend, because I don't want you to get hurt. Don't forget the saying, 'The gun always shoots the bird whose head pops out first.' You have become the most conspicuous bird on campus. If something goes wrong, the foreigners will go home, but you will suffer for the rest of your life. I am sure you do not need to be reminded of what happened in 1957."

I did not need to be reminded of 1957. My own aunt, Shen Xia, was among the victims of the sudden reversal of Party policy. In a democratic gesture, the Great Leader encouraged intellectuals to criticize the Party. But a few months later when the intellectuals responded in earnest and demanded more freedom, the Great Leader abruptly declared the intellectuals enemies of the revolution. "I was just playing a game with them," he said at the Party's Congress, "to lure the vicious serpents and venomous monsters out of their dens, so that we can exterminate them once and for all." In one fell swoop, he rounded up half a million intellectual "monsters" and sent them to labor camps.

I thanked Clever Zhao for his caution and told him that I had taken precautions to protect myself: I had stopped going to her apartment to do translation work. And since we were not meeting in private anymore and were going to movies less frequently, I thought that would be enough to remove all suspicion. But I was wrong.

I received another warning two weeks later. My parents, who rarely wrote me, unexpectedly sent me two letters in quick succession. In a very roundabout and puzzling way, they asked me to be careful of foreigners. Nothing specific was mentioned. Although I was irritated by the tone of their letters, I could sense something was wrong and I had better heed their caution this time. I decided to cut back further on my outings with Jacky. I could not have known, however, that my self-censure and precaution were too little and too late to alleviate the suspicion of the secret police, who had been watching me for some time.

The first time I became suspicious of someone following us was at a movie with Jacky. When the movie ended and people started to file out of the theater, I noticed a man in faded gray uniform standing behind us. He looked familiar. I had seen him during my walk with Jacky two days earlier on the banks of the Yellow River. The man was wearing an old green army overcoat then, but his blubbery face was unmistakable. But later I dismissed the encounter as a coincidence, for Lanzhou was not a very large city.

Then came a bolt from the blue. One day I received from my sister an outdated issue of *The Chinese Youth*, the official magazine of the Communist Youth League. In it I discovered a tiny piece of paper, extremely thin and small, taped on an inside page. On it, in faint pencil marks, my sister wrote:

> Two plainclothes men from the Security Bureau from Lanzhou have been here for the last few weeks. They first went to father's superior to investigate you and our family. They then had a long talk with father. I don't know the details of the talk, but it was certainly about you. Father and mother were greatly frightened, and they were not allowed to tell you about the visit. That is why they sent you those letters in the past few weeks. Be careful with your American teacher. Burn this letter.

As I was reading the letter, my heart sputtered like an old Soviet Gus-69 diesel engine and every part of my body tensed up. I had heard horror stories about the secret police before, and knew I was in great danger again, perhaps even greater than the danger I had faced in prison a year earlier. That night, after I burned the letter, I acted as if nothing had happened and went to bed early, to think about my situation. I tried very hard to recall what I had said to Jacky, every single detail. I knew I had never mentioned anything to Jacky about my experience in the military factory or my father's position in the army. But my word would probably never convince the secret police.

To eliminate the possibility of further suspicion, I suggested to Jacky that we stop going to the movies altogether because I was too busy with my studies. The measure appeared to have worked. In the following weeks, I received no more letters from either my sister or parents and the danger seemed to have passed.

In July, Jacky and her husband finished their one-year teaching assignment and were getting ready to return to their home in America. On a Sunday before their departure, we met for the last time in her office. It was an uneasy meeting for both of us. We talked about our joint project and our future plans. And then, Jacky took my hands and told me that she loved me. I had a feeling that she would say this, but I did not know how to respond. I accepted her kiss, my first kiss on the mouth from a woman, but I was more frightened than happy, for I half expected the door to crash down that very moment and the secret police to rush in and seize me. She sensed my hesitation and did not press it further. The next day, I felt a sad sense of relief when the van transporting her and her husband to the airport pulled out of the courtyard. I thought my political trouble was finally over.

I went home to Beijing to spend the summer, fully expecting endless lectures on political caution from my parents. This time, however, I was resolved to suffer their preaching in silence, as a gesture of compassion and compensation for the fear that they had suffered because of the secret police's visit. That was all I was prepared for. I should have been prepared for a lot more.

On the third night after my arrival, my father said to me after dinner: "Let's have a word in my bedroom." My mother and sister did not seem surprised. Father's grim face told me right away that something very serious had happened. All my life, my father had never had anything so secret to say that he had to call me to his bedroom and close the door.

"Two uncles from Lanzhou will have a talk with you tomorrow," he said in a hushed, irritated voice. Calling men of my father's age "uncle" is a Chinese custom, and I knew he meant the secret police. "I cannot tell you anything more about the talk. I want you to be cooperative and frank with them. Tell them everything you know. We want you to trust the Party's policy, and if you did anything wrong, you must confess. The Party will forgive the mistakes of a young man."

There was no warmth, no protective anxiety, not a hint of sympathy in his voice. His tone told me that he had drawn a line between us: if there was any possibility of wrongdoing, he was prepared to give me up to the authorities, to disown me, to condemn me if necessary. I resented his tone but did not show my anger as I nodded my head and accepted the tacit message. I knew he was trying to protect himself and I could not blame him. That was what many Chinese revolutionary families would do.

Nothing else was said between my father and me that night. I tensely waited for the coming encounter with the secret police.

The next morning, on our way to the New Star Hotel near Princess Tomb, my father and I said little. Upon entering the hotel lobby, he finally broke the silence. "Remember what I told you last night? Tell them everything you know. Don't hide anything. Remember what you say will affect not only yourself, but also your family. As long as you tell the truth, the Party will treat you fairly."

I nodded impatiently. He sounded a lot like Mr. Breakwind now.

We walked directly to a room on the second floor and saw two middle-aged men standing by the door, waiting for us. We shook hands with them awkwardly. It was like shaking hands with ruthless gangsters—one never knew what would come after the handshake. I was a little surprised by the banal looks of the secret agents; they did not look as heinous and frightful as their counterparts did in movies. Neither was strongly built. One was actually thin and small, probably in his forties, with a rough and dry face. The other was tall but blubbery, and looked slightly younger, perhaps because of his crew cut.

My father made the introduction. The small man was Uncle Qi, and his partner, the tall and blubbery one, was Uncle Liu. Somehow, the latter looked familiar, but I could not recall where I had seen those squinting eyes before. We sat down around a small coffee table by the window. Uncle Qi pulled out a pack of cheap cigarettes, but my father quickly put his hand on the pack and smiled broadly. "You must try mine," he said, pulling out a pack of Great Chinas, the most expensive brand on the market. Father used to smoke Front Gates, which were half the price of Great Chinas.

The two uncles were delighted. They each carefully extracted a cigarette from the pack. My father casually tossed the pack on the table, in front of the agents. For a few minutes, the three of them enjoyed their expensive cigarettes and commented on the hot weather in Beijing. Uncle Qi said that he missed the cool breezes off the Yellow River in Lanzhou, and Uncle Liu, Mr. Blubbery Neck, said that he missed Lanzhou's honeydew melons, which were in season now. Father nodded affably while I waited nervously. Finally, Uncle Qi finished the cigarette and turned toward me.

"We think you know why we came to talk to you," he began in an official monotone. "To quote a saying, *let's open the windows and put words in broad daylight*. We have found that the American teacher Jiekelin . . ." he struggled to pronounce the transliteration of Jacquelyn's name in his Lanzhou accent. "We found that she had some problems. You know what I mean. You have been very close to her. Your relationship with her is, shall I say, unusual. To protect you and your family, we have come all the way from Lanzhou to talk to you. We could have talked to you at the university, but we didn't. Why? To protect you. We did not want anyone in school to know about this. I think you can see that we came all the way for your benefit." He turned to Uncle Blubber, as if seeking confirmation from his partner.

Uncle Blubber smiled and nodded his freshly cropped head. Both my father and I nodded and smiled stiffly to show our appreciation of the Uncles' consideration.

"Did you watch the Egyptian film *Going to the Abyss* that was shown a few months ago in Lanzhou?" Uncle Blubber asked.

I nodded. Now I remembered where I had seen that blubbery face. He was the man in the dirty army overcoat who had sat behind us in the theater and had followed us at the riverbank.

"Good," said the blubbery face. "If you are not careful, you could wind up like the Egyptian girl in the film: trapped, used, and then destroyed by foreign agents. I think you know the consequences. Now, think it over, and tell us everything you know about this Jiekelin. It's no use to try to hide anything. Actually we know everything about her, the Party knows everything, but we want to confirm the facts with you first."

It was standard police tactics again. Even though I had been through it before, I was surprised by how powerful it was, how it was still able to rattle me and stir up great fear. Even though I did nothing wrong, any slight discrepancy between what they knew and what I said would arouse suspicion and could end up ruining my future prospects. But I did not have much time to figure out what was safe to say. Any hesitation or apparent deliberation would be an immediate cause for suspicion.

"My contact with Jacky was mostly going to movies and doing joint-translation work," I said. "As a student, I could not refuse her requests. She was a professor. She was studying Chinese and needed an interpreter at the movies. We watched quite a few movies. After the movies, we normally walked down Fishhead Street, going through the farmer's market—from the farmer's market, oh, by the way, there was an old woman selling thousand-year-old eggs, so I would stop and buy an egg . . . and then we would turn on Jasmine Avenue, and . . . turn to the right on Oyster Street which goes straight to the Riverbank. Oh, we also saw the Yugoslavian movie. What was the name of it?"

I was a little surprised that words just rumbled out of me before I was aware of them. They came out in droves like legions of flies. In my mind, I could almost see the dirty little insects land on the uncles' smiling and nodding faces. I told them about one movie after another, and made sure to digress in all sorts of directions as I did so. While my mouth was babbling away, my mind was spinning to recall all the details of those movies and walks. I had to get every detail right. We had been followed during the walks and I must not omit a single detail, no matter how insignificant.

"Good," said Uncle Qi, lighting another cigarette. "What else did you talk about besides movies?"

"Oh, we talked about literature, too." I prattled on quickly and pleasantly. "You know, Shakespeare, Hemingway, and O. Henry. The Foreign Language Department was rehearsing a play by Shakespeare, and

Jacky was the director of the play. So we talked about that. Oh, we also talked about the books that Jacky and her husband were donating to the university. It is really astounding to think of them as spies. But what do I know? I have never seen a spy. Actually everybody in the department liked them, even Mr. Breakwind—I mean Comrade Pi. Even Comrade Pi liked them, he said so himself."

On and on I rambled, for a long time. I told them everything I could think of. But, predictably, the uncles insisted that I tell them more.

"It seems to me that you have not told us everything," said Uncle Qi, glancing at his notebook. "I don't think I need to remind you how serious our conversation is. This is the only chance that the Party will give you and you must not squander it. You won't get another chance. Now, did Jiekelin ask you about Chinese politics?"

"Actually, she never did." That was the truth but I knew they would not believe it.

"But we know there is something she said that you have not told us," persisted Uncle Blubber, with a fixed smile on his plump face.

I was tired of the game now. "I have told you everything I can think of," I said, my eyes raised to meet the squinting eyes of Uncle Blubber. "If you know there is more, you can tell me what I missed."

"If it comes to the point that the Party has to tell you what you missed," said Uncle Qi slowly and menacingly, "it will be too late for you. You'd better think it over again. We will not wrong an innocent person. When we ask you to think some more, we know there is more." He had just picked up his sixth or seventh cigarette. The red packet on the table was almost empty.

By this time, I was exhausted and almost committed a fatal mistake. "I have told you everything about Jacky and her husband," I said in a surly voice. My cheeks were burning and a dangerous anger began to well up in me. "I can't tell you things that I do not know, can I? Do you want me to invent something against her so that you will be satisfied? *Is the Party blind to the fact that I have been telling the truth?*"

They were a bit taken aback that I had the nerve to say that to them.

"THE PARTY BLIND?" Uncle Qi echoed in mimicry that upset my father more than it did me.

"Don't you talk to the uncles that way!" my father reprimanded me in a harsh tone, and with an equally harsh look. Then he turned to the agents with an apologetic smile.

"We do all this for your own good," said Uncle Qi. "The Party would never mistreat a good man. But it will never let a criminal slip through."

He turned to Uncle Blubber, who nodded his smiling face. "All right," he continued. "We'll call it a day now. Let's meet here again tomorrow. In the meantime, we want you to reflect on what we said about your future and your family's future." Uncle Qi tipped his head toward my father, and my father smiled stiffly. The point was not lost on either of us.

Uncle Qi stood up and took my father aside and conversed with him in a low voice for a few minutes. Father nodded eagerly. Then Uncle Qi came back and walked me to the door. "Try to remember all the things that you or Jiekelin said or did. Remember, small things can often lead to big things. Don't neglect any detail."

After dinner that night, my parents retreated to their bedroom, and it was a long time before my father reemerged to speak to me. "Your mother and I," he said in a morose tone, "we think you should use the time tonight to think hard about the things that you did. If you have done something wrong, you'd better tell the uncles. That's the only way you can correct your mistakes. You must trust the Party."

His tone said it all: they did not believe in my innocence. Like most Chinese, they thought that a person was almost surely guilty if the authorities were investigating him—there wouldn't be any waves if there hadn't been any wind.

"I've told them everything I know," I said to his father, my voice defiant and resentful. I knew, however, that nothing I said would convince them.

I slept badly that night and had the old dream again, the flying dream. I woke up before daybreak, tired and depressed.

"Thought of anything new?" Uncle Blubber smiled the next morning as we sat down at the coffee table again in the hotel room. That damned smile never left his plump face. He took a cigarette from a new pack of Great Chinas that my father had brought. There was something nasty behind that smile. The smile confirmed what I had realized since yesterday: the truth, my truth, would never be enough to satisfy them. They would not stop hunting until they had torn me apart and chewed the last of my bones dry. These two were much worse, much more persistent, much more malicious than the two I had faced in prison. While smiling mechanically toward the officers, I began to see myself as a fox locked in vicious combat with a pair of hyenas, and a new tactic occurred to me.

I charged my enemies with a burst of stupidity.

"Yes, I did think of something new to tell you . . . actually, a lot," I said. "I forgot to tell you yesterday that the day we watched a Pakistani movie, I found a man sitting behind me and he looked very suspicious. I don't know how I could have forgotten this important information. But he looked and acted very suspiciously. He stared at the American and I felt almost certain that he had something evil in his mind. Anyway, at the time, I thought he might be a thief. The man looked a little bit like you, especially his eyes." I paused and looked at Uncle Blubber. "He was about your height, and his face was also fat, but of course, his face wasn't as handsome as yours. Anyway he had a fat, ugly face, and just by his looks I could tell that his belly was full of evil water. Anyway, after the movie, Jacky and I walked to the bank of the Yellow River—did I tell you what we saw on our way there—through a small village? Anyway, after the village, we arrived at the bank of the Yellow River, and I saw the ugly man again. He was wearing a green army coat. He pretended that he did not see us, and I pretended that I did not see him. But he acted so suspiciously that I could immediately tell that he was a foreign spy. I think he was trying to pass some secret to the American. Anyway, he must have something to do with what you are looking for. You must investigate this man."

I rambled on with joy. Fear had left me and in its place was insolent amusement. But all the while, I kept a straight face. Uncle Blubber had begun to perspire profusely, and his fat face and neck seemed to be turning the color of a cherry tomato. Uncle Qi, on the other hand, was taking notes furiously.

Unlike the first day, I did not wait for their prompt to think more. The two agents were astonished by the sudden burst of my ardor.

"Another thing just came to mind that I think is very suspicious about this man," I continued. "I think you might use this to catch him. When he sat very close behind us at the movie, he had really bad breath. He also had a big yellow tooth jutting out—" I pretended that I did not see that Blubber had just closed his mouth to hide his teeth, and went on with the utmost sincerity: "Anyway, there is another thing about this man—"

"Good, good. Are there any other men that seemed suspicious to you?" Blubber interrupted me and tried to redirect my report. But I would not let him.

"Yes, there are. But this man, the man I saw in the movie theater and by the Yellow River, is the most suspicious of all. No doubt about it. I was going to tell you that there was something peculiar on his coat. It was a large, white, irregular mark on his breast, but I suspect that it is some secret sign of contact. I've heard that some foreigners used white roses as a sign during a war—was it the War of the Roses? Anyway, of course, I know nothing about this sort of thing, I mean, spies and espionage. I'm sure you know a lot more about this than I do. Anyway, you said yesterday that small things can lead to big things."

Both Uncle Qi and Uncle Blubber nodded in agreement as they pulled on their cigarettes. "Yes, yes, small things can lead to large things," Uncle Blubber mumbled. "You said there were other men that you thought were suspicious?"

"Yes, there is a man at the Security Department in Lanzhou University. I think his name is—yes, his name is Zhang. Although he is the deputy Party secretary and director of the security, I would not trust his loyalty to the Party. Why? Because I saw him speaking in a hushed voice to Jacky's husband on the day they left for America. The stories you told me about all those foreign spies have opened my eyes, and I now see many suspicious things that I did not pay attention to before. Anyway, when he spoke to the American, he had a silver cigarette case in his hand, and come to think of it, it could be a secret sign of some sort, don't you think?"

I was surfing. I had caught the right wave, and I cruised along with joy. When I wrapped up the report on Zhang, I went up to another possible spy, the deputy director of the university's Personnel Department, who was in charge of monthly meetings of the Communist Youth League. All of a sudden, the list of suspects was endless. I had no trouble supplying each story with details and descriptions, most of them mundane, and therefore credible, but a few of them outlandish, to explain why I had noticed something amiss in the first place. Had the agents been familiar with Balzac, O. Henry, and Maupassant, they would have found bits of their work mixed up in my reports. At the end of the day, I promised to think things over during the night and to bring them more information the next day. The uncles looked at each other dubiously and seemed a little reluctant to accept my offer, but how could they refuse my eager cooperation? My father appeared confounded by the sudden flood of stories, not knowing whether he should be glad or afraid.

Early the next day, we knocked on the hotel room door before the appointed time because I told my father that I had thought of something urgent and must tell the uncles as soon as possible.

No sooner had the uncles sat down than I picked up where I left off the day before: more suspicious things about various officials at school. I was now resolved to stay there and tell them stories for as long as they could bear it. The stories began to bore the uncles, but I pretended not to notice a thing.

"Good, good, this information is very useful. I think we can wrap it up now," Uncle Qi said, looking at his watch. It was past eleven o'clock and they had not had breakfast yet, but I, the simple-minded informant, ignored him and rushed on, as if dragging two reluctant dogs for a walk in the hot sun.

Finally, the dogs revolted and refused to move. Late in the afternoon, Uncle Qi stood up and put an end to my report. "The information you provided is very valuable to us and we are quite satisfied with it. But we have to end here. We have some important things we must attend to to-night. But I want to remind you that you should not tell anyone about our meeting."

"But I have not given you the full report on Comrade Pi yet," I said, appearing greatly disappointed.

"We will have to hear that another time," said Uncle Blubber, forcing a tired smile.

Inwardly, I breathed a sigh of relief, thinking the dogs had finally had enough of my nonsense and would never bother me again. But I was wrong.

"One more thing, before you leave," said Uncle Qi. "Let's keep contact when you return to the university next month. We want you to continue to report to us. You must call this telephone number every month. Remember, never use a telephone on campus. After you dial the number, don't ask to speak to us. Ask 'Is this the bookstore?' We will tell you where to meet us later. Again, for your own protection, you must not tell anyone about this. We have spoken to your father and he agrees with us."

Father nodded and turned to me. "You must thank the uncles for the trust they are placing in you."

My heart sank. I knew it was not trust but a new trap the agents had laid for me. I had no choice, however, but to play along.

At the dinner table after the interrogation on the third day, my father proudly declared that he had arranged a car to take the uncles sightseeing in Beijing for the next three days. Obviously relieved, he opened a bottle of red wine for the meal. "Never, never again get involved with a foreigner," he warned me at the table. "Next time, you may not get off so easily."

After returning to campus in September and knowing I had no choice, I dutifully made the first call to the "bookstore." The man at the other end of the line was Uncle Blubber. "We have been waiting for your call," he said. "Let's meet this afternoon at two o'clock in Room 714 at the Lanzhou Hotel. Come to the room directly; don't stop at the front desk."

The luxurious hotel was on the corner of Fishhead Street, two blocks from the campus. At two o'clock, I stepped into the smoke-filled suite on the top floor and saw three figures huddled at the far end of the large sitting room. An older man, with thinning white hair, was slouched in a sofa by the window. Facing them on the couch were my old friends, Uncle Qi and Uncle Blubber. Uncle Blubber nodded to let me sit on the couch. The older man on the sofa was introduced to me as Director Nu. Clearly he was the Big Boss. When he spoke, the other two leaned forward and listened attentively and respectfully. Director Nu spoke haltingly, wheezing all the while as heavily as a blacksmith's bellows. That was fitting, for the room was filled with smoke. He told me that he had read the briefing by the agents and was impressed by it and therefore came to hear my report personally.

To be frank, I was a little apprehensive at first; I did not know whether the Big Boss was any smarter than his troops. As before, I transformed myself into a zealous informant on the spot, and immediately began my report. I poured out juicy stories about Mr. Breakwind, Director Zhang, and other school officials, as though I had been deliberately collecting information for them. The Big Boss seemed beguiled by my information.

After warming up, I gave an elaborate report on a young political adviser, a hated Party loyalist who was called "Smiling Scorpion" by the students. Smiling Scorpion had been hired by Mr. Breakwind to supervise political studies. I launched into a long and desultory report about Smiling Scorpion's lecherous smile and her seductive way of addressing the Canadian teacher, who had just arrived to replace the American couple. Then the romantic intrigue segued into a love story involving Mr. Breakwind. I made sure that the drama involved all sorts of suspicious signs that would be of interest to the agents. At first, the story was a hit with the Big Boss, who rhythmically moved his fat chin up and down in encouragement. But as the story got more complicated, he began to show signs of fatigue, the inevitable result, I thought to myself, of having to move his chin so frequently. After two hours, he struggled to raise his arm to look at his watch two or three times, an obvious suggestion that I cut my story short. I ignored the hint, of course. My face all earnestness, I happily prattled on. I was Virgil guiding my listeners on a journey into deep nonsense, and I wanted to make sure they stayed with me for the entire trip.

Finally, thoroughly bored, the Big Boss bailed out. He mumbled that he had to go to a meeting and would look forward to my next report. He never showed up for any later meetings. At the door, I held the Big Boss's fat hand and said warmly: "Director Nu, it is such an honor to work for you and for the Party. I am proud of the trust you placed in me, and will devote all my energy to furthering the Party! Anyway, Uncle Liu, Uncle Qi, and I originally planned to meet once a month, but I would like to meet more often. I can meet you every two weeks or even once a week. Anyway, there's so much to report that once a month is not enough. Anyway—" The Big Boss escaped before I could launch into another story.

What I did not understand was how the agents could endure the errant nonsense I poured out month after month and not terminate my visits sooner. For more than a year, I met them every month, and without exception, all of my reports consisted of long, winding, silly stories starring Mr. Breakwind and Smiling Scorpion and other Party officials that had no real connection to anything of importance.

In my sophomore year, however, the meetings ended. Uncle Blubber summoned me to a hotel and told me one day: "You have done a good job for the Party, but we have to end our relationship now. You don't have to contact us anymore. From now on, we want you to concentrate on your studies. But be careful; you should never tell anyone about your contact with us. If you do not tell, we guarantee that this thing will never in any way affect your job assignment and your future. In the meantime, we want to you to keep an eye on the democracy movement that is going on at your school now. If you see anything suspicious, any foreign influence, report to us at once."

Appearing reluctant, as if parting from good friends, I said goodbye to the uncles. I pumped their hands long and hard, and promised that if they ever needed me again, I would be there instantly. I had finally— and triumphantly—gotten rid of my unwanted "relatives" and could live a normal life again. I never expected to see them again. But fate has a funny way of dealing with us, and ironically, more than a year later, it was I who desperately needed their help and eagerly sought them out again.

## 25  "Clever Zhao's Missing!"

The Democracy Wall Movement, which Uncle Blubber wanted me to spy on, started quietly in Beijing in 1979, like a hungry mosquito landing noiselessly on a content, unsuspecting pig. In January, to commemorate the late premier Zhou Enlai, who had died in the year of double Augusts, some people put out posters and wreaths on a stretch of wall in Xidan, a busy commercial district in Beijing. The brick wall, barely the length of a basketball court, attracted thousands of passers-by every day. The commemorative posters, however, had a political undertone from the beginning. The mourners, mostly young students and factory workers, cleverly played off of and expanded on the Communist Party's latest official policy—the "Four Modernizations"—to modernize industry, agriculture, the military, and science. The posters suggested that China need modernization in a fifth area, democracy. The posters struck a chord in people's hearts. Within a few weeks, the Democracy Wall became a nationwide movement. People began demanding free speech and free elections for student unions and trade unions.

Being fifteen hundred miles from the capital, Lanzhou University was slow to catch on to the democracy movement. But when it arrived, it exploded with a violent energy. To me, the spring of 1980 was almost a carbon copy of the spring of 1966 when the Cultural Revolution began. Hundreds of big letter posters appeared overnight on building walls, parades were held daily, and like the Red Guards, people soon separated into two opposing camps: the Official Election Committee headed by the Secretary of the Communist Party, and the Independent Student Election Committee headed by a lanky economics student, Song Pingtai. The latter's campaign headquarters was in a dormitory room, next to mine. Revolutions have a way of picking unlikely heroes. Few could have imagined that Song, a quiet and shy man, would be the hero who dared to run against a candidate picked by the Party.

When the Party consented to the demands of the Independent Student Committee to hold a debate before the election on campus—the first that anyone had experienced—the Democracy Movement became a euphoric festival. Perhaps because of my recent dealings with the secret police, I had a strong desire for political reform and I eagerly participated in Song's campaign. My roommates Clever Zhao, Six-Finger Huang, and Squirm also got involved. We wrote posters, printed handbills, and collected donations. The day before the debate, I spent the whole night writing a speech for Song. The next day, at the debate, our hero trounced the Party candidate. Song won the election by a landslide, capturing seventy-eight percent of the student vote and becoming the first freely elected president of the Student Union.

A month later, he ran for the District People's Congress against another Party candidate, who was none other than Mr. Breakwind. The Party mobilized its members and campaigned hard for Mr. Breakwind. But Song, with Clever Zhao as his campaign manager, again won handily. We were ecstatic. In May, we saw Song walk into the auditorium of the District People's Congress, and we could feel tremendous excitement and tension in the hall. All the gray heads of the Party delegates turned toward the door silently, as our man sauntered down the aisle in blue jeans and a blue jacket. "He is *The One*," we heard the gray heads say, and we knew what they meant. Song was the one who upset the tradition, the one not appointed by the Party, the one who was not one of them. There was anger among the roomful of tenured Party appointees. It was plain that to them the Democracy Movement had gone too far.

For five weeks, it was a wonderful spring. At the height of the euphoria, however, I had a nagging fear at the back of my mind that the Party would step in sooner or later and extinguish the flame of the free election because I knew how closely the secret police had been monitoring the democracy movement. But still I never expected the Party to put an end to the Democracy Movement so quickly and so brutally. Just three days after Song's triumphant march into the People's Congress, the police tore down all the democracy posters in the university and declared that the Independent Student Union was illegal and was banned. In Beijing and in other cities, we soon heard, the police had arrested many activists of the movement.

"Another Victory for the Democratic Dictatorship!" declared the headline of an editorial in the *People's Daily* a few days later. "The so-called Democracy Movement is actually an 'anti-revolutionary move-ment' aimed at undermining the socialist dictatorship, and it has been mercilessly crushed." In just a few days, as all signs of the democracy movement disappeared, Mr. Breakwind, with freshly-taped spectacles, resurfaced victoriously on campus and ordered a special two-week workshop for all students, to clear our minds of any thoughts of democracy.

"No one should doubt the Party's resolve," he said firmly to us on the first day of the workshop. "You young people often forget who brought liberation and freedom to China. You must remember that our freedom is socialist freedom, our democracy is socialist democracy, and they must be under the guidance of the Party. You must never forget that on top of democracy there is the Party. The Party hears the people and decides what's best for them. This is what the Great Leader called democratic dictatorship. The Party will forgive most of you for what you have done as long as you confess your mistakes. But those who led the charge against the Party will be remembered and dealt with."

Mr. Breakwind's words were no empty threats. All the leaders of the democracy movement were punished upon graduation two years later and were sent to the most remote regions. Song himself was sent to the Xinjiang Uighur Autonomous Region (China's Siberia), and none of us heard anything from him again.

In the days after the crackdown of the democracy movement, I was very fearful. I knew Mr. Breakwind would not easily forgive me and my friends, who did so much to help bring about his humiliating election defeat. I kept a low profile on campus as much as possible. Again, I spent most of my time on White Pagoda Mountain, seeking peace and refuge in books.

On a hot night in July, I came back to the dorm very late, around midnight, to disturbing news: Clever Zhao was missing! Earlier that day, someone saw him walking toward the swimming pool, but he had not returned. The school had been notified and several groups of students were setting out to search the campus for him. I went with a group to the swimming pool, which had been closed since eight. There was no sign of Clever Zhao by the pool or in the locker room. All lockers were empty. But I noticed a small bundle of clothing up on a high windowsill and recognized that it was Clever Zhao's.

We went out and searched the pool immediately. The pool was murky, with a yellowish mist hanging over the water. We stepped into water, joined hands, and began slowly walking up and down through the water. It was Squirm who stepped on Clever Zhao's body. As soon as the body was pulled up, I performed frantic CPR on the limp body, forcing a few drops of water and blood out of Clever Zhao's mouth and nose. But it was plain from the moment I touched the body that it was far too late.

The body was cold and stiff, and utterly devoid of life. Clever Zhao's face was livid, and without the thick glasses that were always perched on his nose, his face looked distorted and puffy. I did not cry at the pool, for I was too shocked by my best friend's sudden death. Clever Zhao was a good swimmer. How did he end up at the bottom of the pool? It remains a suspicious death to me to this day.

Clever Zhao's funeral was held at the White Pagoda Crematory, not far from the Park where he used to come with me on some weekends. All the teachers and the students of the Class of '82 from the Foreign Language Department went. It was a typical revolutionary funeral, reminding me of the one for Bean Sprout at the aircraft factory. An old record player played slow and pompous revolutionary funeral marches, the same ones that were broadcast over the radio whenever a national leader died. Mr. Breakwind, representing the Party, read a eulogy, full of the very same revolutionary clichés that were always trotted out on such occasions—Clever Zhao "was a good son of the Party . . . He will live in our hearts forever . . . We will transform our sorrow into strength and carry on the revolutionary cause that he has left us." As I knew how much he hated Clever Zhao, his eulogy sounded especially distasteful to me.

After the eulogy, we walked past the picture of Clever Zhao on the table, each bowing three times. I thought of my friend's family, who had such high hopes for Clever Zhao, their proud son, the only one from the village who had ever gone to a university. He was so close to bringing glory to the family. But not one member of the family came for the funeral; they lived far away and were too poor to afford the travel expenses.

After the funeral, we were told that we were allowed to observe the cremation. So a few of us accompanied the body to the basement of the building where there were three large furnaces.

The room with the furnaces was actually a long hall. Through the openings in the grate, I could see that two of the furnaces were burning. Every now and then, there would be a loud crack and some sparks would shoot through a grate and then drop to the floor. The floor itself was covered with a fine layer of grayish ash. At the far end of the room, close to a furnace that was not burning, was a stretcher. A young woman's body lay on it. She was so small that I suspected that she was no more than thirteen or fourteen years old. Evidently she was pregnant for her belly was very large. I could not see her face, which was covered with a dirty handkerchief.

Two workers laid Clever Zhao's body on a metal grit on the floor near the middle furnace. He was wearing his best clothes, a padded gray winter jacket (even though this was summer), and he looked much larger. I joined the others around the stretcher for a moment of silence. When it was over, I placed a small bowl of pork rind—his favorite food—by his body. People started chatting quietly about how the body would burn. Someone said the body would twist three times and jump up once before it finally succumbed to the flames.

I suddenly felt a lump form in my stomach. Why did Clever Zhao have to die? I was only twenty-five, and had already seen so many deaths. I left the room quickly and walked out of the gate of the crematory. The sun was setting, shedding golden light on the White Pagoda on the top of the hill. As I climbed the hill, I started to cry. But who was I crying for? For Clever Zhao? For Bean Sprout? For the patients I could not save? For China? For myself? I did not know.

Clever Zhao died in the second semester of our sophomore year, and so did my interest in politics. Never get involved in politics again, I told myself after his funeral. More than ever I sought refuge in books; I became particularly interested in English novels and began writing a novel myself. Because of my interest in novels, I was quite excited in my junior year to hear that our next course, on the English novel, would be taught by a new professor, an old lady who had been educated in the United States. The fact that she was the only member of the faculty who had a degree from a U.S. university was not the only reason that excited me. What was most interesting about her was that she was a Christian nun who had just been released from prison after serving a twenty-seven-year sentence. Six-Finger Huang even claimed that she was the *only* nun left in the entire city of Lanzhou.

When Miss Zhou first walked into the classroom, the room was completely silent. There was an atmosphere of awe in the room when we looked at the famous former prisoner as she handed out the syllabi for the course. She did not look the way I imagined a longtime prisoner would look. With fair skin, few wrinkles, and hair with just a touch of silver, she looked to be in her early fifties even though she was in her seventies. Nor did she look like a nun. She wore a black sweater on top of a white shirt and dark blue pants, both neatly pressed, and the way she dressed made her look more like my mother than a nun. I knew what a nun should look like. I had seen real nuns once. Before the Cultural Revolution had closed all the convents in Beijing, I once encountered two nuns on the street. This must have been in the early '60s, for I remembered that I was very small and still in kindergarten. I was walking with my father, who had on his colonel's dress uniform, and as we turned a corner toward Wangfujing Street, the busiest shopping street in Beijing, we almost walked into the two nuns. Both of them were foreigners, tall, with big noses, and they wore those black-and-white gowns that now can be seen only in movies. For a few seconds, both my father and I just stood there and stared at the rare and fascinating creatures. The nuns stopped, too, and in unison—as if they had rehearsed it beforehand—bent their knees slightly (which I figured was some kind of salute), and stepped quietly to the side to let my father and me pass. They held their heads straight up and, with faint smiles on their faces, floated by, not saying anything. That was how a nun should look. Nuns were supposed to be foreigners, and they should wear those black gowns all the time.

But Miss Zhou looked too ordinary and too kind to be a nun. She was not aloof; in fact, she smiled too much. Her soft voice and her well-modulated speech reminded me of the best kindergarten teacher that I had in the Big Courtyard. There was one thing foreign about her, however: her distinct American accent, different from that of all the other professors, who spoke with the standard British accent. Ordinary as she appeared, she was an engaging teacher and no professor in college captivated me as she did in that first class. As far as I was concerned, the only thing that was slightly disappointing about her was that she never talked about herself, her religion, or her life in prison. How could someone who had just been released from prison after twenty-seven years be so cheerful and so peaceful? After a class one day, I could hold back no longer, and asked Miss Zhou point-blank: "Is it true that you are a nun? Is it true that you spent twenty-seven years in prison?"

Two or three students, who were nearby and overheard the questions, edged closer.

A faint smile surfaced on Miss Zhou's face. She did not seem surprised at all. Her large eyes looked straight into mine, and she nodded her head. I recognized the smile as definitely a nun's, a smile that was confident and serene, unlike the smiles on ordinary people's faces. I admired her poise. "Yes," she said quietly, but clearly she did not want to elaborate. I knew this was a touchy subject and I should not press it. But still, I had many questions I wanted to ask Miss Zhou: What did you do all those years in prison? Did you have a Bible to read?

A few weeks later, Six-Finger Huang told me that there was a Christian church in the city now, just restored and reopened. The church was restored as a result of the Party's new policy toward religion. "Guess who is the minister?" he asked me. "Miss Zhou!" I guessed. Who else could it be? "How did you know?" he said. "Of course, that's just a rumor. I have not been to the new church, if there really is such a church." I felt an irrepressible curiosity to see the church and to see Miss Zhou as the preacher, but I said nothing. It would be political suicide to be caught going to church. I still remembered how churchgoers were persecuted and belittled a few years earlier. Like a child's whim, the Communist Party's tolerance toward churches today could change in a matter of minutes and without notice. I could not afford to get myself into political trouble again after my ordeal with the secret police, which had just ended.

The next Sunday, I slipped out of the dorm after breakfast, telling my roommates that I was going to a downtown bookstore. I found Goldfish Lane not far from the commercial district. The lane was barely two shoulders wide; it was little more than a dark and damp alley.

At the end of the lane I saw an entrance, a large black door with peeling paint. The door was open and I entered the yard that evidently was once the backyard of a large church. The tall main building, with its pointed spire and weather vane, was now sealed off from the yard. The sound of rumbling machinery could be heard in the main church building, which was probably a neighborhood factory. The small building in the yard looked like a one-room schoolhouse, built with red bricks and gray roof-tiles. Brown paper imperfectly covered some of the windows, which were apparently broken.

I walked into the quiet church. It was even smaller than it appeared from outside, with only six rows of pews, which were really narrow benches without backs. There was no elevated altar. At the front of the room, next to the wall, was a long table with white tablecloth, and on it, a small statue of Jesus on the cross, the size of a large doll. On each side of the statue burned a candle in a white marble candleholder. Their flickering flames were barely visible, and looked as if even the slightest gust of wind blowing in through a hole in a window would extinguish them. There was another small table on the right, also covered with coarse white cloth, which served as an altar. About a dozen people were sitting on the benches and two or three were kneeling in front of the altar and praying. All of them were older people, wearing drab gray or black cotton clothes. There was hardly a sound in the room as I entered. I could hear my own soft steps as I walked carefully across the brick floor. Several heads turned slightly toward the unfamiliar sound, and surprise flickered in their eyes; and then, almost imperceptibly, the heads dropped back down and resumed the posture of quiet worship and meditation.

I sat down on the last bench. I could feel the uneasiness that my presence caused in the room. An old man sitting next to me kept darting furtive glances at me. I understood their fear. With my student outfit, I looked too much like an official or a secret government agent. I looked around and saw a thin volume with a dark brown cover lying next to the woman in front of me. Several other people had similar volumes in their hands.

"Could I borrow this for a moment?" I leaned forward and whispered, touching the woman's elbow lightly. The woman shuddered. Without looking back, she sullenly said, "Yes."

I took the volume. Its pages were stitched together by hand with coarse thread, and the edges of the paper were frayed. The cover was made of brown kraft paper, now almost black, with greasy stains. On it, "The New Testament and Holy Songs" appeared in small handwritten characters. I opened the book. Inside, the words were mimeographed on thin, brittle white paper, and were so small and faint that they were barely legible in places. But the characters were also elegant and flowing, and slanted slightly to the upper right in a vaguely familiar way. As I flipped through the first few pages, it suddenly dawned on me why the handwriting looked familiar: it was Miss Zhou's! That was the way she wrote on the blackboard.

It was not clear when or from which direction Miss Zhou entered the room. But the people in front of me suddenly stood up and Miss Zhou was standing behind the altar.

The service began with songs. There was no organ or piano or any musical instrument to accompany the songs. With each song, Miss Zhou started the first line, and the rest of the congregation followed. They sang earnestly and quietly. Above the low droning voice of the congregation, I could distinctly hear Miss Zhou. She pronounced the words clearly, just as she did in her lectures. I did not know any of the songs, but I liked the soft melodies, so peaceful compared to the strident revolutionary marches that I had heard all my life. After the songs, there was a prayer. When Miss Zhou asked God to bless the service, I felt strange. I tried to keep an open mind, but I could feel nothing, and I definitely could not feel the presence of God. All my life, I had been taught that there was no God, and I believed it. But there was something mysterious about Miss Zhou, something in her soft voice perhaps, that touched me, and I did not feel awkward or silly there, or experience the uneasiness that I thought I would.

Miss Zhou's sermon was on salvation. I had heard of the terms "salvation" and "baptism" during the Cultural Revolution, when such concepts were ridiculed and denounced as superstition. Some years later, when I tried to remember what Miss Zhou said that day, I could not remember. All I remembered was Miss Zhou's face, a face at once sad, serene, and happy, and the tears that sparkled in her eyes at the end of the sermon.

After the sermon, the congregation again sang hymns. I listened to the songs and was amused by the old man sitting beside me. The arteries on his wiry neck bulged and pulsated in time with his lips, but his singing was completely out of sync with the rest of the people. I was nonetheless struck by the absorption of the man and I could almost imagine that I saw an extraordinary light and energy radiating from his bloodshot eyes. Toward the end of the third song, I was annoyed by a sudden and violent jolt of the bench, as a latecomer, who was apparently heavy and rude, sat down on the other end beside the old man. The newcomer's presence, though no one turned to look at him, immediately sent a chill through the room. The volume of the singing instantly dropped to an almost inaudible level, as if an invisible hand twisted a dial on the radio. I cast a quick angry glance at the newcomer. The man wore a dirty old black cotton overcoat with the collar turned up, and a dark green army cap. The black collar, however, did not cover his enormous blubbery white neck, which contrasted incongruously with the dirty coat and with the rest of brown, leathery faces in the room. The blubbery neck! It took me a few seconds to make the connection, but then I shuddered. It was Uncle Blubber, the agent I had reported to for more than a year! I turned my face away from him as quickly as I could, and held the hymnbook up to my face to obscure it. Luckily, Uncle Blubber was craning his fat neck and peering at Miss Zhou and the congregation. I knew the danger I was in and immediately switched my mind into a high gear. I could be expelled from the university if he reported me. Or worse, I could be arrested and sent to prison as a crypto-Christian like Miss Zhou. I tried to sit still, but I could see the leaves of the book shaking in front of me.

The congregation finished the hymn. Miss Zhou held up a large white porcelain cup and all the people stood up. They then began to shuffle into the aisle and to move toward the front of the room to take a sip from the cup. When the old man stood up and nudged Uncle Blubber into the aisle, I saw my chance. I took a stealthy step backward and then quietly slipped out of the room. As soon as I was out of the front gate, I broke into a run with my head buried in my coat. I did not stop running until I reached the bus stop on the main street.

For the remainder of my time at the university, I did not go near the church. But when I went back to Miss Zhou's class, I seemed to have gained a new perspective on the novels we read. Sometimes I thought that the new perspective was simply due to her voice, the gentle and serene voice that I had heard in the church.

Three weeks after my visit to the church, news filtered back to me that the church had been shut down again, as part of the government's effort to prevent a repeat of the democracy movement that had swept the country a few months before. I was not surprised. A year later, it was allowed to open again. Church attendance soon grew exponentially, Six-Finger Huang later reported to me. (Unlike me, he frequently visited Lanzhou after graduation.) The government finally ordered the factory to move out of the church proper, and the main building was returned to the congregation. Six-Finger Huang went to a service years later and told me that the church was so packed that he had to stand in the back—almost out the door—during the service.

"It felt like half of the residents of Lanzhou were there at the church," an exasperated Six-Finger Huang wrote in one of his letters. "I couldn't even get close enough to say hi to Miss Zhou. Wherever she goes, she is greeted with so much respect that you'd think she was the Pope. As a matter of fact, some people say she may become the first bishop of central China since the Liberation."

My experience with Miss Zhou and her church was brief, but through her I gained a glimpse of Christians, which was quite different from what I had been taught about Christians all my life. My previous idea of Christians came from communist cartoons, which depicted Western missionaries—wearing black robes and long blank faces—who came to China to steal ancient artifacts. But since my visit to her church, whenever I thought of Christians, I thought of Miss Zhou and her smiling face. Her forgiveness, her kindness, her humanness, and above all, her strength in faith, all intrigued me to know more about the mysterious religion, even though I was still an atheist and did not believe in God.

## 27 **The Monster of Ambition**

In my junior year, after the crackdown on the democracy movement and the closing of the church, my life in college reached its lowest point. Ventures into political reform had been thwarted and avenues for exploring the religious aspects of life had been closed. Even with all the books available to me, college was not the heaven that I had imagined. Receiving repeated threats from Smiling Scorpion that I would be sent to Tibet upon graduation if I continued to neglect political studies, I began attending Mr. Breakwind's political meetings on a more regular basis, suffering through the boring sessions as I had at the aircraft factory. But I attended other classes less and less, spending more and more time—sometimes for a good stretch of the day—at the White Pagoda, lying under a poplar tree and reading books from the list that Li Ling had given me a long time ago. More than ever, I missed the conversations that I had with Li Ling in the aircraft factory. Although I had not heard from her since her marriage, I thought about her from time to time and wondered if I should contact her at her mother's address. But I never wrote the letter to her that I had drafted in my mind several times, because I thought it would be improper for me to contact a married woman.

To forget about Li Ling, I tried to date a girl from my class, but it went nowhere. The girl was pretty, but my conversations with her were always dry and boring, and I let the relationship fade after a few months. In those days, besides books, the only thing that could bring me some joy was the occasional letter from Smoking Devil, which usually was full of good news and advice that lifted my spirits for a while. In May, I got a letter from him that surprised me.

"You will never guess what I am doing now," Smoking Devil said in his letter. "I have been promoted to the position of Party secretary of the village of Big Porcupine! I am 'Uncle Cricket II' now! Imagine that! When the next Great Proletarian Cultural Revolution comes along and a new crop of Beijing Kids is sent to Big Porcupine, Uncle Cricket II will show them around. Just like old times. Frankly, it is good to be in a position of authority. Better to be the small king of a village than a pompous minister in a big city like Beijing. Ministers in Beijing are more numerous than hairs on a cow! Didn't I tell you that joining the Party was the future for us? My work is to move my lips: giving orders, answering the telephone (the village got its first telephone last year), and eating at everyone's house in the village (which is the most demanding part of my job, although I like it the best).

"But smoking a good pipe after a good meal is not all that I do these days. I have been busy working on the kang too. I am now the proud father of five Golden Flowers. Five beautiful daughters! And a sixth is on the way. I know you are going to scream about the Party's one-child policy. To hell with that! I am a peasant now, and peasants don't give a damn about the decrees of emperors. As the peasants say: Heaven is high and the Emperor is far away—too far to touch us. My biggest mission right now is to have a son, and I will not let my wife get off the kang until she gives me a son. I have a bet with Broken Shoe, who has four daughters now and is as determined as I am to get a BIG, FAT SON. Whoever loses the bet will throw a banquet for the entire village to celebrate the birth of the other's son.

"Have you joined the Party yet? Take my advice: This is the best way to get ahead in China. Political power means everything—I am not going to tell you all the details, but trust me, it will bring you everything."

It seemed that Smoking Devil was right again. With graduation and job assignment fast approaching, I knew I had better start improving my relationship with the Party secretary or I would be in very serious trouble. I definitely did not want to end up in Tibet after four years of college. Again I contemplated sending Mr. Breakwind an application to join the Party.

One afternoon, as I was drafting an application which I knew was hopelessly a waste of time, my friend Young Einstein paid me a visit. His visit, unexpectedly, brought new hope to my life.

"I need your help," he said without ceremony, holding out a large manila envelope. "I need your help with some English letters. I am applying to some graduate schools in the United States."

He was a top student in the physics department, having won a national physics contest a year before. I was not surprised that he was aspiring to study in the U.S., which was still very rare in China.

In the next hour, I drafted several letters in English for my friend and after I was done, I talked to him about my frustration and fear of Mr. Breakwind and my plan to apply to join the Party.

"Why do you have to go that stupid route to avoid Tibet?" Young Einstein asked. "It may get you there even faster if you are a Party member. Why don't you try applying to a graduate school in the U.S.?"

"It would be nice to study in the United States, but I can't," I replied. "First, I don't have any relatives in the U.S. to sponsor me. Second, you know as well as I do that I don't have money for tuition. As a matter of fact, at this very moment, I have eighty-five yuan in the bank, which won't even buy me a week's worth of food in the U.S., let alone a plane ticket to cross the Pacific Ocean." A one-way ticket to the U.S. cost fourteen hundred yuan, an unthinkable sum to me at the time.

"Even though you don't have any relatives in the States, you can apply for a scholarship," Young Einstein insisted. "That is what I am doing now. You see, I don't have any relatives there either. What have you got to lose? The worst that could happen is that you end up in a Chinese restaurant washing dishes for a year and come back home. But even doing that you can still save a thousand dollars to bring home. You would never be able to save a thousand dollars if you stayed here."

A thousand dollars is three thousand yuan. The money was certainly alluring. I would be lucky if I could save a few hundred yuan in my lifetime. I remembered what my friend Little Lenin told me before he married Meatball in the aircraft factory: His life's goal was to save three hundred yuan to put aside for emergencies, and to reach that goal, he was willing to live very simply and to spend very little, with no eating out, no movies, no new clothes, and no new shoes. And I remembered thinking at the time, what a pathetic goal in life! Young Einstein was right: What did I have to lose?

"All right," I said. "I'll give it a try. And I know who to blame if I get into trouble this time."

But money was not the only reason for my decision. A more important reason, understood but never spoken even among friends, was personal ambition, an unmentionable goal in China because it was a "dirty" word, a taboo term as dangerous as the word "bourgeois" in the communist lexicon. The people the Party officials hated most were those who had personal ambitions. Admitting that one had personal ambitions was practically political suicide. But I couldn't help it; I was never content playing the cards the Party had dealt me.

"Welcome on board," Young Einstein said. "But you'd better hurry.

I'm afraid that we are chasing the last bus now. The door could be closed at any time. I hear that the government is already working on restrictions on studying abroad."

That very day I sent a dozen postcards to universities across the Pacific Ocean, asking for application forms. I had not an inkling of how many little woes and tribulations such a simple action would bring me.

The next thing I had to do was obtain school transcripts. I went to the Office of Records, and from the stony face of the official behind the window I knew right away that there would be trouble. Pouting his lips, the man spoke rapidly in a duck-like voice through the small window: "We cannot issue a transcript to a foreign school unless you have the dean's express permission."

The dean, a soft-spoken, smooth-faced man, told me amiably: "We can't give you permission unless you have permission from the Party secretary of the Foreign Languages Department."

The Party secretary was Mr. Breakwind. For two days, I agonized about the talk that I had to have with him. I had battled the Party secretary for nearly three years and I knew it would not be easy. The worst thing I could do was to show eagerness to study in America.

"Comrade Pi," I opened my rehearsed speech to Mr. Breakwind in his office. "For the past three years, you have taught me a lot of valuable lessons: to love the Party, to serve the people wholeheartedly, to make personal sacrifices for the cause of the country. I thank you for teaching me all these things. I have been thinking long and hard that I must make some personal sacrifices to repay the care that the Party has given me. I finally found a way: I want to take the ultimate challenge, to study in the United States. I know I'll suffer great hardship there, but as you have said, hardship will temper our revolutionary spirit. I'll bring back the knowledge that I learn there, and bring back all the money that I earn there, to give them to the country and the Party. Of course, I'd be very happy to work here for the Party too and do a good job. But I think I can make a bigger contribution to the Party by going to America."

My speech was full of correct Party clichés but it still failed to move the suspicious Party secretary. "Studying in America? In the very pulsating heart of capitalism? This is a very serious matter and I will have to convene a committee meeting to discuss it."

To my complete surprise, however, Mr. Breakwind granted my request two weeks later. "There are two conditions," he said, holding the letter of permission. "One, you start attending the special weekly political study sessions for Party activists and make an effort to join the Party.

Two, you help Feng Xia apply to study in America. You know that she is a good Party member and the committee has decided that it will be better if she goes with you." Smiling Scorpion going with me? How absurd! She was dead last in her class and was probably still an eighth grader, educationally speaking. What was she going to study? Was she going to spy on me?

But time was short and I could not worry too much about her, so I agreed to the conditions and received the precious letter from the Party secretary.

Armed with Mr. Breakwind's letter and closely affiliated with a solid Party member like Smiling Scorpion, I sailed forward with a strong but gentle breeze behind me. In two weeks, I obtained transcripts from the Dean's Office and the Office of Records.

Since Young Einstein, his girlfriend, and I all had excellent academic records, we each won scholarships from American universities. Smiling Scorpion, however, failed to be admitted, due to her poor academic record.

But the academic and financial hurdles turned out to be the lowest ones we had to jump. The real challenge was getting a security clearance and a passport from the Security Bureau.

Before going to the Provincial Security Bureau, we first needed a security clearance from the Public Safety Department of the university. The business of issuing a security clearance was taken very, very seriously; everybody was seen as a potential defector. My application went into the Public Safety Department, but, as the Chinese say, like *a mud cow walking into the ocean*, it never walked out. Young Einstein and I went to the Office of Public Safety every two or three days for a month. Director Zhang bluntly told us that it would be a long wait.

"I have sent letters of inquiry to all the places where you have lived," he said, nodding his head, "to check your political backgrounds. And as for you, Fan Shen, your past is more *complicated*—you know what I mean—and I have sent my personal assistant to Beijing and to Xi'an to investigate. Frankly, the Party has to make sure that it can trust you. You belong to the country, and the country has to be responsible for you. We are prepared to take as long as necessary to do a good job."

One day, however, when Young Einstein and I checked at the office, we were surprised to find Director Zhang in an elated mood. "Have a seat," he said, smiling for the first time. "I have news for both of you. You don't have to come here again." My heart leapt, anticipating an approval.

"The Communist Party has just issued Document Number 14." The

Director picked up a thick manila envelope with a red hammer-and-sickle seal on it and tapped it triumphantly. "It stipulates that all college graduates must work for a minimum of two years for the country after graduation before they are eligible to apply for a passport. So, there you are." He handed us the envelope. We both sank into our chairs.

"I hate this country and I want to strangle that director," seethed Young Einstein after we had walked out the Office of Public Safety. "I have got to think of a way to escape. I am prepared to tape the admission papers inside my swimming trunks and swim across the channel to Hong Kong."

"I can't swim," his girlfriend quickly butted in. "Besides, I don't want to end up in a shark's stomach."

"Few succeed in swimming anyway," I said soberly, though I was burning equally with a strong desire to escape. "Many people drown at sea and most of the few who reach shore are captured and sent back to China. The government sends them to prison as traitors."

"I know that," Young Einstein said, calming down now. "I am thinking . . . maybe we can walk across the mountains of Yunnan and slip into Burma. There's a long border there, and there's got to be some place where we can slip through."

"But we don't know the roads," said his girlfriend, clearly frightened. "There are lots of border guards, and they're very good at capturing people who try to escape."

"Before we take that kind of risk," I said, "let's think of other possibilities. Maybe we can persuade the Party officials in our departments to exempt us from the new regulation."

I spoke to Mr. Breakwind the next day and tried to win his support.

"It's too bad," said Mr. Breakwind after listening to my speech. He seemed sympathetic but was actually overjoyed. "I knew it was no use. But you young people *would not drop tears until you saw the coffin*—pardon me for using the cliché. Now you should settle down and be content to work in China. What's so great about going to America? The Party needs you here. Remember, trying to do anything of your own will always brings you trouble. Only the Party knows what's best for you. If the Party needs you to study abroad, it will call you."

I did not want to give up so easily. It was no use trying to reason with moronic local officials like Mr. Breakwind. Perhaps a more powerful "heavenly sword," a high official in Beijing, might help us get around the new restrictions.

For weeks, Young Einstein and I carefully drafted a letter and searched for a connection in the sky. We were looking for someone, a nephew, a son, a former servant or a guard, who had access to a high-ranking Party official and who could hand in our letters personally. I remembered that my friend Baby Dragon had become a lieutenant colonel at the Central Military Committee in Beijing and he might have connections. So I wrote to him and asked him for help. He agreed to find connections to pass the letters on to an official in the Ministry of Education. Even though our connection to such a high official was extremely tenuous, it was the only thing we could think of, and we clung to our hope for a miracle. But the miracle never happened.

I then tried to enlist my parents' help but received, instead, a series of standard lectures that even Mr. Breakwind could not have improved upon. Obey the Party's orders. Be content with the Party's assignment. Subordinate personal interests to the interests of the Party and the country. I understood my parents' thinking and knew that all the lofty slogans they gave me were not for my benefit, but to protect themselves. Party members all their lives, they regarded my ambition as a potential danger to them.

Throughout the summer, Young Einstein and I continued our futile efforts. We sent numerous letters to the Ministry of Education, the State Department, and the Party's Central Committee, but the letters were all returned to officials at the university. Mr. Breakwind sighed as he waved a stack of letters that I sent to Beijing. "Didn't I tell you it's no use?" he said, shaking his head. "You must believe that the Party has the best interests of you young people in mind when it makes its decisions. You will only bring more trouble to yourself if you try to do things on your own. Trust the Party."

Days became weeks and then months: May, June, July, August. The American universities, upon learning our situation, also sent letters on our behalf to Premier Zhao Ziyang. But the letters were like rocks dropped into the ocean, and they disappeared without a trace. I was so desperate that, feeling like a dead pig no longer afraid of boiling water, I seriously considered swimming across the open sea to Hong Kong.

Finally, our time ran out. The American school year began in September. The battle was lost. We reluctantly wrote letters to the U.S. universities and very sadly gave up our hard-won scholarships for the year.

Now that I had lost the battle to obtain a passport, I had to plunge into the other battle that had been looming in front me: my job assignment. Our class had entered its last semester.

We all knew the importance of the long anticipated event. Some people had been positioning themselves and preparing for the once-in-a-lifetime battle ever since they were freshmen. A job assignment from the Party is more of an order than an offer. Since there were few private enterprises in China in those days, refusing a Party's assignment would leave a terrible political mark in a graduate's file, which would practically ruin the rest of his life. Consequently, few college graduates dared to turn down the Party's assignments, even though accepting them might mean enduring long separations from their families or years of working at jobs they did not like.

In March, after the president of the university had returned from Beijing, where he had attended a national conference on job allocations, as if to prepare us for the unhappiness and shock that many of us would undoubtedly experience upon announcement, the administration leaked word that this year there would be fewer good jobs than in previous years. Many people would not be sent back to their hometowns, which was an unstated priority for every graduate.

In April, three months before graduation, each department formed a committee in charge of job assignments. In the Foreign Languages Department, the committee consisted of Mr. Breakwind, Smiling Scorpion, Professor Dai and Instructor Wu, all of them Party members, which did not bode well for my prospects. Rumors circulating in the dormitory added further to my worries. "There are only three positions in Beijing and one in Shanghai for English majors this year"; "Sixty percent of the graduates will be middle-school teachers in remote rural schools and there is indeed a position in Tibet." Rumors like these kept not just me, but everyone, on edge for weeks; the last thing I wanted was to go to

Tibet. In my department, five of us were from Beijing and two from Shanghai. If the rumors were true, there would not be enough positions in these cities for all of us to go back home. Fear gave way to open and ugly competition for the positions, turning classmates and friends into bitter enemies. Behind the scenes, the campus had become a brutal battlefield.

One particularly ugly fight was between two of my classmates from Tianjin, the third largest city in China. Rumor had it that there was only one position in Tianjin. One of them could not go home. For weeks, each of them went to the job committee and bad-mouthed the other in vicious terms in order to increase his chances of getting the job himself. The bitter battle made them mortal enemies and they never spoke to each other afterwards. Theirs was not a unique case.

In the weeks leading to the announcement of assignments, everyone tried to pull some strings or to find a back door, that is, to favorably influence members of the job committee by whatever means he could. Parents who had influential positions visited members of the job committee on behalf of their children. Those without powerful parents sent gifts.

Following common sense, I paid my share of visits to members of the job committee. It so happened that one of the teachers, Professor Dai, had been my bridge partner the previous year. But I knew that a single friendly ally was not enough to overcome my powerful opponents on the job committee. Mr. Breakwind and Smiling Scorpion had always regarded me as the quintessential troublemaker of the department, and had been threatening for four years to send me to Tibet or Xinjiang, where emperors used to banish their troublemakers. I had to find a way to make sure that it would not happen. Although my father was a high-ranking Party official, I knew I could not count on him. He was too afraid of my making trouble for himself and would probably give me another stern lecture on obeying and serving the Party, instead of visiting the school to lobby on my behalf.

For days, I mulled over possible strategies to improve my chances. Then I had an epiphany: I too had strong and powerful "friends" I could count on. I had the secret police, to whom I had had to report every month until a year ago, and with a little bit of ingenuity, I might be able to redirect their awesome firepower to my enemies. It was an audacious and titillating thought and I made my plans accordingly.

I called the "bookstore" the next afternoon. Uncle Blubber answered the phone. "Uncle Liu, this is Fan Shen," I said in an urgent tone. "I must see you at once. I have something urgent to report."

The two uncles rushed over from the other end of the town and we met at the Lanzhou Hotel. Without much ado, I once again transformed myself into a naïve zealot, silly and talkative to the extreme, and reported in all seriousness the "important information" that I had just uncovered about Mr. Breakwind.

"Mr. Breakwind—Comrade Pi, I mean, has been acting very weird lately," I said breathlessly. "Today, I saw him talking to the Canadian teacher. As I was passing by, he slipped a piece of paper to the foreigner and left immediately after that. Anyway, with the training you have given me in the past few years—you said small things can lead to big things—I could immediately tell that he was trying to hide something. Anyway, I have had my doubts about him all along and this was so blatant that I just had to report to you right away." As usual, I offered an analysis of my suspicions and did not hesitate to embellish my report with juicy details. I felt no guilt about the ridiculous fabrications. In fact, it gave me tremendous pleasure to imagine the iron-faced secret agents grilling a terrified Mr. Breakwind.

I followed the account on Mr. Breakwind with another on Smiling Scorpion, who I suspected was an accomplice of Mr. Breakwind. She was Mr. Breakwind's mistress, as everybody knew. I strongly suspected that the reason he had allowed me to pursue studies in America was to camouflage rewarding her. For an hour, I savored the experience of feeding those two dim-witted but very dangerous secret agents great gobs of tasty nonsense. This would be the last time I was able to do so. More importantly, I knew that my gibberish would have profound effects on my enemies. I meant to bore them thoroughly so that they would do anything to get rid of me for good.

After about an hour, my report started to get on the agents' nerves. That fit into my plan quite well.

Uncle Blubber interrupted me after one particularly long-winded story and said, "Thank you for your report. We will have to go back and study it now. We are satisfied that you are vigilant and loyal to the Party, and we have decided that after your graduation, you need not keep in touch with us any more." I guessed he was beginning to fear that I might call them again and again and inflict more torturous reports on them when he repeated and emphasized his last sentence. "I mean, from now on, you *don't* have to report to us anymore. THIS IS AN ORDER. You must act as if you have never known us."

"But I must remind you," Uncle Qi added in his customary cold and threatening voice, "that you should never utter a word to anyone about our meetings. I think you understand the consequences if you do tell anyone."

I certainly did understand the power they had. That was why I was there. But his last remark also provided me with exactly the opening I had been angling for. I saw my chance and grabbed it. "But I have a problem now. You said last time that you would guarantee that my working for you would in no way affect my graduation and job assignment. But because I have been working for you and reporting on a few people in my department, and they somehow seem to know that I am responsible for the unfavorable reports. Comrade Pi, who is heading the job committee, is now trying to punish me by giving me a bad job. He told me so. He said that, given my absences from political studies, I stood a good chance of going to Tibet. But all those times that I was absent, I was out gathering information for you. I was working for the Party. I need your help. I have worked so hard for you and for the Party. Should I be punished for working for the Party—?" My voice trailed off, accentuating the impression that here, before them, was a submissive servant who should not be treated unfairly. "Could you talk to the job committee and let them know that I should be treated favorably because of my special service? Or should I tell them myself?"

I was amazed at my own boldness. As I was uttering the last sentence, I shrank into the corner of the sofa and did my best to look like a weak, pathetic victim of circumstances. I knew that the simple-minded agents would enjoy exercising their power, especially since they could congratulate themselves for their compassion and justice in doing so. But I also knew that they wanted to make sure that an annoying moron like me never returned, and, most important of all, did not want the fact that they had been spying on the faculty known.

"No, no, you don't want to tell them that," said Uncle Blubber. "We'll see what we can do. You can be sure that we will do our best to protect you. Now, remember, DO NOT contact us anymore."

The day when job assignments were announced was a tense one. I was quite nervous because I did not know whether the secret police had done anything on my behalf, and I did not hold out much hope that they had. At nine o'clock in the morning, the entire graduating class of the Foreign Languages Department assembled in a large classroom. The job committee members, every one of them, sat behind a long table facing the class. They looked very, very serious and the room was very, very quiet. All the anxious eyes were fixed on the white sheet in the hands of Mr.

Breakwind. Standing at the podium, head held high with his round glasses still held together with white tape, Mr. Breakwind slowly surveyed the fidgeting crowd. It was his day and he relished it.

"Class of '82," he began in a triumphant blaring voice. "On behalf of the Communist Party, the faculty and staff of Lanzhou University, I congratulate all of you for graduating from this university. But, as Sun Yat-sen, the founder of the First Republic, said, 'The revolution has just begun, and comrades, you must work harder.' You have acquired knowledge and skills, and now it is time to give back to the Party, to the country, and to the people. Our Great Leader Chairman Mao taught us that we must subordinate our personal interests to the interests of the Party. There have been thousands of fine examples of revolutionaries who answered the call of the Party and went wherever the Party called them." A lengthy speech followed on the honor of serving the Party and obeying the Party's assignment. No one paid any attention, and after a few minutes there was impatient and irritated fidgeting.

"Now, the moment of truth and the test—remember, no matter where you go, it is an honor to serve the Party."

We leaned forward stiffly, intense and anxious as Mr. Breakwind slowly read each name and assignment.

"Zhang Yimin, the Municipal Food Bureau in Changsha." A collective cheer went up for the young man. He was going home. It did not matter what kind of job he would have in the food bureau.

"Hui Tu, the Second Middle School in Fox County, Gansu province." A sympathetic sigh was heaved for the unfortunate quiet girl from Hebei province. She buried her head between her knees and started to sob inaudibly. We turned our faces to Mr. Breakwind again.

"Hua Xinpi, the Department of Transportation at Great Desert County, Qinghai province." Another round of sighs, followed by angry mumbles from the disappointed graduate.

There were far more tears than cheers.

"Qian Le, the Henan Technical College in Zhengzhou." Squirm laughed out loud when he heard his assignment. He turned to look at me. I gave him a thumbs-up. I knew why Squirm enjoyed such good fortune. He had delivered six bottles of the best sesame oil from his native town to Mr. Breakwind and Smiling Scorpion ten days earlier.

"Huang Laishi, the First Lhasa Middle School in Tibet." Everyone turned around and looked at Six-Finger Huang, who had received the worst assignment so far. He was too shocked to show any reaction. As if to prevent an anticipated outburst from Six-Finger Huang, Mr. Breakwind calmly offered an explanation to the class. He did not dare look in Six-Finger Huang's direction.

"Tibet is still a virgin place. It is the place where college graduates are most needed. This is the most honorable job assignment of the year, and of course, the most challenging. The Party committee took a long time deciding who should have the honor and who deserves such trust from the Party. We thought that Huang Laishi would be the best choice for the job. It is a tremendous opportunity. College graduates are so scarce there that you may soon be the Party secretary in the middle school, if you work hard for the school and for the Party. Huang Laishi, please accept the Party's congratulations." The room was silent. I could not look at my roommate of four years.

The girl with the highest grade point average took the only position in Shanghai, her hometown. The two positions in Beijing went to two students with high-placed parents. No one was surprised by their assignments. With these positions gone, I knew I had failed and I was more fearful than ever. How would I react if I were sent to a country school in Tibet? I dreaded to hear my name.

Now that the positions in Shanghai and Beijing were gone, everyone was listening for the third best location, Tianjin. Tianjin is an hour from Beijing by train, and had been the object of a bitter smear campaign between the two Tianjin natives, for there was only one position in their hometown. The whole class waited to find out the outcome of their bitter and nasty battle.

"Zhe Yi, the archive room at the Dry Lake Vocational School, Hebei province." Zhe Yi, a lanky man with long loose limbs, stared daggers at his chief rival from Tianjin. Liang Hao, his rival, gloated. Now it seemed certain that he would be going home. He did not have to wait long to find out.

"Liang Hao, the Second National Machine Tools Factory, in Bitter-Melon County, Hebei province." People audibly gasped. "What?" Liang Hao burst out, not believing his ears. No Tianjin native going back to Tianjin? Was the position in Tianjin eliminated?

Everybody in the room now wondered who had gotten the job in Tianjin. There were only a few names left on the roster. The audience became tense again, anticipating a surprise of some kind.

"Cao Ji, the Red Foundation Middle School in Gray Rabbit County, Yunnan province." Another disappointed graduate. But by now our supply of sympathy had been exhausted. There was little reaction.

My name was the last on the list.

"Fan Shen, Tianjin Institute of Light Industry, Tianjin." Loud applause thundered through the room. At last someone had done better than expected. I could not believe what I had heard. Everybody turned around to look at me, who turned out to be the luckiest man of the day. The two teachers on the job committee, sitting in front, beamed at me.

To quiet the angry murmurs of the two Tianjin natives and the envious mumbling of everyone else, Mr. Breakwind raised his hands and took some time to explain the unique assignment.

"This was a teaching position at a good college," he said, "and we need to send one of our best graduates to show people on the east coast how good our graduates are. Fan Shen has the second highest grade point average in the entire graduating class and therefore he should be appointed. Besides, in the past four years, he has demonstrated his loyalty to the Party and has earned the Party's trust. Let's hope that he will continue to serve the Party well in the new position." I smiled, knowing that it was political manipulation, not my virtue as a student or my supposed loyalty as a communist, that had earned me Mr. Breakwind's praise. I also felt a bit guilty, but only a bit. Neither Mr. Breakwind nor any Party official cared about academic achievement to any great extent, and everyone knew, and responded to, the fact that job assignments were more political maneuvering and bribery than anything else.

That evening, I had to suppress my elation in order to console some of the unhappy job recipients. Young Einstein was assigned to the School of Agriculture in Weeds County, thirty miles from Beijing. Not a good job.

"It's so unfair," Young Einstein said. "The two people at the bottom of my class got the best research positions in Beijing, at People's University, and I am the top student in the department but I have to teach in Weeds County."

I also felt sorry for my two classmates from Tianjin, both of whom had been my friends for four years. I was especially sorry for Six-Finger Huang, and I took him out for dinner that evening. Later that night, lying in bed, I thought of the day's events and still could hardly believe that I came out of this treacherous situation a big winner. The good job, however, was only part of the reason that made me so happy that night. What made me even happier was the thought that my distasteful and humiliating dealings with Mr. Breakwind and Smiling Scorpion were over, and happier still, my dangerous contact with the secret police was over. That night I slept very little and I looked forward to the morning when I would start my journey to a new life in Tianjin.

༄

The poplar trees on White Pagoda Mountain were past full bloom and were shedding their brownish flowers on the ground when I walked along the familiar path one last time in the afternoon. The dark leaves looked like millions of giant earthworms. Treading carefully on what looked like a worm-laden carpet, I found the small stone marking the grave of Clever Zhao. I knelt down on one knee and used my hands to dig a shallow hole in the soft, grassy ground. I then took a large wooden bowl out of my satchel, placed it carefully in the hole, and put a steamed bun in the bowl. *I hope you will have enough to eat now, wherever you are*, I said silently to my friend. He would have been so happy but also so sad on this day, the day after graduation, when we would have had to part anyway.

I sat down under a large alder tree and looked toward the Yellow River and the city next to it. A train whistled in the distance. I could see a beautiful cloud of white steam rising, trailing behind the locomotive as it slowly pulled into Lanzhou Station. It was the daily express that had just arrived from Beijing. It would leave in four hours, at 7:15, and carry me back east.

And we forget because we must,
And not because we will.

*Matthew Arnold*

# 5 Water

After a brief visit to my parents and sister in Beijing, I went to Tianjin on August 1, 1982, to report for my job. The easy one-hour train ride from Beijing to Tianjin was pleasant and fast, and I got off the train in high spirits and boarded a bus, which took me to a place called Hui Dui (which literally means Trash Dump), where the college was located. It seemed that the street was well named. It had a row of small and dirty restaurants on either side of the college entrance and their garbage, rotting vegetables and ashes from burnt coal, was heaped by the curb. The place might have been a real trash dump years before and it seemed still to be trying to live up to its name. In truth, though, I barely noticed the filthy appearance of the street on that bright summer day, for I was still dazed by the narrow, almost unbelievable victory of two weeks ago.

With a light heart I walked into the personnel office on the second floor of the administration building. It was a small dingy room, crammed with wooden desks and tall file cabinets. A man rose to greet me from behind a desk crowded with newspapers and teacups. He was perhaps fifty years old, wearing glasses as thick as a soy-sauce bottle, and his brown, wrinkled face reminded me of the parched insides of the squashes that were drying on the roofs of farmhouses along the train tracks.

"My name's Lang and I am the head of the Personnel Department. On behalf of the Party committee, I welcome you to our college, Fan Shen," he said with a dry smile after examining my papers.

We shook hands. I sat down on the wooden chair by the door. Squash Face came to the point of the interview right away.

"The Party Committee thought very highly of your credentials. You have the second highest grade point average in your class and your graduation thesis is brilliant. Twenty-three new college graduates have been assigned to us this year. We looked at everyone's records very carefully and we are most impressed with your credentials. You are one of the best graduates we've got this year."

I was flattered.

"As the Great Leader said," Squash Face continued, " 'The ablest person should get the most challenging job.' Of course, challenge also means reward. The Party Committee has decided to assign you to the Department of Salt Chemistry in Tanggu as an assistant lecturer. I need to point out that this is a special honor and a reward for a good student like you. That department is the most desirable place in the college. It is located on a small campus in the beautiful district of Tanggu, only forty miles from Tianjin. It is semi-autonomous, and therefore offers a greater opportunity for promotion and better living quarters. We have a shortage of dorms here. But in Tanggu, since they don't have many young teachers, you might get your own room. You will be happy when you see the place."

I liked the idea of "a semi-autonomous campus" and my own dorm room. I had been sharing rooms with five or six people over the past fourteen years, ever since I went to live in a cave-house with the army of Beijing Kids.

"When should I report there?" I asked, impatient to leave Squash Face's smoke-filled den and to settle down in my own room.

"I am pleased that you have accepted the Party's assignment," said Squash Face with a broad smile. "There is a truck to the train station in the next hour. I will call the driver to take you and your luggage there. If you need anything, just let me know. Again, congratulations."

It was quite a change to board the train from Tianjin to Tanggu, for unlike most trains in China, this one was clean and not crowded. I easily found a window seat and enjoyed the forty-five-minute journey. The skyline of Tanggu was dominated by the smokestacks of petroleum and chemical plants, but that did not prevent the city from giving me a pleasant impression as I got off the train and strolled the short distance from the train station to the campus, which was located at the center of the town. Quiet, clean, and with unusually few pedestrians, the shady streets were lined with young maple trees and contrasted sharply with the crowded and barren streets of Tianjin. Not far from the train station I spotted a beautiful park. From the street, I could see tall weeping willows and birch trees along the shore of a lovely lake. There was even a white swan swimming leisurely in the water. But the best thing was, I noticed, that there was hardly anyone in the park! I could picture myself spending many peaceful afternoons there, lying under the big willow tree by the footbridge and reading my "idle" books, just as I did under the White Pagoda in college.

The campus was not large, but was immaculately clean. It had white buildings on all four sides, much like an enlarged version of a traditional four-sided courtyard in Beijing. The yard was paved with lead-colored bricks and, like the streets outside, was quiet and deserted. I thought it was very pleasant.

On the first floor of the administration building, I found the reception room and entered. Inside, it was so bright with the afternoon sun that it took me a moment to make out the furniture and the figure sitting behind the desk. A young woman with a sweet face stood up to greet me, and her voice was like a nightingale's: "You must be Fan Shen," she said warmly. "We have all been waiting for you. You are a famous person here; the whole campus knows that you are coming. Have a seat. Would you like some tea?" She lifted a large red thermos bottle from the windowsill and poured me a cup. "I will let Chairman Zhang know that you are here. He has arranged everything for you." She walked past me toward the side door and flashed me a sensual smile that made my heart throb. She left, but her beautiful dimples and plump red lips stayed behind.

Teacup in hand, I sat down on the couch and looked around. Everything was clean, peaceful, and cheerful. The luck that I had had with my job assignment began to sink in. I felt very fortunate. I thought of all my unlucky classmates who were reporting to shabby remote country schools. I thought of the two classmates from Tianjin who had destroyed each other's reputations and neither of whom got this job. I thought of Six-Finger Huang, who was probably drinking Tibetan horse milk and chewing a half-burnt yak leg now. One moment we were all college friends eating in the same dining hall, and the next moment, we were scattered across the country. A lucky few like me were enjoying the amenities of big cities, while others were suffering the hardships of country villages.

I savored the redolent aroma from the teacup in my hands and heaved a sigh of contentment. A yellow bird was twittering on the peach tree outside the window. Even the birds here seemed happier. A sudden spasm of remorse seized me. I felt sorry that I had done many mischievous things to Mr. Breakwind. Come to think of it, he was not such a bad person, just a small naïve bureaucrat still holding on to the outdated rules and ideals of the Party. After all, he was the one who assigned me this good job. I felt a little ashamed and guilty that I had made up so many stories about him and reported him to the uncles. Once I am settled here, I decided, I will write a letter to Mr. Breakwind and apologize for what I had done and thank him for the job assignment.

I raised the teacup to my lips, and the reverie and benevolent dream ended with one sip.

It was the tea. Something was funny about the tea. Actually, it was not funny, it was revolting. The water tasted like spoiled vinegar with an indescribably foul odor, an odor which instantly made me sick. I felt like spitting out the disgusting brew on the spot. I ran to the bathroom, unembarrassed. After spitting repeatedly, I turned on the water, lowered my head, and put my mouth to the faucet to rinse out the bad taste. The next second, I jerked my head back. The tap water had the same odious smell!

The pretty young receptionist was sitting behind her desk when I came back. When she saw me walk in, still wiping my mouth, she laughed. "You big city people are finicky," she said. "It is not polite to spit out your host's tea. But don't worry, you'll get used to it soon." Her voice was still as sweet as a chirping nightingale's. But I noticed, with a shock, that behind her beautiful plump red lips were two rows of brown, twisted, rotten teeth. The teeth looked like a handful of dried and crushed baby corn. "Chairman Zhang will see you now," she said, still smiling.

Chairman Zhang was all smiles when I walked into his office. He pumped my hand rigorously. "Welcome! Welcome!" He said in a booming voice. "We have not had new blood for some time and we desperately need young people like you. Sit down." I sat down in a wooden chair facing him, and he beamed at me as if he were appreciating a piece of newly acquired furniture. He was perhaps fifty-five, with a large, meaty face and thick lips. Perched above the lips I saw two small, oddly-shaped moustaches. I took a closer look and realized that they were not moustaches at all, but long, black nose hairs protruding from his nostrils.

Basking in the sunshine coming through the window, Chairman Zhang settled back in his chair. "See what a beautiful day it is to welcome you here. On behalf of the Party committee at the Salt Chemistry Department, I welcome you. Later, I will show you around and you will meet all the dedicated Party members. You will find that they have overcome many difficulties and have given themselves to the cause of the Party. I am sure you will learn from them and devote your youth to the . . ." As he spoke, his front teeth reflected the sunshine and shot golden rays around the room. Then I saw something in his mouth that made my heart skip a beat: beside his golden front teeth were several black and brown rotten teeth in all shapes and sizes, just like the pretty receptionist's. Something was wrong with this place, I thought, looking at the Chairman's terrible teeth.

Later that afternoon, I met several other people, including the math teacher and the cook in the dining hall. Both were Tanggu natives, and both had rotten, twisted teeth. The encounter that made the strongest impression on me, however, was not one I had with adults, but with the math teacher's four-year-old daughter. She was a lively little fireball. The moment she saw me, she took an immediate liking to me and showed me her drawings and sang the songs that she had learned at kindergarten. As she laughed and sang without self-consciousness, all I could see was little black rotten teeth jumping up and about in her lively mouth.

That evening, alone in the small faculty dining room behind the kitchen, I managed to eat my first supper—steamed bread and stir-fried celery with tofu—but I barely touched the egg-drop soup, which tasted like spoiled vinegar. The cook came over to chat with me, bringing with him a pail of frozen sea bass to work on. He was a heavyset man in a sweat-stained shirt, and walked with a limp. In no time I turned our conversation from the frozen fish to the smell of water.

"Didn't you know?" He asked in surprise. "Everybody knows that the water in Tanggu is bad. It rots your teeth, softens your bones, and if you stay here long enough, sooner or later it will break a bone or two of yours. Three people from the department have fractured bones this year. I had a bad fall three years ago and broke my hip. It did not heal properly and I still have a lot of pain when I walk. Some people get cancer too. An English teacher died two months ago of pancreatic cancer. She was only forty-three." He eyed me suspiciously as if I were one of the dumb frozen fish he had just slit open. "How did you end up here? Did you volunteer to come? You've got to be crazy if you did. Everybody here is trying to leave, you know, including the chairman himself. I have been trying to transfer to another place for fifteen years." I was dumbfounded by the terrible secret of the place.

That night I met my roommate (I did not get my own room, as Squash Face had promised) and, not surprisingly, found that he had rotten teeth too. He was an old bachelor, by the name of "Bookworm," who taught biology. There were books piled everywhere in his half of the room—along the wall, on his bed, and under his bed, and a large pile on the shared desk that blocked almost half of the window. Except for a polite nod, the tall, stooped man took no notice of me and went on with his reading as I hauled in my things.

I unpacked quickly. I felt exhausted and went to bed early. But that night, tired as I was, I could hardly sleep. Every now and then when I dozed off, the pretty receptionist's smiling face would appear and then change into a gigantic mouth full of monstrous, jagged teeth, swaying like hands, waving and beckoning me to go in.

After two days of nightmares and unbearable thirst—for I had swallowed hardly any water—I knew I could not stay there and had to get out. But I soon realized that it would be a Herculean task. Rejecting the Party's assignment was a cardinal sin, a political crime, and financial suicide. I mentioned my desire gingerly to the cook and he laughed. "Transferring out of Tanggu?" he snorted at the mere mention of it, as if I were suggesting that we stir-fry the moon for lunch. "You don't know what you are talking about: no one in the past twelve years has been transferred out of the campus. The department knows if it approves a single transfer, it will trigger an avalanche of requests. The policy of this department is that no one ever leaves this place."

From other staff members I easily confirmed the cook's information, and I also discovered that many people in the department resented violently anyone who harbored the wish to leave. No one embodied such resentment better than Mr. Gao, the faculty coordinator and my immediate boss. The people in the department called him "Medicine Jug." He had a frail and lanky frame and because he had a perpetual cold and a cough regardless of the time of year; he carried a mug of dark herbal medicine wherever he went. I could smell it halfway across campus, and the odor was as disagreeable as it was strong.

No sooner had I mentioned my desire to transfer than Medicine Jug eyed me deprecatingly and sneered: "You want a transfer? That's news to me. No one ever leaves this place. I was assigned here in 1960 and for twenty-two years I have been trying to get out. No one has, as long as I can remember. If you can get out of here someday, you will have single-handedly launched a satellite on this campus." He took a sip from the dark medicine mug and spit the words through his gold teeth. "You will have to get my permission first, and the answer is and will always be—" Medicine Jug stopped spitting and chewed on the last syllables with relish: "FORGET IT."

Medicine Jug had good reason to be bitter and hateful. Twenty-two years of political exile had reduced the once robust Shanghai native to a toothless walking skeleton. He had been branded an anti-revolutionary by the Communist Party in the late 1950s and banished to Tanggu, which was then no more than a sweep of arid wasteland. Twenty-two years of political degradation had finally drained the last drop of hope from him. He had given up on returning to his hometown, and the only positive emotion left in him was the bitter and vicious enjoyment he derived from seeing people trapped in Tanggu with him. But Medicine Jug was far from unique on the campus in that regard—in fact, as I later discovered, he was far from unique in the entire town.

## Watery Stool, No Bacteria?

I must have caught a cold after my conversation with Medicine Jug that night. Dejected and exhausted, I walked for hours through the deserted streets in a chilly breeze mixed with drizzle, thinking about my bleak future. The next day, my fourth day in Tanggu, I had diarrhea. I went to the local hospital. The doctor had my stool examined and, finding nothing serious, handed me some pills and dismissed me.

I gulped down the pills and set out to the department to request a transfer back to the main campus in Tianjin. I first presented the formal request to Chairman Zhang. The chairman's nose-hair moustache visibly shook when he heard the word "transfer," as if I had issued a personal insult.

"Well, I'm afraid that it will not be possible," he said. His friendly voice had instantly switched to a bureaucratic monotone. "If people could go anywhere they wanted to go, our department would have emptied out a long time ago. Yes, there are some problems here, but the Party has been working hard to solve them, and it is our duty to obey the Party and serve the country." He gave a long, standard speech explaining why the Party needed us there. It was a well-organized and well-rehearsed speech, one that he obviously had been giving for years. Finally, patting me on the shoulder and walking me to the door, he added soothingly, "Work here for a few years. The Party will make things better for you. I guarantee it."

I met the same response from the Party secretary. Secretary Zuo, the co-leader of the campus, had a plump, benevolent face like that of the smiling Buddha on the White Pagoda. The Party boss nodded very sympathetically as he listened to my request. His triple chin shook gently like almond tofu.

"Yes, I understand your concern," Secretary Buddha said affably. "Don't worry. The Party cares very much about people's health. We have known about the water problem for several years and the Party has taken measures to correct it. You see—" he pressed the arms of the leather chair and struggled to his feet. Walking to the window, he pointed to the west. "You see—in that direction, the Party has already drawn up plans to build a pipeline to bring sweet water from the Hai River to Tanggu. When the pipeline is finished, we will no longer have to drink bitter water any more. Let me show you how it works." He dipped his finger into his teacup and drew a sketchy map on the glass top of his desk to show me how the more healthful water would be brought to Tanggu. "Wait for a few years. Things will be better." The Party boss ended the semi-formal presentation with a jolly smile.

"Don't believe that smoke-screen plan. Bah!" The cook spat on the ground emphatically to show his contempt when I asked him about the plan to bring better water to Tanggu. "Everybody knows the plan is a sham. It can only fool children. They have been talking about that pipeline for years now, and no one knows when it is going to be built. Besides, according to the people at the municipal water bureau, the planned pipeline is too small to begin with, and the little water we would get from it will have to be mixed with the local water anyway. With more pollution from the chemical plants now being built, the water from the pipeline won't even be enough to offset the new pollution. The water will only get worse."

Within three days, I visited all the local officials. Besides Medicine Jug, Chairman Zhang, and Secretary Buddha, I went also to the vice-chairman and the deputy secretary of the Party. I tried anyone who might have a little power and it was apparent that all the officials knew the seriousness of the water problem, and all had the same standard, pat answer to requests like mine.

Disheartened by the futile visits and realizing that I would get nowhere in Tanggu, I took the weekend train back to Tianjin. By dinnertime, I found Squash Face's apartment in the college-owned apartment building near the campus. It was a small two-room flat, with the sitting room also doubling as a dining room.

Squash Face was not pleased when he opened the door and saw me. "No, you cannot come back to Tianjin," he interrupted my plea testily. "First of all, it is not in my power to transfer you back. Only the president and the Party secretary of the College, with the consent of your department, can make that decision. The Party did not make the decision casually and it will not change it easily. I have sympathy for you, but there's nothing I can do." He stood up and walked toward the door. Holding the door open, he added, "To give you a piece of friendly advice so that you won't waste a lot of time, your department and the College will never agree to the transfer. Remember I told you it is an autonomous campus? They have their own autonomous power. They have had a lot of trouble getting people there, and people there do not come back here."

"But why me? If you knew no one wanted to go there, why did you tell me it was the most desirable place to go?" I argued, standing still, trying to make a last stand.

"I was merely obeying the orders of the Party," he said coldly. "And if I were you, I would think twice before disobeying the Party's order."

I shuffled to the door. My blood pounded so loudly in my ears that I could hear it. But angry as I was, I knew that the Party's order was like an emperor's edict, and I could not criticize the Party under any circumstances. I bit my lips and left.

That night, on the empty train heading back to Tanggu, I gazed at the dark, desolate fields outside the window, not knowing what to do next. The frightening possibility seemed more likely than ever: I was trapped in that dreadful town just like Medicine Jug; and I would die with twisted teeth and crumbled bones. I shuddered even when my mind would allow me to only half focus on the thought. I thought of resigning. But being rational, I knew the idea was absurd. In those years, by disobeying the Party, not only would I lose my city residency, housing assignment, and food ration, but I would become a political outcast.

Transfer was the only way out, even though I doubted I would ever pull it off.

I was awakened from a brief nap by a dull pain in my abdomen and had to rush to the train's toilet. The diarrhea had come back. At the toilet, however, a plan suddenly hit me. It was a plan only vague in outline, a plan without details. It was no more than that, but at least it was a plan.

The next day, I went to the hospital to have a second examination, hoping that the doctor would find something seriously wrong so that I could be hospitalized, which would give me a reason for transfer. But the lab report was disappointing. It showed only a few red blood cells but no bacterial infection in the stool. The doctor glanced at the report, assured me that nothing was serious, and sent me away with a few more diarrhea pills.

Even though the attempt to get out of Tanggu through a hospital door was thwarted, my basic plan was still intact. I knew that only a medical condition would enable me to leave. In the following week, I paid another round of visits to the homes of the five decision-makers of the department, and informed them of my "persistent diarrhea." None of the officials, however, was impressed. They heard my request, reiterated their faith in the Party to take care of the people, and showed me the door within ten minutes. The new hospital that the Party had just built for Tanggu, Secretary Buddha added confidently, was well equipped and would be adequate to cure my illness.

I may have had a plan, but I had almost no confidence. In the course of the first month, instead of curling up with a book on sunny afternoons under the willow tree in the park as I had at first envisioned, I had spent many nights walking around the darkened, deserted park like a ghost, wondering if I should give up and resign myself to my fate, as traditional Chinese wisdom advised me to. Like Medicine Jug, should I be happy to know that when I died with brittle bones that at least I was not alone? But one night, as I passed through the dark shadows of the trees, I heard faint whistles from the train station. It was the last daily commuter train leaving for Tianjin. The sound stirred up something deep in my heart, something unreasonable and indomitable. I could not give up so easily. I would fight to the end. In my heart that night, I declared a secret war against the Party.

The war would start with letters. Dragging my tired body back to the dormitory late that night, I turned on the bed lamp, pulled out a writing pad from under the pillow, and started writing.

The first volley of my attack was to every member of the college's Communist Party Committee, the president, the two vice-presidents, the Party secretary, and the deputy secretary. I knew I should not expect much and I was right. The first round of letters brought back standard replies, printed on the stationery of the president's office:

Comrade Shen,

We have received your letters. As people's servants, the Party committee is very much concerned about your illness and it wishes you well. The committee is studying your request now. As soon as we reach a conclusion, we will inform you. In the meantime, please remember Chairman Mao's words: the revolutionary spirit will overcome any human disease.
With the Highest Revolutionary Salute,
The Communist Party Committee,

[RED SEAL].

For the next few weeks, nothing came out of the "study." I fired a second round of the letters, and then a third round a week later. But no further replies came back.

Since the college officials no longer bothered to respond to my letters, starting on the fifth week, I added national leaders in Beijing to my list of targets—the Minister of Education, Premier Zhao Ziyang, and Deng Xiaoping, the leader of the Communist Party.

This time, I adopted new tactics to attack the dangerous opponent—to shoot my enemy with sugar-coated bullets, to kiss the enemy to death. It was the only safe way to deal with the Communist leadership. In each letter I first praised the Party lavishly for its "dedication" to the welfare of the people. In the second part, I complained tactfully to the Beijing leaders about the local officials' failure to care for the suffering of the people—with myself as an example. At the end of each letter, I added plenty of pompous revolutionary slogans to show them what a good revolutionary I was: "I trust the Party with all my heart! Long Live the Great Communist Party of China! Long Live the Revolutionary Spirit!"

In short, I wanted to praise the Party vehemently in order to bend it to my advantage.

Sometimes, in the small hours of the morning when I finished letters like these, I would sarcastically chuckle at their pomposity. Several weeks after I had sent the letters to the leadership in Beijing, Squash Face called. "We have received the letters that you sent to Beijing," he said in a very annoyed voice. "They have been sent back to us. Actually, the letters were unnecessary. We have not forgotten about your case and have been studying it. We will make a decision soon. But since you have asked for it, why don't you come down to the First People's Hospital in Tianjin to have a checkup tomorrow, to see if you still have persistent diarrhea."

There was a pause and then a malicious, forced chuckle. "That'll help us make our decision. By the way, don't write any more letters to Beijing."

The invitation caught me by surprise. I had not had diarrhea for some time prior to that day and if the lab result showed as much, my whole effort to transfer would come to nothing. Even worse, I would be branded a troublemaker and be persecuted politically. But I had to go. I went to Tianjin the next day. It was cold, and the wind was blowing fiercely when I stepped off the bus at the Trash Dump. The temperature had plunged to below zero in the morning, but I hardly felt it as I trudged to the Bald Donkey Inn, the cheapest hotel near the college campus. I was in a panic.

I checked into the small, empty hotel. The room was unheated and through its second floor window I could see the bus station and the few travelers in heavy cotton coats stomping their feet, waiting for the next bus. I threw my bag on the nightstand and dropped down on the bed. The cold sheet felt damp. An hour before my scheduled appointment at the First People's Hospital, despair sent me reeling. I prayed that some miraculous illness would strike me immediately: Please God, save me, make me really *sick now!* If I don't get sick fast, I'll be dead politically anyway. MAKE ME SICK, GOD, PLEASE!

In a desperate attempt, I stripped off my clothes and sat naked by the window. The bitter Siberian wind was howling through the cracks of the dusty windowsill. Within minutes, I started to shiver violently, but I did not move. I sat for as long as I could bear. When I finally set off to the hospital, I felt weak and dizzy, but I also felt a "pleasant" growling in my abdomen. In the hospital, to my relief, I had to hurry to the restroom; and there, watery stool rushed out. The lab report showed that there were a few red blood cells in the stool. Seeing the report, I was relieved. I had managed to save myself for now.

The precious lab report, however, exacted a heavy price from me. I have never had a very strong constitution, and for more than a week after my desperate escapade I suffered from a severe cold and lost ten pounds from a bad diarrhea.

The day after my self-induced diarrhea, I sent the lab report to Squash Face. Sitting behind his huge stack of newspapers and his teacups, he perused the report carefully. Finally, obviously disappointed, he raised his head.

"The lab report," he said, throwing it on the desk, "is inconclusive as far as your disease is concerned. We will have to study it further and report it at the next meeting. For now, you should go back to Tanggu and see if the diarrhea goes away in a little while."

Although the lab report brought no immediate results, the incident provided me a valuable lesson. I realized that I did not have to have diarrhea all the time: I could induce it on demand. Ten days later, just as I was almost fully recovered from the self-inflicted cold and diarrhea, Squash Face called to see if I was still sick and asked for another lab report. The Party Committee wanted to make sure that mine was a chronic disease, he said. They needed the report by Friday. This time, however, I was reluctant to replicate the feat in the hotel. The price was too high. I was still too weak to risk losing another ten pounds. Racking my brain for two days, I still had no idea how to produce diarrhea without risking my life. On Thursday morning, Squash Face called again, asking for the lab report. I could wait no longer. Having no choice, I walked nervously to the hospital that morning. As usual, in the doctor's office, I was told to submit a stool sample to the lab. I went to the restroom, but the stool was solid and dry. I did not know what to do. Obviously, I could not give the sample to the lab—that would lead to disaster. But it was too late to strip off my clothes to produce a cold and real diarrhea even if I wanted to.

What could I do? The only remaining option seemed to be to slip away without submitting the sample and come back another time when I was "prepared."

I turned to leave the restroom. But as I was passing the dirty washbasin on my way out, an epiphany occurred—one of those bolts from the blue that people say strike them like lightning. I went to the rusty faucet and turned, but it was broken and no water came out. So too were the other two faucets in the restroom. I ran outside and hurried along the corridor to find running water. On the third floor, in a restroom marked "Staff," I found a faucet that worked. I casually lingered in the room, washing my hands slowly, until the last person left. Then, I carefully let a few drops of water drip into the wax box that held the stool sample, and with a discarded burnt-out match I found on the floor, stirred the stool to make it look natural. The warm, yellowish pulp looked repulsive and the thought of it was even more sickening—a college teacher and a grown man playing with feces. But I put a quick halt to such thoughts. This was not a time to be overly concerned about my dignity. I threw my head back, and with my eyes averted and my hands trembling with disgust, I stirred the concoction with the defiance that a proud political prisoner musters when facing a firing squad.

I never expected that the feeling of revulsion would turn into irrepressible wicked joy when I looked at the puzzled face of the doctor who read the lab report: "WATERY STOOL, NO BACTERIA OR RED BLOOD CELLS." The disease would baffle many more doctors, to my delight. After discovering a safe, revolutionary stool-making technique, I put it to good use at least once a week and my crusade took a quantum leap forward. Before long and without any pain, I accumulated a stack of lab reports, which provided me with a steady supply of ammunition to press for a transfer as a sick and slowly dying patient. Week after week, though my sick pay was barely enough to cover the postage, I kept sending lab reports and pleading letters to the Party leaders in Tianjin and in Beijing. My vague battle plan had been filled in with some important details, but I would need another epiphany or two to win the war and leave Tanggu.

But no matter how hard the battle was, I had become more determined than ever. To the wall by my bed, I nailed a sheet of paper with the Great Leader's famous quotation: "Harden our hearts, fear not sacrifices, overcome ten thousand obstacles, to achieve the ultimate victory."

It had now become my battle cry against the Communist Party.

## 31 A Stinking Stone from the Outhouse

Shortly after my letter-writing campaign, I opened up another front in my secret war against the Party. I started a weekly visit to each of the heads of the Tanggu campus. I knew that obtaining local consent was crucial. Squash Face had made it clear that the college would never approve my transfer if the local officials staunchly opposed the move.

This battle, I knew from the very beginning, would be the most difficult, as my early visits had shown. But I had one advantage against the Party officials: secret determination and hatred, the intensity of which they could never imagine. I laid out my battle plan carefully. I drew up a schedule of visits and hung it by my bed. Each evening after sunset, I checked the schedule and, like a vampire bat coming out of its cave in search of a meal, slipped out of the dorm to visit the home of one of the officials. I started each week with Chairman Zhang.

As soon as I entered the chairman's apartment, I transformed myself into a dying patient. My eyes went into a daze, my breathing became labored, and my mind began to suffer memory loss. Having set the proper mood, I started my speech. The first five minutes I fired a volley of sugar-coated bullets at the petty bureaucrat. "Chairman Zhang, I don't know how to thank the Communist Party for doing so much for us ordinary people. As the Great Leader said, you are the true servants of the people. You work hard day and night for the welfare of the people. You are always concerned with the illnesses and suffering of the poor. China would not have become such a great country if it were not for the leadership of the Communist Party. The more I think of what I have today, the more I am grateful to the Communist Party."

Practice makes perfect. After several performances, I reached a point of delivering these pat-the-horse's-behind flatteries without blushing, and with such sincerity that I could move a heart of stone. But Chairman Zhang's heart was harder than stone. Although continually bathed in warm, luxurious praises, he had hardened his heart and was resolved to guard the gates of the department. He would let no one out.

I swallowed hard, eyes drooping wearily, and allowed a meaningful pause. Then I began again. It was time for launching the second volley, the outpourings of the frustrated heart of a revolutionary youth. "Chairman Zhang, you know, I long to dedicate my life to the cause of the Communist Party. If only I were not sick. But, you know, I have been sick since I got here. You have seen my lab reports. My diarrhea—"

"Yes, I know about your diarrhea. You have told me. The Party Committee has discussed your situation." Chairman Zhang attempted to cut short my familiar speech. But I was in a trance now and paid no attention to his efforts to stop me.

"My diarrhea is getting worse now. I am very weak, as you can see, and I think—" my voice becoming fainter and barely audible, "I think I am . . . going . . . to die." I allowed another pause. My head sank to my breast as if I were in the process of sinking into oblivion before the thirteen-inch TV.

After a moment's silence, I raised my head slowly as though trying to perform a final act of defiant courage and strength—the last show of fortitude and moral rectitude by a dying hero, a fatally shot cowboy in an old American movie—and turned with an angry gaze at the chairman. It was the gaze of a dying man who was no longer afraid. "Do you really care about people's suffering? Are you a true member of the Communist Party? The Party cares about people's suffering, but you don't seem to care!" Growing louder, my voice rasped with a twinge of hysteria. "What have you done for the people? Living comfortably in your little house, smoking expensive cigarettes and drinking expensive tea, is that what you call caring for the people? Did you really take an oath when you joined the Party? Or did you sneak into the Party for some despicable selfish reasons?"

No one had ever dared to speak to the chairman that way, and I was clearly out of my mind, desperate and scared by my disease. Even so, the chairman could not let such wicked accusations go unanswered. "Of course I am a true member of the Communist Party," he protested loudly. "I joined the revolution when I was sixteen and joined the Party when I was eighteen." He had fallen into the trap I laid for him. I ignored his claims and attacked him personally once again.

"If you are a true communist, if you really followed the teachings of Chairman Mao, you would not have neglected the people's suffering as you have. You told me every week that you were discussing my case with the Party Committee, but you have never intended to solve the problem. You don't care if I die or not, do you? I am going to tell the Central Committee of the Communist Party what you have done, and let everybody else judge whether you are a true communist or not!" Working myself into a rage, I stood up and began shouting at the top of my lungs. Then I bent over and grabbed the back of the armchair as if trying to support my shaking body.

"This is getting out of hand. I told you that you must obey the Party. It is not my decision; it is the committee's decision." The Chairman was angry now, frustrated, unable to answer the accusations. "You are not going anywhere. That is the decision of the Party. Frankly, we could not grant your request. And never will. The Party needs young people like you here." The Chairman's smoldering anger finally burst into flame. That fit perfectly into my plan.

"You are a hypocrite! You pretend to care about people. You only care about your job. I will . . . Oh, Chairman Mao, where are you? Please, help me!" My hands sweeping in the air in wild gestures, my mouth foaming, my eyes blank, I became incoherent, loud, and hysterical, choking on emotion.

The drama had reached its scripted climax. Last was the deus ex machina, bringing deliverance to the deadlocked opponents.

As I had expected, out scurried the Chairman's wife from the kitchen. I needed her to complete my assault on the Party official. "Please," she said, "please . . . please speak quietly. Comrade Fan Shen, I know Chairman Zhang cares about you and if you will, please, sit down. Will both of you please sit down and talk this out quietly and peacefully? Shouting will not solve any problems." She put her hands on his arm while he shook with rage. Encouraging him to sit down, she turned to me and pleaded, "Please sit down. Would you like some tea?"

With the wife's soft voice, sense returned to me. I sat down as asked, and nodded my head. I could use some tea now after all the shouting. When the tea came, I received it with both hands, and with genuine gratitude, addressed the wife: "I don't know how to thank you. I am so sorry that I've disturbed the peace of your house. Please forgive me. It was . . . it was my illness that made me lose my head. I am so terribly sorry." Turning toward Chairman Zhang, I looked at him with appealing, sad eyes and made my voice quiver a little with regret: "Comrade Chairman, I must apologize to you for being so disrespectful. I don't know what I am doing at times. My illness . . . you know. Can you forgive me? I know communists like you are caring people and I know you have been working hard to help me. I should thank you instead of shouting at you. Would you please accept my apology? I know you have a generous heart."

What could the Chairman do? Could he refuse such a generous apology and hold a grudge? Never. Especially not in front of his wife. With an effort, he relaxed the muscles that were distorting his face, and forced himself to produce a contrived smile.

"Don't worry, I have been doing this for sixteen years," he said. He looked at his wife, who nodded encouragingly. "I fully understand your emotions and I accept your apology. I will not hold this against you. In fact, I should apologize a little to you for losing my temper."

"Oh, Chairman, I don't know how to thank you," I said. "You are indeed a generous person, a true communist. I know I can put my trust in you. I know you will help me to solve my little problem." I was leading the drama in a different direction at that point.

The Chairman then appeared uneasy again, as if he were an old catfish trying to remember whether this was the hook that he had bitten before. I knew he was thinking of how to get rid of me as fast as he could. "Yes, yes, I will try to bring your problem up with the Party Committee at our next meeting. The Party will do its best to help. But of course, there are many more urgent problems on our campus and we have to deal with them by priority. You must be a little patient. But when the issue comes up, you can be assured that I will try to help you."

I listened attentively and calmly, seemingly persuaded by the Chairman's promise. He seemed relieved that the unpleasant visit was coming to an end. Seeing my obedient face, he made the mistake that he would regret next week. He added the standard official line for closing a conversation with his constituents: "Let me know if you have any other problems. I am always available."

"Thank you, Chairman, thank you, Mrs. Chairman, for your time. I won't take up your offer to bother you again unless I have new problems. I know how valuable your time is. After working so hard for the department day and night, you deserve some rest. If I have only minor problems, I will just endure them myself and not bother you. Unless . . . thank you, thank you . . . " Mumbling and bowing, I reached out my trembling hands and grasped the Chairman's sweaty hands. After shaking them, I backed out the door with shuffling feet and downcast eyes.

The play was performed five times a week, for a different audience each night. Monday was for Chairman Zhang and his wife; Tuesday, for

Secretary and Mrs. Buddha; Wednesday, for Medicine Jug and his wife; Thursday, for the vice-chairman and his wife; and Friday, for the deputy secretary and his household. As time went on, the visits had evolved into psychological melodramas, full of emotional twists and turns. The setting of the play was invariably the official's living room-cum-dining room, a pleasant mise-en-scène with one or two sofas, several chairs, a small television, a dinner table, and on the wall, a large portrait of the Great Leader wearing an olive-green jacket and a Red Guard armband, smiling and waving encouragingly to the actors. The time of the play: dinnertime. The cast: a young teacher as the tragic protagonist; an official as the villain; and the wife as the knight in shining armor.

The play always started with a long monologue by the young hero, who praised the Communist Party for caring for the people. In act two, the young hero accused the official of not carrying out the Party's mandate and not caring about his illness. The antagonist, the Party official, would attempt to respond with vehement denials in act three. Act four featured the young hero working himself into a rage—appropriate behavior for an impassioned, desperate, wrongfully treated man, a sort of a "dying Bartleby" striking back for once in his life. His raised voice and wild gestures have succeeded in working up his foe and igniting his anger. The shouting brawl ended in act five with the annoyed wife, the white knight, descending from the kitchen upon the combatants. The young protagonist would promptly simmer down, apologize for his angry words, and ask for forgiveness. Before his wife, the official would be obliged to be gracious and would invariably forgive the young man. The curtain went down when, confident that the official's dinner and sleep that night had been ruined, the young man took leave of the fuming official, but not without first extracting a soon-to-be-regretted promise that he could come back if he had any other problems.

I always had other problems, of course. The next week, we would all faithfully play our parts again. My previous training with secret police and other bureaucrats served me well as the star player and the director. I had learned how to appear weak, how to shoot daggers with my angry eyes, how to be on the verge of collapse, how to drop an occasional remorseful tear—all without emotional involvement. Like a skilled puppeteer, I knew how to manipulate my puppets' behavior and emotions with delicate nuances. After weeks of honing my skills, I could tell from certain facial expressions and body postures the exact moment when each of my puppets had reached the desired critical point—the threshold of helpless rage. It was like pumping up a balloon: at a certain point the skin of the balloon makes a squeaky sound when even slightly touched. Given even a little more air it will burst.

In the midst of the endless but futile hospital visits, lab reports, and letters to officials, my evening visits to the petty officials were a small tactical triumph for me. After four months of house calls, it was easy to see the psychological toll that my visits had exacted on the officials and their families. There were quarrels in some of the families, I heard, and swollen eyes revealed numerous nights of troubled sleep. Chairman Zhang's small moustache had started to turn gray. Secretary Buddha had amassed another sizable layer of fat on his stomach and had more trouble getting in and out of his chair. Medicine Jug was visibly thinner (some insolent people even began calling him "Bamboo Stick"), even though he had doubled his intake of the vile brew he drank. For them, I had become a dreaded sight, a proverbial stone in the outhouse—hard and stinking. Without consulting each other, they had reached the same conclusion: the stinking stone must be kicked out at all costs, even if that meant the demoralization of the entire Tanggu campus and a deluge of requests to transfer. But merely hating me with a passion was not enough. They needed an official reason, a strong medical reason, to get rid of me. That I still needed to supply, although I didn't know how yet. But it did not take me long to overcome this last obstacle.

Despite the euphoric effects of my nightly performances, the psychological warfare was not without toll on me as well. It was hard not to be genuinely angry with the stone-hearted bureaucrats. Sometimes my anger at being held as the collateral of their misery and my fear of being trapped for the rest of my life would keep me awake all night. Each time I dragged myself before the officials, knowing full well what the outcome would be, I felt like a frog jumping against a brick wall, a senseless animal throwing myself against a barrier without being able to budge it. They needed an excuse to get rid of me, and I could not give it to them.

In those months, I had to lead a double life, in order to achieve my goal. The minute I stepped out of the dormitory room, I was a tortured invalid, slowly wasting away from diarrhea. Wearing a dirty old brown cotton jacket and walking slowly around the campus, I greeted people with a silent nod and vacant stares. Sometimes I doubted whether I was merely acting. I had lost my appetite and often felt weak; and when I spoke incoherently and wildly in front of the officials, it sometimes felt so natural that I was afraid that I might actually be going mad.

Whether I could endure the isolation and depression and sustain myself physically and mentally would ultimately decide whether I would outlast the officials. They had seen many people before me start a fierce battle only to be worn down by the political machine and resign themselves to a dismal life in Tanggu. Medicine Jug, for example, was a healthy young man when he first came. For two and a half years, he fought a brave battle for transfer before he lost his health and spirits and succumbed to fate. So did the cook, who struggled gallantly for three years before he finally gave up. Compared to the power of the gigantic political machine, human efforts were inconsequential. To combat depression and sickness, to keep my sanity, and to compensate for what I could not do in public, I had to change myself into another person the moment I stepped into my room. In my sanctuary, I tried everything to keep my spirits high. I sang my favorite revolutionary song "Harden Our Hearts," did pushups and sit-ups, listened to music, and read novels.

In those gloomy days, the only comfort of human contact I had came from conversations with Bookworm, my roommate. It took some time to break the ice, but once I gained Bookworm's confidence, I discovered that he was the most eloquent man I had ever met. He could talk for hours, quietly, intelligently, knowledgeably, about any subject. From his dusty, frayed brown jacket and black cap, few could have guessed that he was once a well-known surgeon in the Missionary Hospital in Beijing. He lost his job in 1957 during the Great Leader's campaign "to lure snakes out of their dens," and was sent here to teach.

Bookworm was the only person who knew what I was doing, and I knew that he would keep my secret. We never talked about it. The only time he spoke to me about my battle occurred one day after I came home from a visit, disgusted and discouraged. I collapsed on the bed that night, and did not get out of bed the next morning. Before leaving for his classes, Bookworm walked to my bed and said quietly, "Don't give up." I did not open my eyes and pretended to be sleeping as he silently placed something beside my pillow and left. As soon as he was gone, I picked it up and saw that it was Jack London's "Love of Life." I sat up and read the thin book in one sitting, and the extraordinary tenacity of the man in the story, who did everything he could to stay alive, including killing and eating a hungry wolf, lifted my spirits and renewed my hope to beat the bureaucratic wolves.

The weekly letters, visits to officials, and lab reports continued into the fifth month. There was no progress. I had heard nothing from Squash Face since I last submitted lab reports, and had gotten nowhere with Chairman Zhang and other officials. More than once, in the middle of the night, I wondered whether Medicine Jug was right after all: "One person wants to launch a satellite? That's like a filthy toad lusting after a swan!"

Then one morning Squash Face called. "The Party is still studying your request," he said, "and it has decided that you need to obtain a definitive diagnosis from the Tanggu General Hospital before we can consider the matter further. Get a definitive diagnosis as soon as you can." He hung up before I could protest. I still did not have a complete plan, but now I was forced into a do-or-die situation.

I went to the Tanggu General Hospital the next day and asked the head of internal medicine for an appointment.

"What do you need a definitive diagnosis for?" the head doctor asked, smiling, but showing pitifully brown and reddish gums. All of his teeth were gone, except for three blackened rotten stubs, like three charred skeletons after a forest fire.

Without thinking, I blurted out, "I need it in order to transfer to Tianjin."

The doctor looked up sharply at my face. For a few seconds, he studied me with a fascination as if he were studying a rare deformity. "So, you want to escape from here, eh?" asked the decrepit-looking doctor. His tone quickly changed and his smile faded.

In a split second, I knew I had made a fatal blunder.

"Everybody wants to leave Tanggu," he said coldly. "I want to leave Tanggu, too. I have been here since I graduated from medical school. Nineteen years next month. But we don't do diagnoses for that reason. It's the policy of the hospital and the Party." With a loud smack, he slammed my file shut and passed it to the nearby nurse. Argument would clearly be useless.

I was crushed. I now had *two* massive problems: getting a definitive diagnosis and having a diagnosis that would enable me to escape Tanggu. Without a definitive diagnosis, the Party would have a good reason to deny my request and pay no attention to me in the future. But even with a definitive diagnosis, my condition had to be more serious than watery stools.

Two agonizing weeks went by, and, finding no way to get around the problems, I decided to give the hospital another try. I had little hope, but to avoid being recognized and rejected out of hand, I decided to disguise myself. Before I went the hospital, I put on an old greasy jacket that I borrowed from the cook. The jacket was so old that its original blue color had faded to gray and its dirty condition was repulsive and bound to elicit pity and contempt. I also borrowed a pair of dark-rimmed glasses from Bookworm. In the office of the head doctor, I meekly submitted my request for a definitive diagnosis. It seemed a miracle that the doctor did not recognize me nor remember my previous request.

"What do you need a definitive diagnosis for?" he asked again with the same smile, showing me the same three black and rotting teeth.

I had an answer ready this time. In a sheepish voice, so as not to appear too eager, I said, "I want to transfer to the Dagang District." The Dagang District was notorious, a barren expanse of salty marshes and reeds. Besides a few oil rigs and an infinity of mosquitoes, there was nothing there. The residents of Tanggu often comforted themselves with the thought that at least they were better off than the poor souls in Dagang.

"Why do you want to go to Dagang?" the doctor asked, obviously taken by surprise. His voice implied a different question: "Who the hell wants to go there?"

"My fiancée is there. She works for an oil company. I have to be with her. And you see, I am sick here all the time," I said in the weak voice becoming a pitiful and helpless patient.

The doctor straightened his back, looked at me through squinting eyes, and smiled: "All right, if that's what you want. Tomorrow afternoon at 2:30, two other doctors will join me to give you a definitive diagnosis. Before you come to our meeting, you need to submit a stool sample to the lab first."

The next afternoon, before the 2:30 appointment, I went to the restroom to prepare the stool sample. There, like a smart student taking an exam in his favorite subject, I proudly concocted the desired watery specimen one more time. By that time, I knew the precise amount of water needed for the sample, and I knew how to stir it slowly to perfection. The yellowish pulp was no longer repulsive to me, and preparing it was no longer a source of shame. On the contrary, doing so had become the symbol of hope and deliverance in my war against an impersonal machine: the warm yellow pulp against the cold blank faces of the Party. It had also become a source of joy—the thought of how the yellow stuff would utterly baffle the doctors elated me. I just wished I could see their puzzled faces.

Full of good spirits and the kind of professional pride of a master magician performing his favorite trick before a packed house, I presented the lab report to the three doctors. On examining the latest lab report and the stack of previous reports, the doctors were predictably baffled. I laughed inwardly, though my face was expressionless. The young doctors looked up to the head doctor who, struggling to come up with a possible disease, began to scratch his balding head with a pencil. I tried to keep a straight face. For several minutes, the young doctors and I waited. But, although they did not know it, if they could come up with nothing, I would be able to help them. I had had another epiphany. I knew the last part of my plan. I knew the name of my disease.

I had coined a good name for my disease, a name that would sound like an incurable condition, a name that could be tied to the local water, a name that meant "transfer." But I had to feed it to the doctors slowly and cautiously so that I would not wound their professional pride.

"Last week, I went to a doctor in Beijing," I began hesitantly, lowering both my voice and eyes in humility. The bald-gummed doctor looked up from a book he was consulting. "A well-known doctor from the Missionary Hospital, Dr. Jia, suggested that my condition appeared to be—uh—*neural-allergic intestinal inflammation*. He said it was most likely related to certain chemicals in the water. Of course, I don't understand what he means." Looking up at the head doctor with the utmost respect, and with a voice quivering just slightly to suggest ignorance and respect, I added, "Is it possible that I have this *neural-allergic* something? You must understand what he means."

They all appeared to be enlightened. "Er—that's quite possible," said the head doctor as he nodded knowingly. The young doctors nodded with him. "But of course, we have to eliminate other possibilities first. You can leave the room now and wait in the hall. We will have a discussion of your case and will call you back soon."

Fifteen minutes later, I had a copy of the definitive diagnosis in my hands. I especially liked the look of the hospital's big red official seal on it. It read:

*Definitive Diagnosis*

THE PATIENT SUFFERS FROM
NEURAL-ALLERGIC INTESTINAL
INFLAMMATION, LIKELY
CAUSED BY DRINKING WATER.

*Dr. Pu Yi*, Head Doctor
*Dr. Hu Zongnan*
*Dr. Jian Nanxiun*
Tanggu General Hospital
[SEAL]

I sent a new round of letters with copies of the definitive diagnosis to the college leaders in Tianjin and the Party leaders in Beijing, and I paid a new round of visits to the departmental leaders. I pointed out that the "neural-allergic disease" was incurable with any medicine and that I had no choice but to leave the area.

Ten days after the letters a call came from Squash Face. His greasy voice sounded very upbeat and friendly.

"I have good news for you. Don't write letters to Beijing or to us any more. The Party Committee of the College has intensely studied your case. We have decided to transfer you to the main campus in Tianjin. You should report here next week. But! *Don't* talk to anyone in Tanggu—you know what I mean. You know your case was a particularly hard one and there was a lot of opposition in Tanggu to your move."

Hearing the news, I knew I should rejoice; but I was too exhausted and too numb to even smile. I could hardly believe it was over. For six long months, I had been telling lies, pretending to be sick, manipulating people, living a double life, and concocting pulpy stool specimens—all for this day. But when the end finally came, I found I could not laugh the hearty laugh that I had dreamed of so many nights.

The news of my transfer to Tianjin, however, exploded on the campus instantly like a small atomic bomb and shook every corner. To many at the Tanggu campus, it was an astonishing feat, an incredibly swift and complete victory. Everybody said I "had launched a satellite." I was the first person to leave Tanggu in twelve years.

"Congratulations!" said Medicine Jug when he burst into my dormitory room the next morning. He smiled broadly with his rotten teeth, grabbed my hand, and shook it feverishly. His stooped back seemed to have straightened up a little. "You have rocked the entire department and shattered morale here. Now everybody's going to send in his request to transfer. You know, I always knew that you were different, that you would do something big. I have tried to help you as best as I could. You cannot imagine how stubborn all the other people on the committee were about your case. When you are at the main campus in Tianjin, would you put in a word for me?" He wanted me to thank him and to tell him the secret of transfer. So did all the other departmental heads, including Chairman Zhang and Secretary Buddha, who became extremely humble and flattering in my presence. I was the hero of the department.

"Would you come to my house and have dinner with us tonight?" Chairman Zhang asked. "My wife is rather fond of you and she insists that I take you home tonight, or I'll be in big trouble. Would you please come? She's making Kung Pao chicken tonight. She bought a young hen today." His swarthy face looked so helpless and human that I could not bring myself to say no.

"We will miss you so much," said Secretary Buddha warmly as I came in for the transfer papers. "You are the most promising young teacher we've had for a long time. But the department will honor the Party's directive. The Party needs you more at the main campus in Tianjin and so we will have to give you up. I feel honored to have known you. By the way, will you have time to have lunch at my home tomorrow? My wife is a very good cook and she was saying that it was a shame that you had not had a chance to try her cooking." Again, compassion for fellow sufferers overwhelmed me and I accepted the invitation. I was not someone who liked to hold a grudge and I was finding it hard to continue to despise these officials. They were as trapped and desperate as I had been.

The only person on campus who said nothing and who seemed not to have heard the news was my roommate, Bookworm. As I was busy packing, Bookworm spent the entire day in the library, coming back only late at night. The next day, the day of my departure, Bookworm disappeared early in the morning before I got up, and did not come back to say goodbye. I was very disappointed but I understood that my departure must have hurt him very much.

To me, the victory that shocked everybody seemed rather senseless. I knew why I felt no joy, because it was a victory over a battle that should not have been fought. I had wasted more than six months of my life just to get to where I had started. That morning, I just wanted to slip away quietly and quickly. When the morning train chugged out of Tanggu, I felt that my mind was surrounded by a vast fog, much like the veiled, desolate cornfields outside the train's windows.

I bent down and slipped my hand into the satchel under the seat, looking for a book to read. What I pulled out was a thin volume with a black leather cover. The book was not in my bag when I packed it in the morning. It was an old book, with yellow and brittle pages, and a title printed in gilt characters so faint that they were no longer legible. Turning to the inside cover, I saw the familiar words: "Love of Life" by Jack London. I knew who gave me the valuable parting gift.

## 33 "I'm the Only One Who Reads Your Letters"

If I was surprised that I single-handedly "launched a satellite" in Tang-gu, I was even more surprised when I bumped into Li Ling in the National Art Gallery in Beijing, just a month after my transfer to the main campus. I had not seen her since we left the East Wind Aircraft Factory nearly five years earlier, and we had lost touch after her marriage.

She had not changed much. She still had her unique way of dressing elegantly but not extravagantly. She wore an unusual dark green short-sleeved blouse and a cream-colored skirt. She was examining a modern painting and I called her name.

"Fan Shen?" she asked, turning and drawing closer. Her eyebrows arched a bit, but her voice was calm and even. She did not seem surprised. "You have changed so much that I would not have recognized you on the street. With your glasses, you seem a much more mature person now, not like the little boy who once sat in my dormitory looking at my stamps." I blushed a little at the mention of that memorable moment.

"You look taller and thinner now. A bit too thin. Were you sick?" she asked.

"Yes, but I am fine now," I answered. "It's a long and interesting story. I will tell you about it someday. But how have you been? You haven't changed a bit."

"Nonsense. I am much older now," she said, smiling. "But a woman has many tricks to hide her age. And I am not going to tell you about them."

I felt my face grow hot. Changing the subject, I asked, "Do you come here often? I bet this is a place you frequent. I remember how much you loved art at the factory."

"Yes, I spend a lot of time here, almost every weekend, just by myself," she said matter-of-factly, which surprised me a little.

"I heard you were married," I added. "How is your husband? Is he always busy on weekends?"

There was an awkward pause, which made me regret the question.

"He has other interests," was her terse reply. She sat down on a bench by a bronze bust of the Great Leader. All of a sudden, she looked tired. I sat down by her.

"I have always wanted to thank you for all the books that you lent me during those years," I changed the subject again, not wanting to embarrass her. "They helped me a lot during those crucial, difficult times. Remember the book by the German composer Schumann that you lent me? I still carry quotations from the book everywhere I go."

It took her a moment to remember the book. She had read so many books; it was natural that she had to search her memory for a few seconds to remember it. But when it came to her favorite books, she always had a perfect memory.

"Are you still reading Nietzsche? Are you still studying German?" I knew her twin passions and how mention of them would always relax her and excite her.

"Yes, I still read Nietzsche," her face brightened up. "More than ever these days. It is difficult to be a woman, especially in China. And, ironically, Nietzsche gives me the strength to be a real woman."

I understood what she meant by "ironically." Nietzsche seemed to have contempt for women in general.

"Men just do not understand what a woman has to go through in life," Li Ling started to talk in the familiar tone of a philosopher. "Most women don't understand themselves, either. That's why Nietzsche belittled women."

As often happened, her words soon started to fly past me, uncaught. When she spoke, I was frequently more fascinated by her facial expressions than by her words. When intellectually engaged, she spoke slowly, testing each word before setting it free. In the Gallery that day, she was engaged. Her white face started to flush, and her eyebrows arched upward one at a time. I could not take my eyes off her, and absorbed her image and her tone more than her words. I had not read much Nietzsche since leaving the aircraft factory—and even then, I read just enough to be able to converse with Li Ling. That was why I felt inadequate once again in the Gallery, just as I had many times before.

"I think Chinese women deserve to be treated this way, myself included." Li Ling's words floated by. I wondered what she meant when she said that men did not understand women, and what exactly she thought it meant to be a woman. But I did not ask. She seemed so certain about these things, as if they were obvious and common knowledge. It was a habit that sometimes irritated me, a habit of briefly mentioning thoughts that she had been contemplating for a long time as though they were merely reminders to her audience.

"Does your husband understand you?" I asked.

"He is a man," she answered.

Conversations with Li Ling were always like this, I reflected. Enchanting, frustrating, and tiring. She had a way of meaning more than what she said. She liked to speak in riddles, to have people guess, perhaps as a way to challenge them to argue. But few people dared to.

Since I had to get back to Tianjin that afternoon, we parted at the museum gate with too many things still to talk about. It was strange that we picked up our conversation so naturally after five years. And since I had read many books and was more her equal now, our conversation became even more interesting.

After our meeting at the Art Gallery, we started to write each other. The letters became frequent. Li Ling wrote long and complex letters. As in our conversations, we wrote mainly about serious subjects: art, science, history, and literature. I remember letters on the Big Bang theory, plate tectonics, game theory that had gained currency in both politics and computer science, and Stendhal, Hegel, and Goethe. My letters were generally shorter than Li Ling's, as I was mostly the listener and questioner, the same role I had played during the factory years. Li Ling was mostly the speaker. Once, in answering a simple question on *yijing*, a notion in Chinese literary criticism, she wrote two long letters, one sixty-nine pages and one eighty-one pages. They were not so much letters as brilliant booklets. I was dazzled by her knowledge of ancient Chinese authors. Previously, I had thought that she much preferred Western authors to those of her native country.

Once a month, whenever I could spare the time and money, I would go back to Beijing and meet Li Ling and spend an afternoon talking. We usually met at a museum—the Natural History Museum, the National Museum of History, or the Museum of Chinese Military History. As in the aircraft factory, our meetings were always platonic; we never hugged or kissed or touched, except for a brief handshake when we greeted each other.

Only once did circumstance press us closer. On New Year's Eve 1983, when all the museums were closed for the holiday, we met in a subway station near Tiananmen Square. For two hours, we stood leaning against a marble pillar and talked. We watched trains come and go and looked at people jammed against the windows in the train. We watched but did not comment. Both of us concentrated only on each other and our conversation. She was wearing a large, fluffy coat and a maroon scarf, and her soft pretty features were half-buried in the high collar and scarf. It was warm underground, and her white face gradually turned crimson.

It was already dark when we finally walked up the stairs to leave. I went with her to the bus station. It was rush hour, and the station was packed with people carrying shopping bags filled with fresh meat, live chickens, fruits, and vegetables, anxious to get home and prepare their New Year's Eve dinner. The large, extended buses came every ten minutes, but they were almost full when they arrived and could take only a few people. The crowd was angry and impatient. Some young people in the back pushed hard when a bus came and arguments broke out. I hardly noticed. Pressed hard against each other, I could feel my body touching Li Ling's, and through the thick winter coat, I seemed to be able to feel her soft warm body. We remained silent and still. Li Ling did not like to talk in crowds. Her beauty always drew stares, and speaking, I think she figured, would only make the situation worse.

When Li Ling was finally about to board the bus, she turned to me and said quietly: "Next time you write me, you don't have to say 'give my regards to your husband.' I'm the only one who reads your letters."

It was very odd for her to say this. I guessed that there must be something wrong with her marriage, but I did not ask.

## 34 The Campaign for a Passport

After winning the transfer battle and settling down in Tianjin as a teacher, I began to transform myself into a new person. There was no need to pretend to be an invalid any more. To regain my health, I threw myself into a rigorous exercise program: running four miles every morning, lifting weights, and playing volleyball with a varsity team. In a few months, I gained back the lost weight and my strength. During the fall semester, I taught freshman courses with great enthusiasm and conscientiousness. I loved teaching and tried a number of innovative techniques. But, as usual, I hated the political seminars that the faculty had to endure one afternoon a week.

Despite the joy I got from teaching and my letters from Li Ling, I did not lose sight of my larger goal. It had been a year and half since my graduation from college and soon I would be eligible to apply to study abroad. As the semester ended, I decided that it was time to start a new campaign, to apply again for a passport. I had kept in contact with the American university, and the graduate chairperson had informed me that they would grant me a new scholarship next year.

I asked Squash Face about the process of obtaining a passport and found out that it was just as difficult as it had been in Lanzhou University. Here, it required at least three approvals—one from the college, one from the Industrial Ministry in Beijing, and one from the Bureau of Public Safety in Tianjin—and I knew each one would be a formidable obstacle.

The Monday after I handed in final grades, I began my campaign. At the college's office of Internal Security I handed in my application to obtain an approval. Even before I went to see Director Zhou, I had heard from my colleagues that the security director was the most dreaded bureaucrat on campus. A retired commissar of the People's Liberation Army, Director Zhou wore an unusually large, gold-plated pin of Chairman Mao prominently above his breast pocket and was known as Director Pinhead; he was the only one at the college who still wore the emblem of the Cultural Revolution.

My interview with him went badly from the start. As I sat in a wooden chair facing the dreaded director, he slowly flipped through my file, and I sensed trouble every time the muscles of his face twitched, reminding me of a horse's behind stung by a horsefly. I knew what sorts of things in my personnel file would set off alarms in the Director's mind: my father was a commanding officer in the army; I was arrested once in connection with a convicted and executed anti-revolutionary; and I had suspicious contacts with an American teacher while in college and had been investigated by the secret police. On top of all this, I wanted to go to the United States, the bastion of capitalism. Even before he reached the last page, I knew from his grim face what conclusion he had reached.

"What can a young man hope to learn in America?" he asked but did not wait for me to answer. "Certainly not revolutionary ideas. Young people all want to go there for money. They all say that they will come back to help build the communist future, but who are they kidding?"

He raised his eyes and scrutinized me for a few seconds before speaking again. "Frankly, I see serious problems in your application and I will have to conduct a thorough investigation first before I make my decision."

"Thorough . . . investigation?" I asked. "How thorough?"

"It may take a few months," he said.

I knew what he was doing. My application was for the fall semester, which was nine months away. If he sat on the file for a few months, my application would be as good as dead. Getting a passport from the Bureau of Public Safety alone, they say, would take at least six months.

"But the investigation is not the most important thing," he said.

"Not the most important thing?" I was surprised. Was there something worse waiting for me?

His twitching face confirmed my suspicion. "We need to talk first about the Party's policy of sending young people abroad. How will you serve the Party?"

From his tone I knew a long lecture was coming.

"The Party, as the Great Leader said many times, needs a lot of intellectuals and experts. But we need *Red* intellectuals and experts, not *White* intellectuals and experts."

"As a young intellectual," Director Pinhead continued, "you must work hard first to make sure that you have acquired a pure Red heart before you spend time on other studies. I saw that you once applied to join the Party. In fact, I have eleven applications in your file that you wrote when you worked at the aircraft factory. They were good applications. That's the sort of thing a young man like you should be thinking of doing now, instead of going to America. As an experienced old revolutionary, I can tell you that there are a lot of temptations in America, bad temptations, bad elements that will corrupt you if you do not have a solid Red heart. You don't want to be corrupted, do you?"

I blinked, shook my head, and smiled blankly. I knew I had met another Mr. Breakwind.

Director Pinhead had a lot of time and never tired of educating a young man like me. During the next few weeks, whenever I went to Pinhead's office to inquire about my application, he would give me a tedious lecture. At the conclusion of each lecture he would tell me that my application was still being studied and investigated. It was already March. Despite all the torturous lectures, I continued to visit Pinhead and methodically and doggedly pursue his approval. It was exactly the same sort of thing that I had done with Chairman Zhang, Secretary Buddha, and Medicine Jug in pursuing a transfer from Tanggu. Here, though, antagonizing officials was out of the question and medical tricks would get me nowhere.

Just as I thought I could take no more of Pinhead's verbal torture, my friend Young Einstein called and told me that his passport application had just been approved. It was just the kind of success story that would renew my hope.

"Don't give up, my friend," he said in his usual upbeat manner after hearing my depressing tale of Pinhead's lectures. "Remember, the coldest and the darkest moment of the day is just before sunrise. I'll tell you how I got my passport the next time I see you. You'll be shocked to know how cunning I have become. Fight them. Don't have mercy on those Party bastards. They are not human beings." It was always somewhat frightening to listen to Young Einstein. He was too blunt and too bold, too ready to speak dangerous "blasphemy." I wanted to tell him how my friend Fountain Pen died because of his loose mouth, but I was afraid that the phone might be tapped. So I made an excuse and cut the call short.

But his phone call rekindled my burning desire to succeed. Doggedly, I continued my visits with Pinhead. My efforts must have moved Lady Luck—or at least Daughter Luck—who intervened on my behalf a few weeks later.

One afternoon, as I was lying in bed recuperating from one of Pinhead's longer lectures, Squash Face paid an unexpected visit to my dormitory room. Grinning from ear to ear, he greeted me with the sort of respect and warmth that immediately alarmed me.

"The Pink Luck of Lotus! The Pink Luck of Lotus!" Squash Face said. "Guess what? You have become the luckiest person on campus!"

"Only if I'm the only person on campus," I said sullenly, slowly rolling over to sit up. I thought Squash Face must have been bored this afternoon and decided to drop in to torture me. "Pink Luck of Lotus" means luck in sexual encounters.

"Believe it or not, the Pink Luck of Lotus has fallen on your head. The daughter of President Jiang told her father that she has a crush on you! Who could have thought that! President Jiang has asked me to be the official go-between."

I rolled to my feet, shocked. The girl was well known throughout college. Dark and fat, Lulu very much took after her father. I had seen her once or twice on campus, rushing about like the wind in her brown army boots—she had just been discharged from the army after serving five years. Despite her appearance, people said that she had a very sweet temperament and was a good cook. Her father was also the president of the college and owned a spacious four-bedroom suite, so conventional wisdom—Chinese conventional wisdom—had it that she was a good catch. "Of course you need to consider this proposal very carefully," I heard Squash Face say. "Don't refuse an offer from President Jiang casually. Lots of people dream of having such an opportunity. Besides, as far as your political future is concerned . . ." He left the sentence unfinished, quite sure that we both knew what he meant.

To Squash Face's surprise, I readily consented to meet Lulu. A plan had instantly occurred to me.

My first date with Lulu was a dinner at President Jiang's home. The meal was good. After dinner, President Jiang excused himself and went to his office to make phone calls. His wife served us tea and fruits, and left to do the dishes. My conversation with Lulu went very well. I found her to be well read, sincere, and honest. I told her about my plans to study in the U.S., and Lulu was delighted with the idea. She said that she would like to study in America, too.

The second date took place the next Sunday in the People's Park. I was surprised by how much we thought alike. We both loathed the phony political study sessions, and we both longed to have more freedom. Although we did not mention it, I sensed that Lulu also shared my fear, a deep-seated fear that found its voice only in my dreams. Perhaps because she had been in the army, Lulu was unusually straightforward, even blunt.

"I hate being the president's daughter," she said, sucking a popsicle. "I hate the phoniness of those suitors who visit me because they want access to my father's power. But who can blame them? We all use whatever power is available to get what we want, don't we? I am not above playing that game either. I know you are applying to study in the U.S. and you need help. Pinhead will sit on your application until it dies. But I am thinking of studying in the U.S. and I need help, too. I don't know how to apply and my English is not good. That's why I asked to meet you. I'm sorry that I had to use a go-between, but I can't stand this country anymore and I want to get away so much. Would you help me so that both of us can go to America?" She extended her hand.

I took her hand and sealed the pact with Lulu. It turned out we had the same plan. I would help her with application letters and tutor her in English, and she would have her father influence Pinhead to help me get security clearance. We would pretend to be boyfriend and girlfriend for the time being.

"Let's have a toast, comrade-in-arms," Lulu said, raising a bottle of orange soda.

"May we both succeed," I said as I solemnly touched my bottle to hers.

A few days later, Squash Face told me that President Jiang had said that the dates had gone satisfactorily and he and his family approved of the relationship going forward. "Congratulations," said Squash Face, smirking and squinting. "I never imagined that you were such a fortunate and charming person. First getting out of Tanggu, and now getting hold of President Jiang's golden apple. By the way, I have sent a word on behalf of President Jiang to Director Zhou about your application. It will be processed soon."

By the end of the week, Pinhead had stamped the office's seal on my application. I had no doubt that he did so with reluctance, but President Jiang had made him an offer he could not refuse. Bypassing two dozen people with more seniority, the president offered him a three-bedroom apartment in a new residential building, a reward for "his exceptional service to the college."

I took a train to Beijing the same day to obtain the second approval, that of the Industrial Ministry. No time was to be lost. I had already written to all my friends in Beijing, asking for any connections to the Ministry. Strangely enough, of all my friends, the one who helped me the most was Old Brother, my onetime fellow prison inmate. I had run into him a year before at a farmer's market in Beijing; he had just been released after serving four years for manslaughter and was running a watermelon stand on Boxer Street. Old Brother had many useful street friends in the city, so I went directly from the train station to Old Brother's watermelon stand for help.

"Don't worry," Old Brother said, handing me a big slice of watermelon. "I know a friend at the electricity bureau who knows people at the Ministry."

At ten o'clock the next day, I met Lao Fu, the friend Old Brother found for me, at the first floor entrance of the Ministry.

"Your problem is nothing," Lao Fu said. "I know someone who works in the deputy minister's office. He will do this favor for you, but you'd better do something to thank him." He put out his hand, with all five fingers stretched toward me. I nodded. Five cartons of good cigarettes was not an unreasonable price.

At the Sea Dragon restaurant that evening, I handed Lao Fu seven cartons of Great Chinas; the two extra cartons were for Lao Fu himself.

"It was a piece of cake," he said, stashing the cigarettes into his brown canvas bag. From his breast pocket he carefully took out a piece of paper and passed it to me. It was the official letter of approval, complete with a big red seal. "You know how Shrimp got the seal for you? He walked into the office when the secretary was out to lunch. He knew the key was in the drawer, so he helped himself to it, and stamped your application himself. You are very lucky. Otherwise, you would have had to pay the secretary as well."

Back in Tianjin, I handed in my application, along with all the letters of approval, to the office of Passport Control at the Municipal Bureau of Public Safety. It was the third and last approval I needed for my passport.

"You can go home and wait now," said the official behind the glass window without raising his eyes. "From what I see in your personnel file, to be honest, you may have a long wait. In the last few months, the relationship between China and the United States has deteriorated, as you know. The approval process may take six to twelve months. We will inform your college if you are approved."

In the small waiting room, a young man in a fashionable brown leather jacket confirmed what the official had said. "My application was handed in eight months ago and has not yet been approved," he said. "Yours could be an even longer wait." It was July already and I knew that if I were delayed another year, I would lose my scholarship. I could not sit and wait, I decided. I had no choice but to declare a second war on the Party's bureaucrats.

Against the bureaucrats in Passport Control I immediately launched a tenacious campaign. I liked the military analogy. My battle involved many of the elements of actual warfare: determination, courage, risk, strategy, and weapons. For the assault, I employed all the conventional Chinese "weapons" for such a battle: hand grenades (bottles of liquor), twenty-gauge shotguns (cigarettes), bangalore torpedoes (smoked sausages), and time bombs (smoked chicken), all very effective in this kind of close-range, hand-to-hand combat. Of course, the specific ordnance differed for each encounter, but with a little reconnaissance, what was needed could be easily ascertained. Before I moved in on the enemy, I always found out what brand of cigarettes or liquor the target liked, or in the case of someone who did not smoke or drink, what kind of meat he liked. Occasionally, I encountered "incorruptible" officials, who had a reputation for not accepting gifts. These were dangerous hidden strongholds that had to be captured in devious ways. In such cases, I would target best friends or superiors first. Few people will refuse a favor requested by a best friend or superior, no matter how incorruptible they might otherwise be. As an experienced general and tactician, I planned each of my moves carefully. I did not want to obliterate the enemy, but only to bend it to my will.

As before, the first step was to mobilize my network of friends in order to find connections that would lead to the official in charge of Passport Control, an Officer Ke. The chain of connecting links began with Lulu, who introduced me to a friend of her mother's, Dr. Mu of the Third People's Hospital downtown. This was an important connection. In the game of networking in China, two kinds of people are most useful, as characterized by their instruments: a stethoscope (a doctor) and a steering wheel (a professional driver). They were the ganglia that connected the nerves in the social network. Dr. Mu agreed to help.

Among Dr. Mu's patients who owed him favors was Ms. Zhu, the personal assistant to the deputy mayor of Tianjin. Dr. Mu had written sick leave slips for her in the past whenever she wanted some vacation time. Armed with gifts and a generous introduction from Dr. Mu, I visited Ms. Zhu in her office. "No problem," Ms. Zhu said, smiling amiably after reading Dr. Mu's letter. "Dr. Mu's friend is my friend." She sat down at her desk and quickly flipped through a big notebook filled with names and phone numbers. Then she picked up the phone and dialed a friend at the mayor's office.

The friend, Ms. Ji, owed a big favor to Ms. Zhu. Ms. Ji knew a Captain Cai who had just been promoted to the position of chief of traffic control.

Several dinners later, I got acquainted with Captain Cai. The final connection was soon made: Captain Cai knew Officer Ke at Passport Control; in fact, he had recently taken care of a traffic ticket for one of Officer Ke's brothers. Captain Cai agreed to speak to Officer Ke to expedite my application. All this networking was expensive but I had no regrets. After my last dinner with Captain Cai, I found that I had three yuan and twenty cents left in my pocket. I had exhausted all my savings.

Two weeks later, at the end of September, Pinhead told me to report to the office of Passport Control at once. There, a smiling Officer Ke greeted me in the reception room. "Why didn't you tell me earlier that you were a good friend of Captain Cai?" he rebuked me amiably. "It would have been much easier if I had known. Here is your passport. You got really lucky. We have just been ordered to suspend the processing of applications to America."

That evening, I received another piece of good news: Lulu, with my help, had been accepted at an American university and granted a fellowship. She had just started working on her application for a passport. With her father's connections, she did not expect much trouble.

At that point, all I needed was the visa from the U.S. Consulate, or so I thought.

## 35 "Savor It"

I had seen very little of Li Ling in the past few months, having been busy pursuing connections in order to obtain my passport. When I finally saw her in October, after I received the passport, I was shocked to see how pale and thin she was. She was practically a skeleton, wearing a loose-fitting dress.

"I have just come back from death," she said calmly. "Don't be so shocked. I am OK now. There is one good thing about losing a lot of weight. Your hair grows a lot faster. I have always wanted to have longer hair, and now I have it. See," she said, and turned around. Her black hair now reached her waist.

In the quiet hall of the Military Museum, we sat on a leather bench facing an old cannon. I listened quietly as Li Ling talked in a flat tone about her latest near-death experience and her troubled marriage.

"I have never wanted to tell you about the troubles in my marriage, because I am ashamed of them. I even have trouble talking to my mother about them. I did not want to admit that I made a mistake. But since you want to know what I have been through in the last few months, I have to start with my marriage. You know that we got married hastily, right before we separated to go to different colleges.

"The marriage was troubled from the start. One issue was children. Long before I got married, I decided that I would never have a child. My family and I have suffered so much that I couldn't bear the thought of bringing another life into this miserable world. But my husband was the only son in his family and he was determined to have a child bearing his family name. After the marriage, he tried to force me to get pregnant. He forbade me to use birth control devices or pills, and frequently searched my belongings to see whether I had hidden anything. Each time he found birth control pills in my various hiding places—under the mattress, in the cracks in the floor, even among my underwear—he would throw them away and raise hell with me.

"In the last four years, despite my efforts to hide the pills and take them whenever I could, I got pregnant three times. The first two were normal pregnancies and I ended them with abortions. My husband was mad about it, but I did it anyway. When I had my third pregnancy, he vowed to watch me every minute. He forbade me to go to a clinic. But the third pregnancy was an abnormal one, which was not discovered until the growing fetus broke an artery in my fallopian tube. One morning in May, just as I was stepping out the door, I collapsed on the stairs. Fortunately, my neighbor, a taxi driver, found me and brought me to the emergency room. By the time I got to the hospital, I had lost so much blood that the doctor said that I would have died if I had come in half an hour later. The day after emergency surgery, I was nearly killed again by a careless nurse. She was supposed to insert a tube into my bladder to drain the urine. But she did not insert the tube far enough, and by evening I was so sick and bloated that I nearly passed out. My husband, meanwhile, refused to call a nurse. He thought I was just complaining for no reason. At midnight, a second nurse noticed that something was wrong with my pulse and that I was semiconscious, and she called in the doctor. They reinserted the tube, which saved my life."

She took a deep breath, as if trying to decide whether to continue her story. I waited patiently.

"But the troubled pregnancy was only the beginning of the end of the marriage. A month after my discharge from the hospital, I got an anonymous call at work, urging me to go home early. I did and discovered my husband in bed with another woman. I never found out who placed the call, but it did not matter.

"I had always tried to maintain our marriage, even through all the arguments that I had with my husband, because I was taught to honor marriage no matter what. But adultery was the last straw, and I finally filed for divorce and moved back to my mother's home. I am still feeling ashamed that I failed to save the marriage. I felt it was my fault. But I am glad that I can spend as much time as I want on my books, my writing, and my painting now. My first short story has just been published. It is about my experience in Shaanxi as a Beijing Kid."

She spoke without emotion, her beautiful face completely calm. But I could sense great emotion in her heart, and I was shocked by her story. I never imagined that a strong woman like her could be so weak in her marriage.

I had just one question, a question I had wanted to ask her years ago. "Why did you marry your husband in the first place?"

"Certainly not for his looks," Li Ling replied tiredly. "I don't care much about the appearance of a man, as you already know. My husband was not good-looking by any means. I married him out of a sense of obligation: his parents and my parents were good friends. He was my classmate throughout my high-school years and he was my most devoted admirer. During the Cultural Revolution, after my father died, he was the only one who dared to speak to me; and in my desperate loneliness, his love was the only comfort I had. In 1968, we were both sent to the same village in the countryside that you were. Because of all this, when we were about to go to college and he asked me to marry him, I felt that I had an obligation to do so, even though I did not love him. I was too traditional and weak. I did not want to disappoint my mother and his parents, who naturally expected us to get married. I felt that I could belong to only one man, the man my mother had chosen for me. The marriage turned out to be a total disaster from the start. He had little interest in books and arts, and he drank and smoked excessively. When he was drunk, he would sometimes abuse me verbally. That is why I spent so much time in museums, the only places that I could find peace and comfort. It took me many years and nearly cost me my life to finally muster the courage to break the cycle of pain. But I am glad it is over now."

At the subway station in front of the museum later that afternoon, we parted as friends, just as always, but I had the feeling that there was something more that she wanted to tell me. For a moment, I wondered whether I loved her, or could love her. But I dismissed the idea quickly, as I had during the factory years. She was too superior and too beautiful for me.

In the next few weeks, we saw each other more frequently as I worked to obtain my visa from the U.S. Consulate in Beijing. When I was not in Beijing, we wrote each other frequently.

On the first Monday of November, I received a letter from her. Judging from its thickness, I thought she must have hit upon another intellectual subject she felt passionate about. I let the letter lie on my bed and waited till evening, when I would have more time to read and ponder her lengthy discourse on some weighty matters. And weighty matters indeed! But not what I had expected. There was a copy of her short story and with it was a short letter.

The letter read:

I have just finalized my divorce. I know you are going abroad in a month or two and therefore whatever I say will not change anything important between us. But I have to say it before you go, because I have kept it inside for many years and cannot do so any longer. I want you to know that I LOVE YOU! I have loved you for the past twelve years. I did not tell you this before because I was not sure if you would be interested in a woman who was seven years older than you. But I loved you all the same. I loved and respected your ability and tenacity, the real strengths of a man.

I have started a new life for myself too. I am applying to a graduate program at Beijing University to study microeconomics.

I do not expect you to say anything to what I have just said, other than to know my true feelings for you.

Strangely, something in Li Ling's letter had thrown a switch in my mind, connecting her heart to mine. And it surprised me that my feelings for Li Ling, suppressed for so many years, emerged so strongly after I read her letter. There was nothing else I could do. I took the 9:47 train to Beijing that evening and proposed to her.

We got married the next week. Our wedding was a simple one: registration at the City Hall and a modest dinner at a small restaurant near Li Ling's home. My parents, as expected, were opposed to the marriage and did not attend the wedding dinner. Li Ling, my mother said, was a nice girl, but she was not from a revolutionary family and would be political trouble for the entire family. My father refused to allow Li Ling to visit their home, and my mother cried and begged me to reconsider. It felt like I was leaving a funeral when I left my parents' home.

At the office of registration, Old Brother was the witness and best man. At the dinner, the restaurant owner, a buddy of Old Brother, presented us with a bottle of wine, and Old Brother practically drank the whole thing. "The day you have good wine is the day you must get drunk," he said each time he filled his glass.

We did not exchange rings at the wedding: neither of us could afford it. We decided to exchange books instead. After dinner, I opened the gift from Li Ling. It was a collection of short stories about the Beijing Kids in Shaanbei. Her story was the second in the collection. My gift was wrapped in red paper. Li Ling opened it carefully.

"Ah! This was my father's book!" she cried. She looked at it for a long time; then a stream of tears dropped on the frayed cover of the book. "I remember I used to sit on his lap and look at this book. He would be so happy to know that it came back to me." It was an illustrated history of Western art, the book with pictures of naked women that I had taken from her house in the early days of the Cultural Revolution. "How did you get the book?"

"I was one of the Red Guards who robbed your family at the beginning of the Cultural Revolution." My words came out laboriously. "I took the book from your father's library. I am so sorry for what I did."

"Shhhh," she put out her hand and pressed her fingers to my lips. "It is all past. I am only sorry that my father did not live to see this day. He was such a learned man. Did you know that he killed himself after the raid?"

"Uh-uh," I lied. I did not have the heart to tell her how her father actually died.

We took a room in Li Ling's mother's two-bedroom apartment. On our wedding night, after we closed the door of our small bedroom, I told Li Ling that I was a virgin and did not know how to make love.

"Don't you worry," she said, dimming the lamp by the bed. The faint light looked like a candle, making the room a cozy Arabian cave. The new quilt and comforters that her mother had made for us took on an inviting reddish hue. "I will teach you. I will make you very happy."

She was true to her words. Never in my life had I been so happy. She was a great lover—slow, careful, and sensual. "Savor it," she whispered, as her hand brushed and touched my body.

The next morning, Li Ling whispered dreamily into my ear: "This is the love that I have been dreaming of all my life. When I was in high school, I once sneaked into my father's library and found a forbidden book, an Indian book called *Kama Sutra* by Vatsyayana." Her memory of long foreign names always amazed me. "The book was two thousand years old, and was about techniques of making love. According to the book, a man's life has three priorities: *Dhama*, which is ambition or career; *Atma*, health; and *Kama*, sexual pleasure. Without Kama, a woman's sensual love, says the book, a man will not be able to achieve complete Dhama or Atma. And only when someone has acquired all three is he able to reach supreme happiness, *Altha*. I think that makes a lot of sense."

As we lay in ecstasy, a sense of regret and guilt crept over me. I wanted to say how wonderful it would have been if we had had the courage to confess to each other earlier. We would have been married ten years ago, in the Aircraft Factory. But what was the use of talking about would-have-beens? I lay still, feeling her warm body, and listened happily to the quiet noises her mother made as she moved about the kitchen preparing lunch.

## *36* **Don't Laugh Yet!**

In late November of 1984 I received my visa from the American Consulate. But I felt no sense of relief. There was no celebration, no looking back, no wild elation. Any such reaction would be bad luck. China was a highly unpredictable country: too many people celebrated prematurely, only to be crushed by political winds that shifted at the last minute. Besides, the Party had just erected a new hurdle for me to jump over; the previous month it had instituted a new policy: after the approval of a visa, a passport holder had to go back to the security bureau to obtain an exit permit.

Even with the passport and visa in my pocket, my heart was heavier than ever. The new regulation had caught many people by surprise. People who had obtained all the permissions, the passport, and the visa, suddenly found that the government had been toying with them. Many people had their passports canceled when they applied for the exit permit, often for completely inexplicable reasons.

This happened to Young Einstein shortly before I received my visa, so I was forewarned. I had invited him to my place for dinner, to celebrate his impending departure for America. Li Ling made "Squirrel Fish," fried carp with sugar syrup, and I opened a bottle of sorghum liquor, a wedding gift from Smoking Devil. After several glasses, Young Einstein told us the story of his adventures and how he spent the last two years trying to obtain the passport. It turned out that his experience was not too different from mine. He finally bribed a security officer with money he borrowed from his relatives. "The devil will push the millstone if you pay him enough," he said, quoting a Chinese saying. "Within a week of the payment, I got my passport. I am going to buy the plane ticket tomorrow after I check in at the security bureau. The longer the night, the more nightmares a person will have, as the saying goes. I will get out of the country as soon as I can. Let's drink to my departure!" We laughed and clicked our glasses.

But it is bad luck to celebrate. Young Einstein did not buy the plane ticket the next day, nor the next week. I accompanied him the next day to the Beijing Bureau of Public Safety to obtain his exit permit. The official sitting behind the desk glanced at his passport for a few seconds and then abruptly threw it in his drawer.

"Your passport has been canceled," he said, closing the drawer.

Young Einstein almost jumped up. "What!? . . . Why? . . . How?" he stuttered, his eyes wild with surprise and fear.

"Your school, the School of Agriculture, belongs to the jurisdiction of Weeds County," the official said, as if explaining a simple arithmetic problem to a first grader. "Although Weeds County is part of Greater Beijing, your passport must be issued by the Weeds Bureau of Public Safety, not by the Beijing Municipal Bureau. So there is nothing I can do. You must go back and reapply for your passport and visa." He sounded very logical, and he seemed to be extra patient with my friend.

"But I spent two years!" Young Einstein cried. "The school year will start in three weeks. How can I get another passport and visa in three weeks?"

"That's not our concern," the official replied in a monotone. "We have to go by the rules. Someone made a mistake when he accepted your application here. There is no point in arguing about whose fault it is. The upshot is that you have to start again if you want to go."

"But it was your office that approved my application and issued me the passport in the first place," argued Young Einstein. "How could the government make me pay for its mistake?"

The official raised his head as his eyes narrowed and his tone turned threatening. "Are you accusing the government? Given the security risks and your family problems, your application should never have been approved in the first place! You will never get out of this country if you have this attitude!"

Shaking with anger, Young Einstein stumbled out of the office with me. That night, he told me that he had devised several schemes to get back the passport and "kill the bastard behind the desk."

"Don't be carried away by the moment," I said, trying to calm him down. "Killing the petty official won't make the slightest difference to the bureaucracy. You have to go the old-fashioned Chinese way, and use the network that will lead to him. Everybody, even a dog, has someone that he will listen to. Let's find that someone. I will let my friends know and we will help you. Let's start right away."

The next day, we mobilized our networks. The first person I contacted was Old Brother, whose Boxer Street watermelon stand was so successful that he was opening two more in nearby streets.

"Your friend's problem is my problem," Old Brother said right away, pointing to his fat bare chest. "My watermelon stand is a superhighway that can lead anywhere, even to the bedroom of Premier Li Peng. I'll get on it today."

Li Ling also contacted all her friends.

Like a wave, our friends contacted their friends. The circle got wider and wider. In two frantic weeks, after many bottles of liquor and cartons of cigarettes, we found a woman whose sister was married to the official who had taken Young Einstein's passport. We gave the woman three hundred yuan and she agreed to deliver some gifts to her brother-in-law and put in a good word. By the end of the second week, four days before Young Einstein's graduate program was to start, he was summoned to the office of the Passport Control. Without expression, the official took the passport out of his drawer and threw it across the desk. "You are very lucky," he said with a dry chortle. "I will be a saint this one time only." Like a thief, Young Einstein snatched the passport and fled the office.

He took the earliest flight he could find and left China two days later. After seeing my friend off, I had an attack of despair on the way back from the airport. Would I be able to join my friend in America someday?

To prevent a repeat of Young Einstein's experience, I again activated my network in Tianjin before I dared to submit an application for an exit permit. With money borrowed from Old Brother, I threw a lavish banquet for Captain Cai and Officer Ke, who both promised to put in a good word for me. I could hardly believe my eyes when I received my passport back two weeks later, with a slip of white paper attached. It was the exit permit. I could not believe that I had been let go so easily. For the next few days, I waited for the Party to pull another trick that would block my departure.

Besides, there still remained one more barrier. The plane ticket from Beijing to San Francisco cost thirteen hundred yuan, and my wife and I had only forty-five yuan in the bank. I did not have relatives who could lend me that much money; nor could I go to my father for it. Even if he had it, my father would refuse to lend it to me. He did not approve of my traveling to the U.S. in the first place; it was a potential risk to his career in the army. Old Brother had pledged all his savings, three hundred yuan, to me and had promised to help borrow the rest from other friends. But that might take a few weeks.

The day after I received the visa, I went back to the college in Tianjin to fill out the many papers needed to leave the country. I had to go to half a dozen offices to resign my position, to suspend my food ration, to suspend my residency, and to get my foreign currency allowance. For a whole day, I rushed from one office to another, trying to finish the paperwork as soon as possible and trying to avoid anyone I knew. But, as fate would have it, as I was leaving the last office, in walked President Jiang, the last person I wanted to see.

"Ha! You are just the person I have been looking for," he said. "I heard you have obtained your passport. Is that your passport? Let me see it." He took the precious booklet from me and carefully examined it. "Come to my office with me," he said and put my passport into his pocket.

I almost jumped on him. Blood pounded in the back of my eyes. The invitation sounded ominous. This could only mean trouble. I had kept my promise and helped Lulu apply to American universities. She had been admitted and her passport had been approved. Did my sudden marriage to Li Ling upset the old man?

"It looks like you are all set to go to America," he said as he closed the door of his office. "Congratulations. That will be beneficial to both of us."

I stood by the large desk, my eyes on the brown-covered passport in the president's hand.

"Relax," said President Jiang. "I am not upset about your marriage, and Lulu is not either. Remember how I helped you to obtain your passport? I can help you again, if you do me a favor. And of course, I can still call the security bureau to reexamine your passport. It's your choice." He paused, taking another look at the passport. "Do you have enough money to pay for the plane ticket?"

"No, I don't," I admitted. "But I will borrow it from—"

"No need for that," he interrupted. "I will lend you the money, and you don't have to pay it back. That is, I will ask the college bursar to give you a loan. But there are two favors that I ask of you. If you can do me these favors, the college will forgive the loan."

I could not believe my ears! A parting gift from the Communist Party! Literary ironies did not get better than this. I consented to the conditions immediately—to help Lulu get her visa and to help find an opportunity for President Jiang to visit a U.S. university as a visiting scholar.

An hour later, I walked out of the cashier's office with a thick envelope. I had never seen so much money in my life.

The next day, I bought the plane ticket. But still, I dared not celebrate. I told only a few friends that I was leaving.

My last dinner at my parents' house did not go well. I had quarreled with my mother. She wanted me to take three extra tubes of toothpaste that she had bought for me, so that I would not have to spend hard currency on something cheap and readily available in China. I refused. My suitcases were packed with books and, if I were within the weight limit, I would rather take an extra book than three tubes of toothpaste. She got very upset. When the dinner was over and I was leaving, she barely nodded her head as a way of saying goodbye.

As I was packing, Baby Dragon and Old Brother paid me a visit. Baby Dragon came in a new army jeep, and was visibly annoyed by the presence of Old Brother, the rough-looking watermelon monger. I was surprised at how much my childhood friend had changed. At twenty-nine, he was already stooped.

Old Brother did most of the talking. He was excited about the new stands that he had just opened and promised me the royal treatment when I came back from America. "Oh, before I get carried away," he said, "I have a small gift for you." He took out a small silk box and put it in my hand. Inside the box was a small snuff bottle with a woman in a traditional dress painted on it.

"This is a Ming Dynasty bottle from my grandmother," he said. "It's probably worth a few hundred dollars. If you are hard up at the beginning in America, you can sell it."

"I can't possibly accept such a valuable gift," I said, deeply moved. "Besides, it's from your grand—"

"You must take it if you don't want to insult me," said Old Brother firmly.

My hand was slightly shaking as I put the box in my shirt pocket.

"I have a gift for you too," said Baby Dragon. "It will remind you of your friends from the Big Courtyard."

Baby Dragon's gift was a small packet wrapped perfunctorily in brown paper. I opened it. It was a red silk armband. I unfolded it and saw the familiar words: "*hongweibing* (Red Guard)—The Great Wall Fighting Team" written in faded gilt characters. Having moved so many times in my life, I had lost my own armband and I was quite emotional at seeing the red armband that marked the beginning of my revolutionary career. Holding the emblem of revolution in my hand, I wondered if it signaled the end of my journey as a Red Guard or just a new chapter in that journey.

Smoking Devil sent a letter to me and wished me well in America. He could not have sent me a better parting gift than the news about himself and other Beijing Kids. "I have been promoted to deputy secretary of the county," he wrote. "But my biggest achievement is that I am the father of six girls, and my wife is due with the seventh in two months. This time, I am certain that I will be the proud father of a son! I can tell from the shape and size of my wife's belly. All the village experts agree with me that it is going to be a boy."

Of our other friends, he told me that Water Buffalo, the only Beijing Kid from our village who managed to return to Beijing, was paralyzed from the waist down and had tried a few times to kill himself with pain-killers, but the expired pills from the state pharmacy were ineffective and only burned a hole in his stomach. Moon Face was doing well. He had just published his first novel and had become a local celebrity.

Little Lenin had also sent me a letter, which brought a mixed bag of news from the East Wind Aircraft Factory. Master Pan had been allowed to transfer to a factory in his native Sichuan province after his daughter died during an outbreak of meningitis which also took six other lives, including Old Revolutionary's. But the biggest news at the factory was that they had torn down the statue of the Great Leader which we used to pass twice a day on our way to work. "In the name of reform," Little Lenin wrote, "they blasted the statue to bits in the middle of the night. The whole factory was shaken the entire night by the explosions. Half of the workers were there to witness and enjoy the historical event. But the Old Man was tough, and would not give up his magnificent post easily. The first few explosions, with smaller amounts of dynamite, made only a few pitiful holes in the pedestal. Finally they tripled the amount of dynamite and the Old Man was reduced to a loud boom and a shower of shards and stones. But those bits and pieces took out most of the windows in the administration building, so he had his small revenge."

After all these years of battling the Great Leader and his Party bureaucrats, I wished I could be there to witness the historical event and to see the Great Leader blown to pieces. It would have been the best parting gift of all.

The night before my departure, Li Ling and I slept very little. Lying in bed, we talked about the latest stories that she was writing, developments in research on the yijing theory, and the economic theories of John Maynard Keynes, which Li Ling had just begun studying. It was odd, I later thought, that we should have talked about such idle subjects on the eve of a long separation. In all likelihood, it would be at least two years before we would see each other again, and we had been married less than three months. As if by agreement, we avoided talking about the trip, the future, and the inevitable moment of saying goodbye. It was just like the old days, sitting on the rough benches in front of the testing bay at the aircraft factory, talking about books and ideas. Both of us, entranced by "useless ideas," knew that night that we were forever joined in our hearts.

Neither of us knew that this would be the last time that we would ever be truly happy and peaceful together. We did not know that Li Ling had breast cancer that had been quietly growing and was about to spread to the rest of her body. We did not know that she had only a few years to live. On that last night, holding each other tight, all we knew was that there was a heaven.

လ

Flight 789 from Beijing to San Francisco took off at 11:28 A.M. and immediately rose steeply into the clouds. The Boeing 747 was packed. Most of the passengers were Chinese dressed in ill-fitting Western suits. There was an atmosphere of general excitement in the cabin, with happy conversations among the passengers and the continual clicking of beer bottles. But I did not pay attention to any of it, and I was not rejoicing alone, in my heart of hearts. I was still living in the last moments at the airport, passing through the gate for international flights and waving quickly to Li Ling, who struggled to wave back in the crowd that tightly encircled the gate. My mind was full of fragmented thoughts and images and I felt very lonely and very tired. I was in a partial state of shock from everything I had been through, and separating from my beautiful wife and flying to America.

Since the plane was heading west, the daylight disappeared very quickly. Less than two hours after takeoff, the sun had disappeared below the horizon. I looked down at the ocean thirty thousand feet below, which looked like a giant piece of gray tofu. Even though I knew we were probably a thousand miles from the coast of China, I still tried to keep cool and would not let my heart get too excited. Having been through so many disappointments, I still could not believe that my troubles were all behind me, and I still thought that getting too excited would be bad luck. I sat back and tried to think of some practical things to occupy my mind so that I would not think too much about actually setting foot on American soil. That possibility was still too far off for me. I raised my hand and slid it into the breast pocket of my shirt and felt one more time the crisp paper inside. All the money I carried to America was this single piece of paper, a hundred dollar bill. Tomorrow, I thought, I would start a new life from scratch with this paper. It would not be easy. I knew one hundred dollars was not enough for my first month's rent and food, and I did not know where I would get more money. But having fought through and overcome countless obstacles, I was confident that I would manage to survive. I thought that I had better start thinking of a plan.

Bending down, I groped in the handbag under my seat and took out my diary, which was a parting gift from Li Ling. The diary was thick. Between the pages was the armband that Baby Dragon presented me. I touched the soft red silk and gazed at the flowing bold golden words on the silk band, "The Red Guard," in Chairman Mao's calligraphy, and thought of the huge fire in the Big Courtyard on that hot summer day so many years ago and the happy faces of my friends when we first wore the red armbands. Looking at the new diary, I remembered the phony diaries that I dropped into the exhaust tunnel of the testing bay. A strange and oddly frightening thought suddenly struck me: from now on, for the first time in my life, I did not have to write down my thoughts in a code only I could understand. I could write anything I wanted in plain language. What a strange feeling it must be to write that way!

I decided to try the new way of writing. I took out a pen and started the first entry in the diary, in plain language. But I only wrote down the title of the entry "My plan in America," and then I stopped. I found I was too tired to concentrate. I closed the diary and dozed off. I did not sleep very long, however, for as soon as I drifted to sleep, I had a terrifying dream, in which I saw Bean Sprout smiling at me and thick black smoke coming out of his mouth. I was glad that a soft voice interrupted the nightmare and woke me up.

"Would you like something to drink?" At the voice, I opened my eyes and saw the smiling face of a flight attendant.

"Do you have bottled water?" I asked.

"Yes," she said with a smile and handed me a bottle with a glass.

After she left, I sat up and slowly poured the water into the cup. I took a sip. The water tasted cool and sweet. Sweeter than any water that I had tasted in my life. All of a sudden I thought of the bitter water in Tanggu, and all the troubles that I went through to get out of that place and to escape the endless reach of the Party, and my sweet wife whom I had left behind, and I could not control my emotions anymore. Tears came to my eyes, but this time I did not try to choke them back as I always did. Through my blurred vision, I looked at the crystal water in my hand and thought of the bittersweet victory that I had won. After trying to escape for so many years—four years in the countryside, six years in the aircraft factory, four years in college, and two years in Tanggu and Tianjin—I had finally done it; I had beaten the Great Leader and I did not have to pretend to be a revolutionary anymore. No more "patting-the-horse's-behind" to get ahead and no more fears of the terrible power of the Great Leader and the Party. I savored the tears that ran down my face: they were not only for all the things and all the time that I had lost but also for all the things—love, freedom, a new life—that I had gained. They were tears of victory.

One after another, the tears rolled down my cheeks and dropped into the cup in my hand. I took a sip of the salted water, and for the first time in my life, I let my heart laugh.

IN THE AMERICAN LIVES SERIES